中国与阿塞拜疆

经济比较研究

裴长洪
[阿塞]纳吉姆·伊曼诺夫 ◎ 主 编

中国社会科学出版社

图书在版编目（CIP）数据

中国与阿塞拜疆经济比较研究／裴长洪，（阿塞）纳吉姆·伊曼诺夫主编．
—北京：中国社会科学出版社，2018.9
ISBN 978 - 7 - 5203 - 3162 - 3

Ⅰ.①中…　Ⅱ.①裴…②纳…　Ⅲ.①经济发展—对比研究—
中国、阿塞拜疆　Ⅳ.①F124②F136.84

中国版本图书馆 CIP 数据核字（2018）第 212197 号

出 版 人　赵剑英
责任编辑　王　茵　马　明
特约编辑　张冰洁　周枕戈
责任校对　沈丁晨
责任印制　王　超

出　　　版　中国社会科学出版社
社　　　址　北京鼓楼西大街甲 158 号
邮　　　编　100720
网　　　址　http://www.csspw.cn
发 行 部　010 - 84083685
门 市 部　010 - 84029450
经　　　销　新华书店及其他书店

印　　　刷　北京君升印刷有限公司
装　　　订　廊坊市广阳区广增装订厂
版　　　次　2018 年 9 月第 1 版
印　　　次　2018 年 9 月第 1 次印刷

开　　　本　710 × 1000　1/16
印　　　张　22
字　　　数　258 千字
定　　　价　89.00 元

目　　录

上　篇

下　篇

上　篇

中国社会科学院王伟光院长的致辞

王伟光[*]

尊敬的阿利扎德院长,

尊敬的魏敬华大使,

女士们、先生们,

上午好!

很高兴来到阿塞拜疆首都——美丽的巴库,参加"中国—阿塞拜疆经济发展与合作研讨会"!首先,请允许我代表中国社会科学院对此次会议的召开表示热烈祝贺!对来自中阿两国与会的专家学者表示热烈欢迎!对会议主办方的辛勤工作表示衷心感谢!

今年是中国和阿塞拜疆建交25周年,也是阿塞拜疆独立26周年。26年来,阿塞拜疆人民在独立国家建设、社会经济发展中取得了巨大成就,我们对此表示钦佩和祝贺。

中阿建交以来,两国关系顺利发展,在双边和国际事务中相互理解、相互配合,互为重要战略伙伴。特别是近年来,

———————

* 王伟光,时任中国社会科学院院长。

两国加强高层接触和对话，中阿关系水平得到进一步提升。

中阿两国虽然相距遥远，但两国人民之间有着悠久的交往历史。2013 年，中国国家主席习近平提出"一带一路"倡议，得到阿塞拜疆积极回应。2015 年 12 月阿利耶夫总统访华期间，两国签署了《中阿关于共同推进丝绸之路经济带建设的谅解备忘录》等系列文件，推动中阿关系进入快速发展的新阶段。

女士们、先生们，"一带一路"是中国在新时期提出的重要国际合作倡议，旨在加强沿线国家在基础设施、产能、贸易便利化、金融以及人文交流等领域的合作，实现共同发展和繁荣，希望通过实施"一带一路"倡议为各国创造共同发展机遇。为此，中国设立丝路基金，发起成立亚洲基础设施投资银行。2017 年 5 月在北京举办"一带一路"国际合作峰会期间，中国又提出一系列促进"一带一路"建设的举措，包括加大资金支持，向丝路基金新增资 1000 亿元人民币，鼓励金融机构开展人民币海外基金业务，规模预计约 3000 亿元人民币；中国国家开发银行、进出口银行将分别提供 2500 亿元和 1300 亿元等值人民币专项贷款，用于支持"一带一路"基础设施建设、产能、金融合作。

阿塞拜疆位于欧亚两大洲交界，是欧亚大陆的"心脏地带"和交通走廊交汇的"十字路口"，地理位置十分重要。在"一带一路"建设中，加强中阿合作对提升整个欧亚大陆的互联互通和促进"一带一路"沿线发展具有重要意义。随着"一带一路"倡议的实施，中阿务实合作将迎来新的发展机遇。目前，中阿不仅在传统的炼油、石化等产业密切合作，也在探索在其他领域拓展合作的可能性。在信息产业、农业、旅游业、交通运输等多领域，中阿都具有良好的合作空间。

中国社会科学院是中国人文社会科学的最高学术机构和综合研究中心，广泛开展对外学术交流是中国社会科学院长期坚持的方针。近年来，中阿在人文社会科学领域的交往日益密切。中国社会科学院与阿塞拜疆驻华大使馆、阿塞拜疆科学院一道，多次共同举办重要的学术交流活动，这对于中阿加深友谊、增进相互理解和信任都具有非常重要的意义。今天，我们两院共同举办学术研讨会，为两院专家学者开展深入交流提供了平台，真诚期待大家畅所欲言、发表真知灼见，为促进中阿友好合作关系的发展做出新的贡献。

最后，真诚祝愿本次学术研讨会取得圆满成功！谢谢大家。

阿塞拜疆国家科学院
阿基夫·阿利扎德院长的致辞

阿基夫·阿利扎德[*]

各位与会代表，

尊敬的各位来宾，

女士们、先生们：

首先，请允许我对各位此次来到阿塞拜疆的首都巴库致以热烈的欢迎。阿塞拜疆国家科学院的圆形大厅见证了无数科学盛事，而今天的会议更是意义非比寻常。今天，我们汇聚一堂，旨在促进阿中两国间的全方位合作，其中经济领域的合作居于首位。

毫无疑问，中华人民共和国是当今世界上最具影响力的经济体之一。我相信，对于阿塞拜疆来说，加强与中国的经济及文化交流具有重要的政治意义。与此同时，阿塞拜疆也在中国的经济发展前景中占有一席之地，一旦中国经济发展达到一定水平，其政治上的影响力也随之而来。因此，我认

＊ 阿基夫·阿利扎德，阿塞拜疆国家科学院院长。

为本次会议的主题具有多边性质。最终，它将不仅仅涵盖经济领域，还会涉及政治、社会和文化层面。我们应在各领域寻求新型合作机会。而在我看来，这正是本次会议面临的最大挑战。为达成这一宏伟目标，我们必须积极开展研究人员、智囊团以及重要科研机构间的合作，这是我们总体合作间不可分割的一部分。即将召开的本次会议，一定会成为向这一合作迈进的重要一步。

正如各位所知，阿塞拜疆与中国间的友好合作关系具有深厚的历史渊源。古时候，伟大的丝绸之路在我们两国的贸易与文化交流中扮演着至关重要的角色。幸运的是，这些历史传统并未丢失，两国关系在当今时代又达到了新高度。苏联解体后不久，两国就开始了双边合作。值得一提的是，在1991年阿塞拜疆宣布独立之际，中国是第一批承认我们主权地位的国家之一。眼下，我们的中国朋友对高加索及中亚地区的一批全球性经济项目展现出极大的兴趣，尤其是交通道路方面的项目，这将能够促进这一广大地区的经济、文化乃至政治合作。

我们的民族领袖、阿塞拜疆前总统盖达尔·阿利耶夫在1994年访华期间，肯定了中国在国际政治及经济事务中所起的重要作用，阿塞拜疆愿意从中国的发展经验中学习。特别值得一提的是，在那次具有历史意义的访问中，阿利耶夫还访问了中国社会科学院，并就当代世界政治和经济问题以及两国在国际舞台上所能够扮演的角色发表了重要讲话。

阿塞拜疆总统伊利哈姆·阿利耶夫成功延续了前任国家领导人的政策，为密切两国社会生活方方面面的联系做出了卓越贡献。他的访华之旅硕果累累，与中国国家主席习近平就重建丝绸之路，即当下的"一带一路"倡议开展了卓有成效的协商。中国政府评价称此次访问是两国关系史上的里程碑。阿塞拜疆在南高加索地区经济领导地位的不断增强，为未来中阿关系发展带来积极影响。总统阿利耶夫强调，他将致力于推动中国企业积极参与到高加索地区尤其是阿塞拜疆各领域的经济发展中去。他还称，政府将全力协助中国商业群体在该地区投资。

阿塞拜疆地处丝绸之路中段，是连接东西亚国际交通走廊的关键所在。这一特殊地理位置是我们的优势，同时也赋予了我们巨大的责任。阿塞拜疆从一开始就积极支持"一带一路"倡议。尽管国际经济下行、石油价格世界范围内下跌以及其他复杂的政治因素，中阿之间的贸易额仍保持稳定增长。目前，中国是阿塞拜疆主要贸易合作伙伴之一。两国在交通、通信、农业、医药、工程及轻工业等方面成功开展多项合作。双边投资也在不断增长。1993 年，两国贸易额达150 万美元，而与之相比，当前两国贸易额已超过 7 亿 7 千万美元，在 25 年间增长了 500 倍！

借此机会，我想再次向中方同事表明，我们对过去二十年间两国成功建立的经济模式感到骄傲。首先，这一模式建立在经济自由的基础上——包括自由竞争、自由定价和自由贸易。当然，它还建立在知识产权保护的基础上。该经济模式连同我国自然资源一道，促使我们在过去数年间展现出令人惊叹的经济成果。现在我们正致力于推动经济及社会发展实现质的飞跃。我们未来的发展进程将在极大程度上依赖人力资源发展和科学教育的进步。要想进一步推动国家发展，我们必须激发国家的人才潜力，建立一个鼓励知识有效利用的体系。

亲爱的同事们，众所周知，当今世界经济的发展与科技进步间存在着千丝万缕的联系。甚至可以说，两者互相起决定作用。一个高度发达的经济体至少会向科研工作提供财政支持，没有完备的技术设施，科研工作也就无从谈起。而科学研究又反过来为经济发展提供新理念、新产品和技术创新，是经济发展不可或缺的动力。

这就是促使我们决定保留科学院的主要原因之一，而诸多苏联国家废除或彻底重建了其国家科学院。这些实验有的相当成功，而还有些则不尽如人意。我们还针对科学院进行了一系列改革，这次转型还在持续进行中。我们的主要目标在于建立并落实一个以成果为导向的科研体系，除了一些必要条件，还需要探索科研融资的新方法。

我们的努力已初获成效。在我看来，科技与经济间愈来愈紧密的联系正是重中之重。目前，阿塞拜疆科学院不仅积极参与国家项目的开发与实施，有时还会在诸多经济领域对国家项目实施检测。这些项目将经由总统审批，是国家发展规划的主要手段。为了履行这方面的责任，我们特地在科学院内设立了创新项目检测与协调委员会。

我们积极同欧洲科研机构展开合作，参与多个欧盟不同领域的研究项目。在发展和引进创新方面，我们致力于从各国宝贵的经验中学习获益。

阿塞拜疆科学院在推动国内创新发展方面起到重要作用。

我们秉持这一目标，建立了科学院的大型基础设施，其中包括一些技术中心和企业孵化器。首先，我一定要谈谈我们的高科技园区。该园区在总统的特别行政令下建立，园区内入驻的所有公司都可享有免税权，称得上是一块我们研究人员所提出的新理念的试验田。

亲爱的朋友们，令我尤其心满意足的是，近几年阿中两国的科研机构在科技领域建立起了极为高效的关系。我们有决心，将这一联系拓展到更多领域中去。

两年前，由副总统哈比贝利带领的阿塞拜疆科学院代表团访问了中国社会科学院。双方签署了重要协议。紧接着，阿中科学关系工作小组在两国科学院主席团的领导下建立。阿塞拜疆科学院下属的中国文学研究中心，为科学院的工作人员及其他各方人员提供中文课程，此乃双方互利共赢的典范。科学院其他部分机构也同样致力于协同中国各方，通过科研项目、会议、研讨会、工作交流等形式开展合作。

怀着愉悦的心情，我想再次强调我们两国经济学家的合作。阿塞拜疆杰出的经济学家、本次会议主要发言人之一萨梅扎德教授，几年前出版了一本有关中国经济的巨作。阿中两国经济学家之间的合作，在穆扎法里教授访问中国后大大加强。他还在访华期间，于中国社会科学院经济研究所做过报告。从他的开场演讲中，我意识到，中方专家对我国研究者衡量经济自由度的方法兴趣十足。我相信，该方法能够为两国开展联合研究打下坚实的基础——尤其在自由经济为双方带来积极影响之际。

我希望在不远的将来，我们两国将进一步加强学术合作。

从这一点来看，今天的会议至关重要。我相信，本次会议的发言和研讨将是丰富多彩、成果丰硕。在此，衷心祝愿各位一切顺利！

中国驻阿塞拜疆大使馆
魏敬华大使的致辞

魏敬华 *

尊敬的阿塞拜疆国家科学院阿利扎德院长，

尊敬的中国社会科学院王伟光院长，

各位专家学者，

女士们、先生们：

很高兴应邀出席由阿塞拜疆国家科学院和中国社会科学院共同主办的"中国—阿塞拜疆经济发展与合作研讨会"。我谨代表中国驻阿塞拜疆使馆对论坛的举办表示热烈祝贺。

中国社会科学院是中国政府的重要智囊，是中国最具权威的智库机构。阿塞拜疆国家科学院是一个大师云集、名家辈出的地方，在阿塞拜疆经济社会发展中发挥着不可替代的作用。此次，中阿两大科学院强强联手，共同聚焦中阿经济发展与合作，定将碰撞出思想火花，为中阿经贸合作注入新的活力。

---

* 魏敬华，中国驻阿塞拜疆特命全权大使。

中阿传统友谊源远流长。早在 2000 多年前，古老的丝绸之路已将中阿人民紧密相连。2015 年 12 月，伊利哈姆·阿利耶夫总统成功访华，与习近平主席共同见证签署两国共建"一带一路"合作备忘录，为双边关系发展开辟了新的广阔前景。

在新的历史条件下，中方提出"一带一路"倡议，就是要继承和发扬和平合作、开放包容、互学互鉴、互利共赢的丝路精神，秉持共商、共建、共享原则，把中国发展同沿线国家发展结合起来，把"中国梦"同沿线国家人民的梦想结合起来，赋予古丝绸之路以全新的时代内涵，推动"一带一路"沿线国家及相关地区实现共同发展、共同繁荣。

阿塞拜疆地处欧亚接合部，是丝绸之路沿线重要国家，是亚投行创始成员国和上海合作组织对话伙伴国。2017 年 5 月，以阿塞拜疆经济部长穆斯塔法耶夫为首的 5 名部级官员参加了在北京举行的"一带一路"国际合作高峰论坛。我们愿同阿方结伴而行，不断深化政治互信，扩大互利合作，增进民心相通。相信通过双方共同努力，中阿传统友谊将会在古老而又现代的丝绸之路上绽放出新的光彩。

最后，衷心祝愿此次论坛活动取得圆满成功。祝阿塞拜疆国家科学院、中国社会科学院为"一带一路"建设、为中阿关系发展多建言献策，做出更大贡献。祝阿利扎德院长、王伟光院长和各位与会嘉宾身体健康，工作顺利。

谢谢！

"钢铁丝路"与"一带一路"
倡议中的科学因素[*]

伊萨·哈宾贝利^{**}

众所周知，就发展水平而言，中华人民共和国位居世界前列，与美国和众多欧洲发达国家比肩。因此，从这一角度看，阿塞拜疆这一独立不久的年轻国家，其发展水平无法与世界大国之一的中国相提并论。然而，我们可以从两国的区域地理位置、地区职能和历史的角度对两国的异同之处做共时性分析。例如，中国是世界古代文明的摇篮之一，中华文明与埃及文明比肩。阿塞拜疆则是高加索地区古代文明的中心之一。在阿塞拜疆的阿祖卡赫洞穴中发掘出了 35 万—40 万年前原始人的下颌骨，阿祖卡赫人正是阿塞拜疆古文明的印记。嘎米嘎雅和戈布斯坦地区的古代岩画反映了我们阿塞拜疆古代人类社会的生活方式。就这层意义而言，阿塞拜疆文明是连接中华文明与埃及文明的重要桥梁。东方文明借此得到发展。数千年来，阿塞拜疆为世界文明做出了伟大的

　　* 本译文依据作者英文原文翻译，作者文责自负。
　　** 伊萨·哈宾贝利，阿塞拜疆国家科学院副院长，院士。

贡献。

阿塞拜疆境内商道的开拓有着久远的历史。这些商道在促进贸易的同时，推动了沿线文化和科学的发展，同时也完善了沿线基础设施的建设：驿站、祭火圣地及寺庙都得以建成。这是一个历史性的发展进程。商道转变成了丝绸之路，也使阿塞拜疆商道的地理版图得以延伸。丝绸之路贯穿欧亚，阿塞拜疆则位于这条古商道的中心和关键地段。经济、商业连同文化、科技一道，通过阿塞拜疆在东西方之间往来沟通。这促使阿塞拜疆的文化和科技融入世界，同时使得世界各地的文化和科技理念通过丝绸之路传入阿塞拜疆。因此，在11—13世纪时期，阿塞拜疆是东方文艺复兴的中心之一。其原因有二：其一，最重要的原因在于通过高加索地区、阿塞拜疆以及古商道沿途的阿拉伯语，复兴了古希腊和古罗马的文化及科技，其二，是这条经过阿塞拜疆贯穿中国与欧洲的丝绸之路。

在11—12世纪，丝绸之路为阿塞拜疆带来了东方文艺复兴。尽管阿塞拜疆文艺复兴是整个伊斯兰文艺复兴的一部分，它仍具有独特之处。阿塞拜疆文艺复兴尤其关注贸易发展中的民族特色，如陶瓷、金饰、铜器加工、纺织等，而这正是文艺复兴文化中最重要的特征；建筑中广泛使用具有地域特色的装饰，这也同样确定了阿塞拜疆文艺复兴的鲜明特征。该现象对阿塞拜疆产生了极大的影响。尼扎米·甘伽维、加特兰·塔布里齐、阿夫扎拉丁·哈加尼、迈赫赛提·甘贾维、阿贾米·纳希切万和纳西拉丁·图西等杰出诗人、学者和建筑师，都为阿塞拜疆文艺复兴时期的文学、科技和文化做出了极大贡献。伟大的丝绸之路从中国一直延展到西方，创造出了许多伟大的文化，因此催生了许多先进的思想，以及这些杰出的人物。同时期内在丝绸之路影响下产生的东西方文明共同构成了社会与文化层面的文艺复兴。在同一时期，丝绸之路使东西方文明得以融合，引发了社会文化层面的文艺复兴。

在东西方的文艺复兴中，中国都是影响力最大的中心及动力之一。古老的丝绸之路在中国扮演着重要角色。由丝绸之路产生的地区融合表明，阿塞拜疆在很久以前就开始了对外文化交流。自独立以来，我国一直在国家层面继续推行对外交流的政策。在阿塞拜疆国家领袖盖达尔·阿利耶夫的倡议下举办的国际科学大会——"伟大的丝绸之路"，正是当今独立后的阿塞拜疆政策的充分展现。如今，在中华人民共和国，"一带一路"工程是国家的重点工程。与此同时，独立的阿塞拜疆共和国建造了 21 世纪的第一条"钢铁丝路"——巴库—第比利斯—卡尔斯铁路，并于 2017 年 10 月投入运营。巴库—第比利斯—卡尔斯"钢铁丝路"经阿塞拜疆，覆盖从欧洲到中国的广阔领土。古丝绸之路是人类伟大文明的缩影，始于公元前 3—前 2 世纪，一直延续到公元 13—14 世纪。巴库—第比利斯—卡尔斯钢铁丝绸之路为亚欧之间的经济文化交流搭建起了新的桥梁，为其伟大发展提供了动力。这一重要的国际工程本着中华人民共和国提出的"一带一路"理念，以阿塞拜疆构建的巴库—第比利斯—卡尔斯"钢铁丝路"为基础，定会将世界各国团结起来。此外，中国是公认的和平国家，不干涉全球及地区的军事和政治冲突。尽管阿塞拜疆共和国被人为地卷入了战争和冲突之中，我们在高加索地区发挥的作用同中华人民共和国相似，倡导在国际法律规范的框架内通过对话解决军事政治冲突。现今，阿塞拜疆与世界各国，特别是高加索地区的国家互相合作，保持着正常的国际关系。

在中华人民共和国，经济改革是国家总体发展纲领的重要组成部分。与此同时，中国自主创业领域也取得飞速发展。自主创业、经济发展和国家开放也是阿塞拜疆的头等大事。有鉴于此，我们认为中阿两国的合作具有重大的历史意义和光明的发展前景。两国间的多领域联系为 21 世纪的相互合作提供了广泛的机遇。中国资本目前正活跃在阿塞拜疆的石油工业、信息技术等领域。

正如中国社会科学院院长在讲话中所说，科学正在国际交流融合过程中占据特殊地位。阿塞拜疆科学院与中国社会科学院于 2015 年签署了多份协议，这正是我们两国科学交流取得更广阔发展的充分印证。特别需要指出的是，在阿独立时期，阿塞拜疆前总统盖达尔·阿利耶夫就已奠定了中阿科学交流的基础。

阿塞拜疆前总统盖达尔·阿利耶夫在 1994 年访问中华人民共和国期间访问了中国社会科学院。他在讲话中表达的观点具有深刻的洞察力，他所提出的责任和义务已成为我们两国在科学方面关系的坚实基础。此外，杰出的国家领袖盖达尔·阿利耶夫所建立的国际关系，在伊利哈姆·阿利耶夫总统任上成功地得以继承，并且决定和促进了阿塞拜疆与中国在包括科学在内的全方位交流融合。中阿科学关系出现新浪潮。萨马德扎德院士出版了一部有关中国经济的深刻专题论著。

在总统的领导下，阿塞拜疆共和国战略研究中心的工作人员编制并出版了一部阿塞拜疆语—汉语大词典。继尼扎米·甘伽维之后，阿塞拜疆科学院文学研究所的工作人员还在 2017 年参加了两次中文考试，并取得了高分成绩。阿塞拜疆科学院开设了孔子中心。阿塞拜疆科学院经济研究所与中国社会科学院有关科学机构建立了富有成效的合作关系。

由中国社会科学院院长率领的多人代表团访问阿塞拜疆，将进一步深化中阿两国科学关系以及文学和经济领域的协调发展。我认为，中国提出的"一带一路"倡议和阿塞拜疆共和国的巴库—第比利斯—卡尔斯"钢铁丝路"将为进一步深化丝绸之路沿线，包括阿塞拜疆在内的各国科学交流做出卓越贡献。

中阿两国将在艺术、建筑、经济和社会文化发展的联合项目框架内，重建并拓展双方的科学交流活动。这将从多方面深化科学因素对中阿两国发展的重大作用和意义。

阿塞拜疆和中国经济：自由经济 与经济调控研究的借鉴[*]

纳吉姆·伊曼诺夫^{**}

尊敬的阿塞拜疆国家科学院院长阿基夫·阿利扎德院士，
尊敬的中国社会科学院院长王伟光学部委员，
中华人民共和国驻阿塞拜疆大使魏敬华先生，
尊敬的各位政府与议会的代表们，
亲爱的各位同僚和媒体代表们：

我很荣幸代表阿塞拜疆国家科学院经济研究所感谢各位
出席这场旨在推进阿塞拜疆和中国经济合作的会议。

这是第一次如此规格和意义重大的会议。根据阿塞拜疆
科学院领导到访中国时达成的协议，2016 年我很荣幸在中国
社会科学院经济研究所进行了一场讲座。我的主要目标是向
中国的各位同行介绍我们的相关研究，即对政府干预经济程
度的测量及界定政府在自由主义与调控主义相互关系中的最
优选择区域。这场讲座被具有相应兴趣的研究者接受，在这

---

    * 本译文依据作者英文原文翻译，作者文责自负。
    ** 纳吉姆·伊曼诺夫，阿塞拜疆国家科学院（ANAS）经济研究所所长，教授。

一年 6 月中国社会科学院经济研究所裴长洪研究员率领的中方高级别代表团到访我所，更加深入地了解了这项研究。我所研究人员也就此进行了一系列展示和陈述。这次中阿经济合作会议正脱胎于那时候进行的一系列详尽的、富有成果的交流讨论中。

对阿塞拜疆的经济学来说，阿塞拜疆科学院经济研究所进行的理论与应用研究能够引起特定的、或许尽管不是那么高的国际关注，无疑是值得骄傲的。正如你们中许多人所了解到的，我们的主要研究问题涉及阿塞拜疆后石油经济时代的社会与经济方面。改进对经济的政府调控，探索经济领域里右翼（自由主义）和左翼（调控主义）之间的平衡区间都是我们研究中必不可少的组成部分。

我认为现代经济学理论史也可以被看作一场自由主义与调控主义的对峙。在当代世界，国家内部的（有时甚至是国家间的）政治竞争往往建立在两种哲学理念（意识形态）之间的矛盾上，而这正是现代世界政治经济起步的主要驱动力量之一。

阿塞拜疆科学院经济研究所在这一领域内研究的独创之处在于我们现在能够做到测量（定量评价）经济自由主义—调控主义的程度。为此我们发展了一套方法并且提出了一个工具，即一个我们称之为经济左翼（右翼）指数的综合指数［简称为 IL（R）E］。自 2014 年开始，这就是阿塞拜疆科学院经济研究所的一项年度发布指标。最近一次发布涵盖了经济发展程度不同、来自世界各代表性地区的 95 个国家。

这项研究的方法论基础是，我们区分了政府干预经济的形式，并将其"模式塑造"的形式分配到一个单独的小组中。建立在不同国家的经济模式是被区分开的，首先是由这些形式的政府干预的程度来区分的，也就是说，任何经济体都可以被认为是比其他经济体更自由或更调控性的，这只是基于对不同干预措施程度的评估。模式塑造型的政府对经济干预的特点主要是两极性：在正常情况下，它们的减少是为了改善商业环境，它们的增长是为了加强民众的社会保障。例如，对外贸易的监管所追求的两个目标，在事实上是相互排斥的，进口自由化和国内市场保护都有存在的理由。它们就像零和博弈中的两个值，即一个值的增加意味着另一个值的减少。从根本上说，不可能增加进口自由化程度的同时，加强对同一商品和服务（或整个国家）的市场保护。

这种复杂性源于这样一个事实，即不存在纯粹的自由主义（即仅基于市场自我调节机制）或完全的国家调控（即完全由政府监管）经济体。这种经济形式在理论上都是不可能的。所有的经济体都位于传统规模的中间点，其左极是经济和右翼的极端调控——极端自由主义。在任何特定的国家与任何特定的时间，经济都获得一定程度的左翼倾向（右翼倾向），这取决于政府干预经济的模型成型形式的程度。政府干预的程度越高，经济越左，反之亦然，经济的右翼倾向就意味着干预的减少。

经济左翼（右翼）指数基于这些方法规定的基础上，并且是次要指数的加权平均：公共财政、价格调控、对外贸易、许可、就业调控和最低工资。需要计算相关次要指数的数据，反过来则又是取自各种重要的国际统计数据。

IL（R）E 不存在任何总体的（适用于所有经济体）最佳价值。从图 1 可以看出，IL（R）E 同经济增长之间的关系在人均 GDP 达到 35000 美元以上的国家（图中的虚线），以及其他国家都是较弱的（图中的实线）。

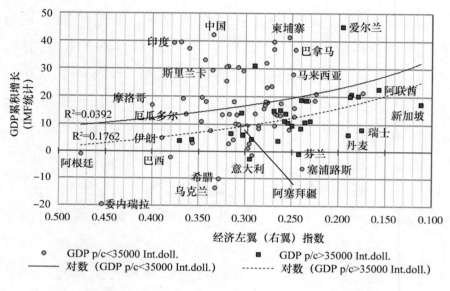

图 1　2012—2016 年 IL（R）E 与实际 GDP 的增长

（95 个国家，2011 = 100% ,%）

经济上采取自由主义取向或者调控主义取向的国家可能取得一样的成功，无论是在经济发展方面还是在公共福利的提升方面。部分国家取得较大的社会经济成功源自于它们的右翼经济，而另一部分则是因为左翼经济政策。此外，由于种种经济和非经济原因，对单一国家而言该指数的最优范围也会随时间而变化。

然而，在任何一个特定国家，多年来的累积经济增长都为确定该国的 IL（R）E 的最优水平有了一定的依据——这种方法被称为"指示性"。它还可以用来评估政府在不同经济部门的监管变化。如果政府在任何的经济部门引入了更自由的（或调控型的）规定，结果将是该行业的发展速度高于其他部门（或高于整体经济增长率），从而使政策选择得当，同样性质的改革得以延续。

在 IL（R）E－2016 上付出的工作与阿塞拜疆经济适应后石油时代基本同期。到那个时候，新的经济改革规划——"国民经济及其主要部门战略路线图"已经开始实施。实际上，所有的"战略路线图"设想下的"模式塑造改革"都有着右翼自由主义的特征。我们最近的研究报告确认了这种性质的改革应当持续推进，因为当下模式塑造性质的政府经济干预偏离了自由主义—调控主义两者之间的"最优选择领域"。经济自由化仍然具有很高的潜力。在当前形式下，自由化的改革是加快经济增长与提高公共福利的必要非充分条件。

所有关于阿塞拜疆和中国的经济的相关问题将在我们的会议上详细讨论。我希望，这种"匹配"的陈述能够引起与会者的兴趣。对于每一个问题，我们都会听到两份报告——一份来自阿塞拜疆，另一份来自中国。这将使我们能够评估阿塞拜疆和中国专家在讨论相关问题上的观点异同。祝愿各位发言者和与会者进展顺利。

经济模式的自由化潜力：中国与阿塞拜疆的比较分析[*]

马伊斯·古拉利耶夫[**]

一 导言

国际经济关系方方面面的迅速扩展是通过全球化对国民经济自由化扩展的影响实现的。国民经济自由化是全球化进程在国内范围的投射。世界贸易组织、跨国公司、国际金融机构和许多其他国际组织要求将各国经济自由化作为全球化的主要手段。因此，现代社会里每个国家都面临着两个相反的选择：通过迎接全球化的挑战来确保本国经济的自由化，抑或是加强政府对经济的调控以保护国内市场。

世界上没有任何一个国家不进行对外经济活动，去走完全自给自足的道路。也没有任何一个国家能借助全球化的呼吁完全透过金融和移民来获得所有类型的商品和服务。对任何国家而言对外经济活动的必要性都是毋庸置疑的。但是，

---

[*] 本译文依据作者英文原文翻译，作者文责自负。

[**] 马伊斯·古拉利耶夫，博士，阿塞拜疆国家科学院经济研究所。

每个国家都力求在充分利用全球化带来的机遇的同时维持其国内市场。全球化进程与自给自足之间的矛盾在国民经济中体现为自由化与国家调控的矛盾。每个国家都力求确保经济的自由程度与商业环境的发展和对国内市场的保护处于同一水平。

经济自由主义与国家调控之间的比例因国家而异。这一比例可能取决于国家的经济发展水平、区域特征、社会的历史发展水平、民族认同和其他决定因素。例如，日本经济中的自由主义水平就不等同于德国或瑞典经济中的自由主义水平。同样，在同一地区的格鲁吉亚和伊朗经济自由化程度也有很大差异。

全球化是民族国家外部的一种法律和政治环境，但与国家之间存在着不间断的联系。这种环境是动态的并一直处于变化中。在这个过程中，两种性质上截然不同的要素之间形成了经济关系。首先，它是任何国家的经济体系与制度之间的联系，并对全球化进程的形成和发展起着关键作用。其次，涉及以种种方式进入世界经济中的国家之间的经济关系。这种环境也鼓励各国不断改进其立法和对外经济活动。这种改进只能通过两种方式进行：增加国家对经济的介入（国家调控）或减少国家对经济的介入（自由化）。经济政策向国家调控或自由主义方向的不断变化是每个国家经济发展史上的常态。通过全球化的扩展，没有任何国家能够做到绝对自由化或明确的国家调控政治。尽管如此，每个国家通过选择"更倾向国家调控"或"更自由化"的经济模式来决定发展方向。这种经济模式影响着国家所有经济活动的有效性，包括对外经济活动。

二　文献回顾

致力于国家干预模式塑造形式宏观经济影响（尤其是国有制经济所占比例、价格管制、外贸平衡、获得许可经济活动领域的管制、最低工资、就业）的研究者们的研究能够在经济学的文献中找到。

经济学文献对国有化与私有化的经济效果与两者的矛盾关系有不同的认识。例如，B. Holmstrom 和 P. Milgrom （1991）、A. Shleifer（1998）认为经由私有化能够确保税收增加，原因是其他社会成本的减少。[①] Guriev 和 Rachinsky 则认为私有化创造了强大的利益集团，这些集团对国家经济政策的制定会产生相当的影响。[②] 值得注意的是，如果一个国家的政治、法律和经济都比较弱的话，私有化影响下产生的利益集团最终将成为私人垄断者。既然如此，为市场经济发展创造竞争的环境也变得不可能了。[③] 尽管如此，在国有制处在支配地位而私有企业居于弱势的经济条件下，即便是民主治理也无法解决效率与社会福利问题。

[①]　Bengt Holmstrom and Paul Milgrom, "Multi-task Principal-agent Analyses: Incentive Contracts, Asset Ownership and Job Design", *Journal of Law, Economics and Organisation*, Vol. 7, 1991, pp. 24 – 52; A. Shleifer, "State Versus Private Ownership", *Journal of Economic Perspectives*, Vol. 12, 1998, pp. 133 – 150.

[②]　Sergei Guriev and Andrei Rachinsky, "The Role of Oligarchs in Russian Capitalism", *Journal of Economic Perspectives*, Winter 2005, pp. 131 – 150.

[③]　Mara Faccio, *The American Economic Review*, Vol. 96, No. 1, Mar., 2006, pp. 369 – 386.

　　私有化政策研究方面的学者可以分为两类：一类学者认为私有化对经济发展和减贫非常重要。这主要是基于 C. Shapiro 和 R. D. Willing（1990）以及 J. Laffont 和 J. Tirole（1991）的理论判断，他们认为与国有制相比，私有制企业的利益冲突相对较少。[①] 在公共部门，国家扮演着所有者、管理者与监管者的角色。此外，国家又为国有企业创造了有利的发展条件，阻碍了市场竞争。

　　A. Boardman、C. Lauren 和 A. Vining（2002）在私有化的效果评估方面的研究证实了在私有化后，商业盈利率与劳动生产率会上升。[②] 在汇总 150 多项公私企业效率和多个国家私有化后果的研究后，B. Villalonga 指出这些研究中有 3/4 是旨在证明私有企业更加有效率。[③]

　　但另一方面，在私有化产生积极经济与社会经济效益的国家，这些影响却可能并非持续性的。在这种情况下，国有化—私有化进程通过某种程度上此消彼长的相互替代成为国家对经济的调控手段。[④] S. Kobrin（1984）分析了 20 世纪

　　① Shapiro, C. and Willing, R. D., "Economic Rationales for the Scope of Privatization", In E. N. Suleiman and J. Waterbury (eds.), *The Political Economy of Private Sector Reform and Privatization*, Boulder, C. O.: Westview Press, 1990; Katz, Lawrence F. and Krueger, Alan B., "The Effect of the Minimum Wage on the Fast Food Industry", *Industrial and Labor Relations Review*, Vol. 46, No. 1, October 1992, pp. 6–21.

　　② Boardman, Anthony E., Claude Laurin and Aidan R. Vining, "Privatization in Canada: Operating and Stock Price Performance with International Comparisons", *Canadian Journal of Administrative Sciences*, Vol. 19, No. 2, 2002, pp. 137–154.

　　③ Villalonga, B., "Privatization and Efficiency: Differentiating Ownership Effects from Political, Organizational, and Dynamic Effect", *Journal of Economic Behavior & Organization*, Vol. 42, No. 1, 2000, pp. 43–77.

　　④ Chua, Amy L., "The Privatization-Nationalization Cycle: The Link between Markets and Ethnicity in Developing Countries", *Columbia Law Review*, Vol. 95, No. 2, 1995, pp. 223–303.

60—70 年代 79 个国家的国有化进程，得出了这样的结论：
国有化进程开始于 1960 年，20 世纪 70 年代初达到顶峰。[①]
在接下来的几年中，这一过程逐渐减弱。M. Minor（1994）
扩展了这项研究，覆盖到 1993 年以及 95 个国家。根据他的
研究，这一进程在 20 世纪 80 年代后期被逆转，私有化进程
取代了国有化进程。[②] O. Manzano 和 F. Monaldi（2008）的研
究则证明，在 2008 年金融危机之后，私有化过程有被国有化
取代的趋势。[③]

　　私有化的支持者认为私营企业的利润增加了企业家和管
理者的效率是这一过程的主要驱动力量。[④] 一些研究者则认
为，即便企业为国家所有，但工人还是更倾向于提高劳动生
产率并刺激积极经营。[⑤]

　　财政政策对 GDP 的影响有不同的研究路径。Ramey 和
Shapiro（1998）在"狭义"上探讨财政政策，并得出公共支
出的变化会对需求产生重要的影响这一结论。[⑥] 他们分析了公

---

① Kobrin, Stephen J. , "Expropriation as an Attempt to Control Foreign Firms in LDCs: Trends from 1960 to 1979", *International Studies Quarterly*, Vol. 28, No. 3, 1984, pp. 329 – 348.

② Minor, Michael S. , "The Demise of Expropriation as an Instrument of LDC Policy, 1980 – 1992", *Journal of International Business Studies*, Vol. 25, No. 1, 1994, pp. 177 – 188.

③ Osmel Manzano and Francisco Monaldi, "The Political Economy of Oil Production in Latin America", *Economia*, Vol. 9, No. 1, 2008, pp. 89 – 103.

④ Radu Vranceanu, "Corporate Profit, Entrepreneurship Theory and Business Ethics", ESSEC Working Paper, Document de Recherche ESSEC/Centre de recherche de l'ESSEC. ISSN: 1291 – 9616. WP1308, 2013.

⑤ UNDP, "Is the Private Sector More Efficient?" A Cautionary Tale//UNDP Global Centre for Public Service Excellence#08 – 01, Block A, 29 Heng Mui Keng Terrace, 119620 Singapore, 2015.

⑥ Ramey, V. , Shapiro, M. , "Costly Capital Reallocation and the Effects of Government Spending", Carnegie Rochester Conference on Public Policy, 48, 1998, pp. 145 – 194.

共支出对行业的影响，并给出了同样的双部门模型。与单部门模型相比，双部门模型提供了更多关于数量可能变化的信息。

其他的研究人员，如 W. Edelberg、M. Eichenbaum 和 J. Fisher（1999）继续采用这种方法，分析了公共采购对美国经济的影响，取得了与 Ramey 和 Shapiro 相一致的结果。[①] 根据 1997 年的数据，他们得出公共采购能够创造经济上的积极改变的结论。研究结果表明，实际收入、国内投资、消费总量均随着公共采购、产品发布、就业、对外投资的增加而减少。实际收入的减少有助于替代商业周期模型。Fatás 和 Mihov（2001）辨别了财政冲击，并将增加政府支出视为对经济的干预。他们得出了这样的结论：在国家干预经济的过程中，私人投资的增加超过了补偿私人消费减少的数额。与宏观经济变量的动态影响相比，他们的财政政策的主要结果之一是，政府支出的增加导致消费和就业的增加。对财政政策宏观经济影响的实证分析表明，政府支出的增加对私人消费的增加有影响，但对投资的增长没有影响。[②]

我们在 Blanchard 和 Perotti（2002）的研究中也看到了同样的结果。因此，财政冲击对产品发布和私人消费总量有积极影响，对私人投资总量有负面影响。[③] Mountford 和 Uhlig

---

[①]　Edelberg, W. , Eichenbaum, M. , Fisher, J. , "Understanding the Effects of a Shock to Government Purchases", *Review of Economics Dynamics*, Vol. 2, No. 1, 1999, pp. 166 – 206.

[②]　Fatás, A. , Mihov, I. , "The Effects of Fiscal Policy on Consumption and Employment: Theory and Evidence", cepr discussion paper#2760, 2001.

[③]　Blanchard, O. , Perotti, R. , "An Empirical Characterization of the Dynamic Effects of Changes in Government Spending and Taxes on Output", *Quarterly Journal of Economics*, Vol. 117, No. 4, 2002, pp. 1329 – 1368.

（2005）的研究表明，财政冲击对国内和对外投资都会有负面影响。[1] 加拿大、德国、澳大利亚和英国等一些国家的类似研究也显示了同样的结果：财政政策对私人消费有正面影响，对私人投资有负面影响，在某些情况下没有影响。[2] 这类研究不能涵盖另一些国家，尤其是美国的经济，这一事实没有考虑到确定财政政策影响宏观经济指标的经验模式，特别是产品发布以及投资和消费数量的影响。开展此类研究的主要困难是在绝大多数国家很难获得关于公共财政的准确信息。

R. Perotti（2004）通过向量自回归方法探讨了财政政策对 5 个经合组织成员国 GDP、通货膨胀和收入规范的影响：（1）财政政策对 GDP 的影响几乎没有影响，只有在 20 世纪 80 年代的美国，这些影响更大。（2）没有可靠的证据表明减税的经济效果比加税对经济的影响要高。（3）增加政府支出的冲击和税收增加对 GDP 及其组成部分的影响正在逐渐减弱。1980 年后，这些影响尤其是对私人投资的影响绝大多数是负面的。（4）1980 年后，政府支出对利率的影响为积极的。（5）政府支出对通胀的影响也很微弱。[3]

De Castro 和 Hernández De Cos（2006）的计算表明，短期内政府支出与总生产量之间存在正相关关系，中长期内政府支出则导致高通胀和总生产率下降。[4] 德国和意大利进行的研

---

① Mountford, A., Uhlig, H., "What are the Effects of Fiscal Policy Shocks?" Hum-boldt-Universität zu berlin working paper sfb#649, 2005.

② Perotti, R., "Estimating the Effects of Fiscal Policy in OECD Countries", University of Bocconi, Working Paper, 2004.

③ Ibid..

④ De Castro Fernández, F., Hernández de Cos, "The Economic Effects of Exogenous Fiscal Shocks in Spain: A SVAR Approach", ecb working paper#647, 2006.

究中获得了有意思的结果。Heppke-Falk 等人（2006）研究了政府支出对德国私营部门总体生产和消费的正面冲击的影响，并得出结论：政府支出的正面冲击增加了私营部门的总体生产率和消费。但也应该考虑到这种增长并没有想象中那么大。[①] Giordano 和其他研究者（2007）在意大利进行的研究也得出了同样的结果。[②] Biau 和 Girard 的研究也显示，公共支出的累积增加不止一类。法国的经验计算表明，政府支出在私人消费和私人投资上的支出是正面的。

D. Barlow（2006）、A. Panagariya（2004）、M. Chui 与其他合作者（2002）关于贸易自由化对经济增长影响的研究也指明这些指标之间关系的本质并非普遍适用的，而是随着一国到另一国与短期/长期的时段而变化。[③]

研究揭示了外贸次指标与对外直接投资占 GDP 比例之间的关系在本质上是依赖外贸的自由主义/调控主义水平的，并且对该水平的变化非常敏感。在那些对外直接投资占 GDP 20% 以上的国家，外贸机制相对自由，外贸次级指数为 0.2。有关贸易开放度对对外直接投资总量影响的研究也表明这些

---

① Heppke-Falk, K. H., Tenhofen, J., Wolff, G. B., "The Macroeconomic Effects of Exogenous Fiscal Policy Shocks in Germany: A Disaggregated Svar Analysis", deutsche bundesbank, discussion paper#41, 2006.

② Raffaela Giordano, Sandro Momigliano, Stefano Neri, Roberto Perotti, "The Effects of Fiscal Policy in Italy: Evidence from a VAR Model", *European Journal of Political Economy*, Vol. 23, 2007, pp. 707 – 733.

③ Barlow, D., "Growth in Transition Economies: A Trade Policy Perspective", *Economics of Transition*, Vol. 14, No. 3, 2006, pp. 505 – 514; Panagariya, A., "Miracles and Debacles: In Defense of Trade Openness", Columbia University, 2004; Chui, M., Levine, P., Murshed, S. M. and Pearlman, J., "North-south Models of Growth and Trade", *Journal of Economics Surveys*, Vol. 16, No. 2, 2002.

指标之间不存在一种普遍型的关系。根据对 1977—2009 年 25 个撒哈拉沙漠以南非洲国家贸易开放度与对外直接投资的研究结果,在特定挑选出来的一些国家中这两个指标之间存在着因果关系。

有关贸易透明度对对外经济活动尤其是进出口总量影响的研究表明,一些国家的贸易自由化对进出口总量的提高具有正面影响。[1] 贸易开放度对总出口量的影响则能够更明显地被预期和感受到。每个国家都乐于扩大出口。对总体进口的影响也是正面的,同样,进出口量变化对贸易开放度的依赖也是一种普遍法则。

在绝大多数国家,最低工资是基于生活水准决定并通过立法予以确定的。在经济学文献中,有很多种方法可用于计算生活水准这种人的基本权利。古希腊的柏拉图和亚里士多德,中世纪的托马斯·阿奎那乃至 18 世纪的亚当·斯密都强调了确定最低的谋生限度的问题。[2]

绝大多数研究者认为较高水平的最低工资对年轻人和低技能工人的就业具有负面影响。一方面,许多研究显示最低工资水平的上升不一定会对贫困人口的家庭人口产生重要的影响。最低工资水平的变化影响着年轻人对中等和高等教育的参与以及他们从大学的毕业情况。[3] 另一方面,最低工资的

---

① Chaudhary M. Aslam and Amin Baber, "Impact of Trade Openness on Exports Growth, Imports Growth and Trade Balance of Pakistan", *Forman Journal of Economic Studies*, Vol. 8, 2012, pp. 63 –81.

② Stabile Donald R., *The Living Wage: Lessons from the History of Economic Thought*, Northampton, MA: Edward Elgar, 2008, p. 176.

③ Neumark, D., "Wasche Minimum Wage Effects on Employment and School Enrollment", *Journal of Business & Economic Statistics*, Vol. 13, No. 2, April 1995.

增加反过来又通过对贫困家庭消费的影响对家庭之间的收入再分配产生影响。[1]

"最低工资"对经济增长、社会—经济发展、对外经济活动与其他领域的影响在经济学文献中受到了特别关注。大多数国家致力于通过干预最低工资水平来减少贫困。人们认为在贫困线以下的家庭收入伴随着最低工资水平的增加而增加。尽管如此，有研究指出利用最低工资水平来减少贫困或许并非有效路径。[2] 最低工资水平的增加对失业率也会产生一定影响。通过增加最低工资，低技能员工的辞职可能导致他们被高技能员工或者中等技能员工取代。[3] Lustig 和 McLeod（1996）以及 Clemens 和 Uither（2014）的研究得出同样结果。[4] Dube（2013）声称在其研究中最低/最高利润使得最低工资对就业的负面影响被降到了最低水平。此外，也要充分考虑这些关系对时间的依赖性。Dube 认为最低工资与失业之间不是一种因果关系。[5]

最低工资、就业与生活标准之间存在直接或间接关系的

---

① Marc T. Law, "The Economics of Minimum Wages", The Fraser Institute, Public Policy Sources, Number 14（https：//www. fraserinstitute. org/sites/default/files/EconomicsofMinimumWage. pd）.

② Card, D. and Krueger, A. B., *Myth and Measurement：the Economics of the Minimum Wage*, Princeton University Press：Princeton, 1995.

③ Neumark, D., "Employment Effects of Minimum Wages", IZA World of Labor, 2014, p. 6.

④ Lustig, N. and McLeod, D., "Minimum Wages and Poverty in Developing Countries：Some Empirical Evidence", Brookings Discussion Papers in International Economics, No. 125；Clemens, J., and Wither, M., "The Minimum Wage and the Great Recession：Evidence of Effects on the Employment and Income Trajectories of Low-skilled Workers", No. w20724, National Bureau of Economic Research.

⑤ Dube, A., "Minimum Wages and Aggregate Job Growth：Causal Effect or Statistical Abstract", IZA DP No. 7674, 2013.

可能性对经济增长也具有意义。一方面，最低工资可能通过
征税和投资给经济增长带来积极或消极的影响。最低工资对
经济增长的影响也可能同最低工资对劳动生产率水平的影响
相互关联。[①] 在另一项研究中，作为最低工资影响经济增长的
机制之一的劳动力成本增加的后果是，产品价格的上涨和利
润的下降对实际 GDP 具有负面影响。另一方面，如果最低工
资增加，低技能员工的收入就会继续增加，与那些失去工作
的人和公司所有者的人相比，GDP 的数量也会增加，因为这
些工人的边际消费倾向会增加。[②]

　　最低工资对国家贸易的影响可能首先会同对劳动力市场
的影响联系在一起。Slaughter（1999）在研究中强调国际贸易
对最低工资的影响。他认为，国际贸易改变了劳动力市场的
需求和工资结构。[③] Freeman（1995）解释了来自低工资国家
的进口活动对低技能劳动力市场压力的增加。[④] 因此，从这些
国家进口的增加减少了该国对低技能劳动力的需求。如果出
口国的最低工资水平（W_e）低于进口国的最低工资水平
（W_i），那么低技术劳动力创造的商品贸易就成为可能。如果
$W_e / W_i \sim 1$，这些国家的这类商品贸易就会下降。

　　Chihiro Inaba（2014）试图通过最低工资对生产高/低技

---

　　① Samuel Kwabena Obeng, "An Empirical Analysis of the Relationship Between Minimum Wage, Investment and Economic Growth in Ghana", *African Journal of Economic Review*, Volume Ⅲ, Issue 2, July 2015.

　　② Sabia, J. J., "Minimum Wages and Gross Domestic Product", *Contemporary Economic Policy*, Vol. 33, No. 4, 2015, pp. 587 – 605.

　　③ Slaughter, M., "Globalization and Wages: A Tale of Two Perspectives", *World Economy*, Vol. 22, 1999, pp. 609 – 630.

　　④ Freeman, R., "Are Your Wages Set in Beijing?" *Journal of Economic Perspectives*, Vol. 9, No. 3, 1995, pp. 15 – 32.

术产品的影响解释最低工资对国际贸易的影响。他认为发达国家（北方）能生产两类产品（高/低技术产品），发展中国家则只能生产低技术产品一类产品。发展中国家最低工资水平的提高促使发达国家倾向减少低技术货物贸易。这种减少又增加了这些国家对低技术产品劳动者的需求。[①]

在 20 世纪中期与后半叶，这些问题都吸引了许多研究者的注意。George J. Stigler（1946）、Richard A. Lester（1960）、Lawrence F. Katz 和 Krueger（1992）、David Card（1992）研究了最低工资对就业的影响。按照 George J. Stigler 的研究，认定最低工资水平不会刺激公共就业的增长，也不会刺激失业的增长。即便如此，Lawrence F. Katz 和 Krueger（1992）发现了国家经济干预还没有增加失业这一事实。David Card 和 Alan Krueger（1993）近年在快餐业内最低工资对就业的影响研究也证实这两个指标间不存在严重的矛盾。更进一步的研究没有发现最低工资水平对就业产生消极影响的证据。[②]

然而，所有研究都表明，国家对经济的干预并不构成企业环境与工人社会保障两极之间的矛盾。正是国家的这种干

[①]　Chihiro Inaba，"Effects on the Cross-country Difference in the Minimum Wage on International Trade，Growth and Unemployment"，Kobe University，Discussion Paper series，July 2014.

[②]　Stigler，George J.，"The Economics of Minimum Wage Legislation"，*American Economic Review*，Vol. 36，No. 3，June 1946，pp. 358 – 365；Lester，Richard A.，"Employment Effects of Minimum Wages"，*Industrial and Labor Relations Review*，Vol. 13，No. 2，1960，pp. 254 – 264；Katz，Lawrence F. and Krueger，Alan B.，"The Effect of the Minimum Wage on the Fast Food Industry"，*Industrial and Labor Relations Review*，Vol. 46，No. 1，October 1992，pp. 6 – 21；Card，David and Krueger，Alan B.，"Minimum Wages and Employment：A Case Study of the Fast Food Industry in New Jersey and Pennsylvania"，National Bureau of Economic Research（Cambridge，MA）Working Paper No. 4509，October 1993.

预倾向于将国家的经济向"右"推（进一步自由化）或向"左"推（国家调控）。从这个意义上说，国家干预的模型塑造形式可以用同样的规模来衡量，并通过综合指数来量化。这种评价方法由 N. Muzaffarli（2014）提出，后来由阿纳斯经济研究院的经济研究小组发展而来。

根据 N. Müzəffərli 等人（2017）的研究，每个国家的经济模式都与国家对经济的干预直接相关。[①] 当国家对经济的干预影响财产关系、社会保护措施和经济行动自由时，这一经济制度的内容将差别很大。经济模式的本质是由自由主义与行政自由的比例决定的。同样的东西将任何国家的经济体系都与其他国家区别开。

应该指出的是，并非所有形式的政府干预经济都有三种影响。例如，政府减少经济腐败的大部分干预措施与国家干预的模型塑造形式无关。

由于国家的经济模式是由国家对经济干预的模型塑造形式所决定的，这些干预总是引起致力于制定经济政策的公共政治团体之间的讨论。有趣的是，不管经济模型的分类如何，只有国家干预经济的模型塑造形式反映了其自身作为政党讨论的主题。

政府对经济干预的"媒介"可能是无穷无尽的。此外，国家干涉任何特定经济领域的事实可能只有两个相反的方向："右"和"左"，或"下"和"上"。这就是为什么国家干预不同经济活动的最终特征矢量将有两个方向。最终矢量的绝

---

① Müzəffərli, N., IS (S) I – 2015: Iqtisadiyyatın liberallıq potensialı-Bakı, "Elm və Bilik" nəşriyyatı, 2017.

对值和方向决定了"混合"经济系统在任何时候的静态位置，表征了发展动态的趋势。

在以混合经济体系中国家干预为特征的"矢量"中，有可能区分国家对人口社会保护和改善商业环境的责任的"存在"或"缺席"。国家及其机构应采取适当步骤确保人民的社会保护，并在必要时干预经济。这种对经济的干预可以通过限制商业环境来减缓经济增长。因此，一些以国家干预为特征的矢量将重点放在混合经济体系"向左"的社会保护方面，以及向"右"的商业环境方向。

国家对经济的干预是可以衡量的。在具有左右坐标轴的一维坐标系中，国家干预的程度及其动态可以通过经济系统的位置来分析。定量测量国家对经济的干预具有重要的方法论意义。这种干预的增加，经济"左"的倾向（或相反，国家干预的减少，"右"的倾向）会导致严重的宏观经济和社会后果。

因此，国家干预经济的模型塑造形式为：（1）通过对人口的社会保护来发展创业精神；（2）国有和私有财产；（3）个人主义和集体主义的二分法。所以，政党试图利用这种二分法来维护自己的政治利益。政治党派不仅将国家干预经济的模型塑造形式转变为讨论的主题，甚至通过增加或减少政府干预的方式形成新的国家经济模式。新形成的经济模式如果能保证国家经济的最优发展，那么这种模式将会持续很长一段时间，否则，它会很快变化。

三　研究的相关性

中国和阿塞拜疆这两个国家被选为研究对象。这两个人口和领土规模有很大不同的国家，有不同的经济发展历史。这两个国家的经济发展模式在本质上是不同的。基于国家经济的发展动态和这些模型的宏观经济影响，对两国经济发展模式进行定量评估，可以使所选择的模型与"优化"的距离更接近。

四　本研究对世界科学的贡献

通过在模型塑造干预形式的基础上建立各国的经济发展模型，可以通过确定发展的特殊性和动态性来确定国家对经济干预的"最优"程度。对存在显著差异的中国和阿塞拜疆两国之间的这种模式进行比较研究，为对其他国家进行比较分析提供了一种方法。在这种分析的基础上，可以衡量国家干预经济的程度以及这种干预对各国经济发展模式的有效性。

五　研究目的

本研究的目的是通过比较中国经济模式与阿塞拜疆经济的自由主义或国家调控水平，来确定国家干预经济对宏观经济影响的有效性。本文回顾了中国和阿塞拜疆经济的特点，中国和阿塞拜疆之间经济关系的一些元素，比较了两国经济干预模型塑造形式的各种组成部分和各组成部分的动态，对两国经济发展模式各组成部分的宏观经济效应进行了计量分析。

六　方法

本研究采用阿纳斯经济研究所经济左（右）性指数的方法。以国家经济干预的七种形式——模式塑造型干预形式为基础：（1）国家所有权在经济中的份额；（2）公共财政总量；（3）价格管制；（4）对外贸易管理；（5）许可贸易的应用；（6）就业监管；（7）最低工资的应用。

应用了一种不同的方法来确定每一种干预形式的水平。公共部门在经济中所占的份额是：（1）公共部门在该国就业人口总数中所占的份额；（2）公共部门在国家主要资金总额中所占的份额；（3）公共部门占该国国内生产总值的比重；（4）公共部门在该国企业数量中所占的份额；（5）综合指数，如"公营部门的规模"，是指公营部门主要资金在全国投资总额中所占投资份额的数值平均值。

七　主要结果

中国和阿塞拜疆的经济增长率与世界平均水平有很大差异。在阿塞拜疆经济的衰退时期（1991—1993 年），中国的经济增长率约为 14%。1995 年，阿塞拜疆的经济改革开始显示出积极的效果。1998—2004 年，两国的经济增长率大致相同。然而，由于2005—2007年大规模履行石油合同，阿塞拜疆的经济增长率高于全球平均水平和中国的经济增长率。近年来，由于世界市场石油价格的下降和石油产量的下降，阿塞拜疆的经济增长率急剧下降。马纳特在2015年和2016年的贬值加速了经济增长率的下降（见图1）。

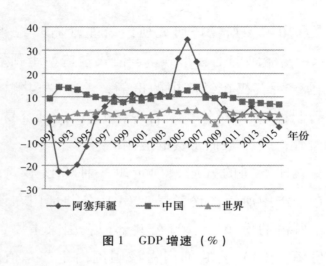

图1　GDP增速（％）

在中国和阿塞拜疆，按目前美元计算的人均国内生产总值与2005年之前相比并无显著差异。2005—2014年，阿塞拜疆人均国内生产总值超过了中国的指标。但在2014年之后，阿塞拜疆远远落后于中国。不幸的是，这一指标在过去三年中有所下降。应该指出的是，两国的人均国内生产总值都比世界平均水平低得多（见图2）。

然而，根据购买力平价的计算，两国的人均GDP都在稳步增长，阿塞拜疆在这一指标上领先于中国和世界（见图3）。

在获得独立后，阿塞拜疆大大扩展了对外经济关系。就

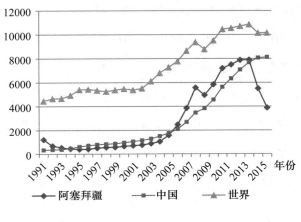

图 2　人均 GDP（美元）

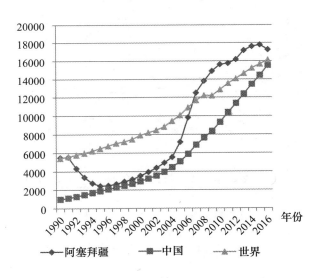

图 3　人均 GDP（购买力平价法，美元）

出口占 GDP 的比重而言，阿塞拜疆是世界领先的国家之一。在某些年份，出口额超过 GDP 的 50%。1992 年增长了 86%，2007 年增长了 68%。1998 年，出口占 GDP 的比重不到 20%，占 GDP 的比重最低。根据这一指标，阿塞拜疆在过去

25 年里一直高于世界平均水平。在中国，出口占 GDP 的比重约为 20%—30%。仅在 2005—2008 年，这个数字在 30%—40%（见图 4）。除了这几年，中国出口占 GDP 的比重低于世界平均水平。把中国和阿塞拜疆之间的严重不同与全球化或自由化程度的差异联系起来是不正确的。因此，石油和天然气在阿塞拜疆的出口中起着重要作用。如果对非石油产品进行这样的计算，就会发现阿塞拜疆的这一数量是非常小的。

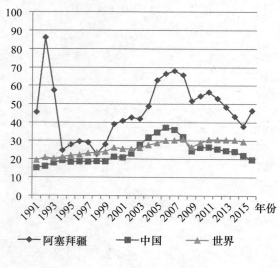

图 4　出口占 GDP 比例（%）

阿塞拜疆对外贸易的进口额也很高。自 2000 年以来，进口占阿塞拜疆 GDP 的比重超过了 40%。这远远高于世界平均水平。不包括 2003—2009 年，中国的这一数字约为 20%，略低于世界平均水平（见图 5）。

阿塞拜疆经济对外贸活动的高度依赖反映在贸易差额在国内总产值中所占的份额。在获得独立后，阿塞拜疆国

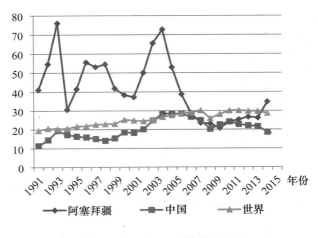

图 5　进口占 GDP 比例（%）

内生产总值中负差额贸易的比重在某些年份上升到 30%
（例如，1998 年）。2005 年以后，对外贸易差额大多为正
差额。在马纳特贬值后，这一数字下降到了 3%，尽管有些
年这个数字超过了 40%。在过去的 25 年里，中国对外贸易
差额占国内生产总值的比重一直是正数，为 0—10%。此
外，这些指标的对比也表明，中国经济对对外贸易活动的
依赖性很小；它拥有稳定的对外贸易正差额。这在很大程
度上取决于该国经济的规模。较小的经济体严重依赖对外
贸易平衡（见图 6）。

　　中国在阿塞拜疆对外贸易伙伴中具有重要地位。然而，
在这方面进口量远远高于出口量。只有在 2008 年，进出口总
额才大致相等。中国的进口额不断增加。出口量比进口量少，
但不是可持续的，而且每年都不同（见图 7）。

　　阿塞拜疆与中国的经济关系比与独联体国家的关系要弱
得多，特别是与俄罗斯的关系。在有些年份，中国在阿塞拜

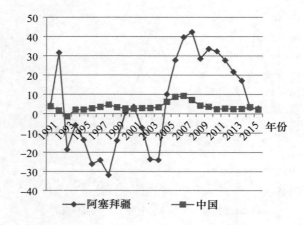

图6　贸易均衡份额占 GDP 比例（%）

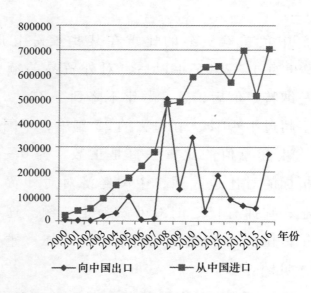

图7　中阿贸易进出口量（千美元）

疆出口活动中所占的比重甚至在 1% 左右（见图 8）。然而，来自中国的进口不断增加。虽然从独联体国家的进口额超过中国，但它的活力正在不断增强（见图 9）。

　　虽然中国和阿塞拜疆的经济规模相差甚远，但根据这两

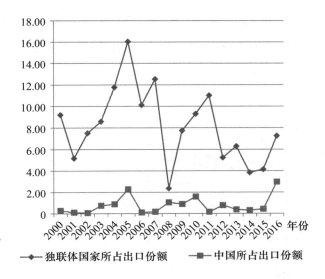

图 8　独联体国家和中国占阿塞拜疆出口份额（%）

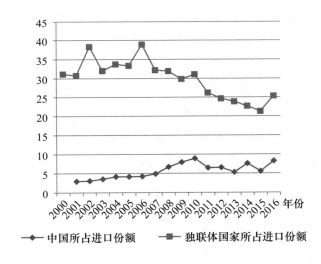

图 9　独联体国家和中国占阿塞拜疆进口份额（%）

个国家的人均国内生产总值和人类发展指数都对这两种经济模式进行了比较分析（见图 10）。主要的兴趣点信息是：（1）这些国家经济产出的紧密程度取决于它们应用经济模型的程度；（2）这些国家采用的经济模式可能会改变经济产出；（3）各国发展现有经济模式的潜力类型，以进一步改善经济成果。

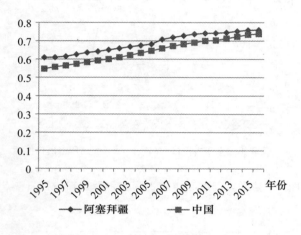

图 10   人类发展指数

让我们首先比较一下基于上述方法的中国和阿塞拜疆经济模型的主要轮廓。正如我们所提到的，当我们说经济模型时，我们指的是对经济进行模型塑造的干预形式的静态系统，这个模型描述了国家在经济中干预的程度。经济的左（右）性指数——IL（R）E，根据六个子指数对两国进行计算，可以在一定程度上表征国家对经济的干预程度。这些子指数是：（1）公共财政子指数；（2）价格监管子指数；（3）外贸子指数；（4）许可贸易子指数；（5）最低工资子指数；（6）就业监管子指数。对于中国来说，2007—2016年这些子指数的估价如表1所示。

表 1　　　　　　　　　中国经济的左右性指数和子指数动态

年份	公共财政	价格监管	对外贸易	许可贸易	就业监管	最低工资	经济的左右性指数
	SF_t	P_t	FT_t	L_t	E_t	MW_t	$IS(S)I_t$
2007	0.476	0.245	0.347	0.588	0.4075	0.439	0.4265
2008	0.482	0.211	0.347	0.517	0.4075	0.418	0.4106
2009	0.527	0.208	0.378	0.458	0.43	0.439	0.4260
2010	0.444	0.196	0.375	0.430	0.46	0.435	0.3987
2011	0.453	0.176	0.380	0.378	0.46	0.422	0.3902
2012	0.458	0.169	0.394	0.323	0.46	0.435	0.3868
2013	0.461	0.165	0.392	0.307	0.46	0.443	0.3857
2014	0.464	0.165	0.360	0.126	0.46	0.463	0.3595
2015	0.479	0.167	0.360	0.126	0.46	0.482	0.3670
2016	0.499	0.182	0.347	0.126	0.46	0.487	0.3739

资料来源：由作者计算。

在基于这些分类指数建立的中国经济模型中，2007—2009 年，对公共财政的经济干预水平略有上升，但 2010 年大幅下降，并在随后几年继续增长。然而，2016 年这一领域的干预比 2007 年有所增加。过去 10 年来，国家对价格政策的干预一直在稳步减少。然而，与 2014 年相比，2015 年和 2016 年的干预水平略有上升（见图 11）。

2007—2012 年，国家对中国对外贸易体制的干预有所增加，但在随后的几年里以大致相同的速度下降。因此，2016 年的干预水平与 2008 年持平。2007—2014 年，国家对许可证制度的干预不断减少，在接下来的几年里，它保持稳定。2007—2016 年，就业和最低工资分项指数略有上升，表明政府在这一领域的干预有所增加。

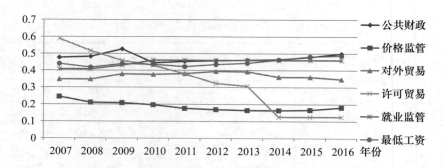

图 11　中国的子指数动态

　　根据中国的这些子指数计算的综合指数——"经济的左（右）性指数"通常表明中国的经济在过去的 10 年中已经实现了自由化。虽然 2009 年、2015 年和 2016 年对经济的干预指数水平有所上升，但与 2007 年相比，2016 年的中国经济可以被认为是相当自由的。

表 2　　　　　　阿塞拜疆经济的左（右）性指数和子指数动态

年份	公共财政	价格监管	对外贸易	许可贸易	就业监管	最低工资	经济的左（右）性指数
	SF_t	P_t	FT_t	L_t	E_t	MW_t	$IS(S)I_t$
2007	0.341	0.317	0.361	0.204	0.272	0.195	0.291
2008	0.360	0.240	0.358	0.178	0.270	0.161	0.277
2009	0.373	0.294	0.358	0.152	0.284	0.227	0.296
2010	0.363	0.260	0.344	0.140	0.230	0.218	0.276
2011	0.374	0.211	0.342	0.143	0.230	0.177	0.267
2012	0.383	0.208	0.333	0.139	0.306	0.190	0.280
2013	0.390	0.210	0.333	0.136	0.360	0.202	0.291
2014	0.381	0.215	0.333	0.139	0.251	0.200	0.274
2015	0.392	0.316	0.337	0.097	0.316	0.218	0.297
2016	0.401	0.439	0.338	0.122	0.378	0.200	0.327

资料来源：由作者计算。

对包括中国和阿塞拜疆在内的 95 个国家进行的研究表明，政府减少对外贸易中的政府干预对经济发展是必要的，但这还不够。换句话说，国家对对外贸易活动的更少的干预不会伴随经济发展。在发达国家，国家干涉对外贸易，但这种干涉不超过一定的限度。对于新兴经济体来说，对外贸易的自由并不总是伴随着经济的发展。过去 15 年来，阿塞拜疆的对外贸易分项指数一直在稳步下降。在阿塞拜疆货币贬值后，采取了一些保护主义措施。然而，对外贸易自由与阿塞拜疆经济增长之间的积极联系表明，保护主义行动可能产生负面影响。[①]

在过去的 10 年里，国家资助的子指数在阿塞拜疆一直呈上升趋势。然而，研究表明，公共财政分项指标与 GDP 总量之间没有普遍的联系，这两个指标之间的关系性质与每个国家的经济特征有关。阿塞拜疆的公共财政分项指数与 GDP 总量之间存在正相关关系。[②]

研究表明，在过去的 10 年里，阿塞拜疆面临着更高的公共财政、就业和物价的管制，并进一步放宽了许可贸易、对外贸易和最低工资标准。由于价格调控水平的提高，“经济左（右）指数”在过去两年里略有上升（见图 12）。

通过对中国和阿塞拜疆经济的左（右）性指数的相互比较，可以看出，与阿塞拜疆相比，国家对中国经济的干预相

---

① Gulaliyev, M. G., Abasova, S., Huseynova, Sh, Azizova, R., Yadigarov, T., "Assessment of Impacts of the State Intervention in Foreign Trade on Economic Growth", *Revista Espacios*, Vol. 38, No. 47, 2017, p. 33.

② Ibid. .

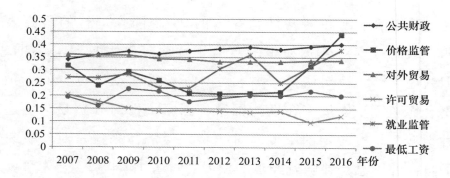

图 12   阿塞拜疆子指数动态

对较高。然而，在过去的 10 年中，中国的干预水平普遍下降。在阿塞拜疆，可以观察到周期性的增长。另一个值得关注的问题是，中国和阿塞拜疆两国经济中自由主义水平的逐渐接近，这两国的经济规模大不相同。中国经济持续自由化的步伐不仅在过去两年有所放缓，甚至出现了"左倾"现象。阿塞拜疆的保护主义改革大大增加了国家对该国经济的干预（见图 13 至图 15）。

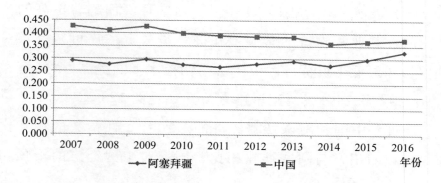

图 13   阿塞拜疆和中国经济的左（右）性指数动态

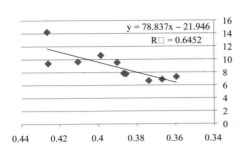

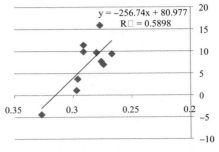

图 14　中国 GDP 增长（y 轴）
与经济左（右）性指数（x 轴）
的相关性

图 15　阿塞拜疆 GDP 增长
（y 轴）与经济左（右）性
指数（x 轴）的相关性

研究表明，中国经济自由化改革对 GDP 增长具有负面影响。在阿塞拜疆，非石油部门的经济自由化水平与经济增长之间的关系是积极的。

八　所得结果分析

中国和阿塞拜疆不能被视为以上述方法评价国家干预程度的先决条件。模式塑造型经济干预形式的本质与国有企业在经济中的权重有关。不足之处是，所提到的方法没有考虑到国家所有权的水平。因为两国不可能获得必要的指标来确定国家所有权在经济中的权重。作为一种方法论，另一个不足之处是，在过去 10 年里模式塑造形式被定义。观察的缺乏降低了两国经济增长或其他宏观经济指标确定其对经济中自由主义水平的依赖程度的可靠性。作为一种方法论，在未来消除这两种短缺可能会提高结果的可靠性。

九 结论

因此，通过分析过去 10 年中国家对经济干预模式的塑造形式的动态，可以得出以下结论：（1）现代条件下的中国经济自由化对经济发展没有积极的影响；（2）在中国，有必要加强一些干预模式的塑造形式。有必要对它们分别进行研究，以确定这些干预模式的塑造形式；（3）由于近年来在阿塞拜疆实施的保护主义措施，经济的"左"倾向对经济增长有消极影响；（4）阿塞拜疆目前的经济状况远低于它所能拥有的"最佳"自由化水平，因此，国家的经济需要进一步自由化；（5）应当对阿塞拜疆经济继续进行宏观和行业层面的调查，以确定是否需要更多"哪种"形式的自由化，以及"多少"自由化模式塑造形式。

中国经济可持续高质量发展：
现代经济体系的构建[*]

兹亚德·萨梅德扎德[**]

全球化的进程打破了国家的界线，信息技术与计算机技术已经将相距甚远的各国家和地区紧密结合在了一起。

中国一个有趣的方面在于，其全球化的进程不是像某些国家那样以惊人的速度一蹴而就的，而是逐渐发展演化的。例如，一些国家是通过经济自由化迅速进入了世界经济。但中国这个大国，则是通过加强其国民经济及保障其经济安全进入了世界经济。1978 年，在改革开放之前，中国的人均GDP 相当于当时的俄罗斯的 1/9。

经济结构的不协调、众多的贫困人口、高失业率以及其他几个低水平的关键性指标，都将当时的中国推入了一个深渊，而这个后果对于整个世界来说都是严峻的、危险的。

上述种种也加剧了当时中国社会的紧张感。正是在这样

　＊ 本译文依据作者英文原文翻译，作者文责自负。

　＊＊ 兹亚德·萨梅德扎德（Ziyad Samadzade），阿塞拜疆国家议会经济政策与工商企业委员会主席，"单向通径经济分析与合作"公会科学主席。

的局势下，邓小平提出了使中国免于崩溃解体的一项大战略。这项战略使中国经济政策发生了根本性的变化，其提出也被认为是 20 世纪发生的少有的大事件之一，并涵盖了中国经济生活的众多领域。

其中一个主要方面在于，在改革进程中增强中国执政党，即中国共产党所发挥的作用，被认为是中国快速发展的一个重要因素，另外，也要对改革的思想基础给予特殊考虑。换言之，即是要在不改变国家政治制度的前提下进行经济改革。

然而中国人没有让老一辈人遭受精神上的打击，他们不是通过喊口号的方式，而是巧妙地运用了从现实中总结出的思想形态和方法，从社会主义经济和市场经济中获益。没有其他的出路了。中国找到了一条有效的改革之路，而不必进行"休克疗法"。

这项复兴计划其实是对中国这个人类文明的古老中心、历史上强大的国家的爱国主义精神的挑战。历史上很多年，中国一直没有将任何国家看作对手，但那之后却开启了半殖民地国家的一段岁月。这项复兴计划符合中国人民的主要诉求，也因此激发了人民投入建设的热情动力。复兴计划成为中国政府与中国执政党实际活动的主线，消除国家经济衰退已成为所有外交和国内政策的主要职责。该项目的长期性也给中国社会带来了历史性的乐观。

总而言之，与其他社会主义国家相比，中国共产党不仅是改革的发起者，同时还是改革实施的保障者和组织者。

在改革的过程中，邓小平还发表意见说："计划经济不等于社会主义，资本主义也有计划；市场经济不等于资本主义，社会主义也有市场。"这种立场也削弱了当时支持计划经济反对市场经济的那些人的诉求。

1978 年 12 月，经过中国共产党十一届三中全会上长时间的讨论，对世界采取"对外开放"的原则最终被采纳了。将分阶段地执行改革也被最终确认了下来。

改革首先从中国农村开始。首先从农业部门开始进行改革实际上与当时西方给出的建议是相悖的，这一举措存在很大的风险，但同时也是非常正确的一步。毕竟，相较城市而言，中国农村的情况甚至更糟。20 世纪 80 年代初，中国农村的贫困率相当高。在城市，人们凭粮票购买粮食；而在农村，有 2.5 亿人口的收入是低于官方贫困率的。因此，中国共产党决定首先在农业部门实行市场关系，并且取得了积极成果。

中国准备加入世贸组织的过程是非常谨慎的。为此，中国深入分析了世界市场的规则，力求在自由市场贸易中生产出更有竞争力的产品，并取得了显著的成效。目前，中国已具备很高的出口能力。描述出口和进口的相关数据清楚地证明了这一点。中国的外汇储备，包括黄金在内，超过了 3 万亿美元，是 2005 年的 3.6 倍。人为地减少货币流通在中国是不允许的，只能刺激国内需求，系统地分析和控制消费者价格指数的变化。

最重要的问题之一在于不允许经济改革中出现激进主义，财产形式也没有得到正视。政府倾向于采取预防性措施，以提高公共财产的使用效力，并根据竞争原则为发展产权形式创造条件。此外，政府还对法律做了相关的修订，防止其权益受到侵害。

我们的研究表明，中国在发展速度、规模和成果方面所创造的令世界惊叹的"经济奇迹"，在很大程度上与其创新型的产权制度相关。

中国人民认为，将在一些个例中显示出的社会经济的失败与痛苦归咎于社会主义制度，是对历史的诽谤、对历史事实的伪造，是对神圣精神、对我们伟大先辈的奋斗与经受过的苦难的失敬与背叛，除此无他。

在我们与中国的科学家和专家的对话与讨论中，其中一个值得注意的方面是，他们没有宣称中国的经济模式是单一的发展模式。他们赞成利用世界经验，不论哪个国家，只要是好的就值得学习借鉴。

世界经验表明，许多不发达国家即便有经济援助，仍然不能确保较快的发展速度。换言之，还没有哪一个曾长时间处于不发达国家阶段，目前进入发展中国家行列中的国家在短时期内取得了像中国这样的进展。

中国一贯奉行经济自由化，并提出保护国家利益，争取社会损失最小化。一方面，政府以拒绝行政主导的方式放任经济；但另一方面，出于对经济的调控的需要，政府也在逐渐向其靠拢。

而中国经验则再次证明，在错综复杂的转型期，"市场解决一切"的想法是极其错误的。那些持有这个想法的人或者不甚理解世界经验，或者认为中国经济复兴方面完全不存在任何问题。

2017 年，中国共产党第十九次全国代表大会上尤其强调的一点是，中国的经济政策和其面临的最新挑战将继续观照世界和国家利益的变化。

中国政府把在经济管理中忽视、拒绝社会主义思想看作一个不可饶恕的错误。

在科学经济文献中，有许多关于"开放经济"的概念。中国政府的经济政策及其成功再次证明了开放经济应该具有一定的局限性。自由经济的发展，如没有任何界限，就会损害国家利益、国家安全和国家独立。

到目前为止，大多数发展中国家都遭受过"开放经济"激进概念的实施和不良竞争方法的应用之苦。相反，如果开放经济的概念能够被慎重地贯彻实施，任何国家都能在世界经济中取得巨大成功。

今天，在中国沿海地区、毗邻地区和内陆地区，已经建立起了多学科的、协调的产业结构，以确保中国经济对外开放，目前在世界范围内还没有其他可与此相匹敌的规模。在发展国外市场导向经济、增加货币收入和引进先进技术等方面，这些地区都扮演着"窗口"和中介的角色。

受惠于成功的"对外开放"政策，中国在引进外资方面已升至世界第二位。

中国已通过了所有规定进出口管理机制的规章文件，以及反倾销和反补贴的规则。这些法律行为有助于完善对外贸易管理机制，在对外经济关系中制定规则，从而提高了中国的国际声誉。

由于"对外开放"政策以及同外方经济合作的迅速发展，中国的经济结构有了显著的改善。中国的外汇储备增加了好几倍，并已成为保证中国国家经济安全的重要因素。

今天，中国是一个对全球经济具有巨大影响的国家。

即便是现在，外资企业在中国经济中的投资仍在迅速增长。中国市场的巨大潜力及其巨大规模解释了外国投资者对于中国市场的巨大兴趣。此外，它们对中国市场的浓厚兴趣也与中国接近亚洲快速发展的市场、低交易成本和政府直接支持出口有关。

总体来说，今天的中国被公认为是一个具有吸引力的投资环境、非常灵活的市场环境的国家，所有这些有利因素都为外国投资者所关注。外国投资者注意到中国有着丰富的文化和悠久的历史，而中国人将始终记得他们的投资者，坚持传统，效忠祖国。

中国政府每年都在简化投资方面的相关规定。中国对包括外资在内的多种组织结构参与下的混合经济活动给予了极大的重视。这些企业是由中国的公司和企业、外方法人或实体建立的经济组织在中国设立的。

中国已经与世界 220 多个国家和地区建立了贸易和经济关系。过去 40 年的经验表明，由于实行"对外开放"的外部世界政策和积极的对外贸易，可以更充分地利用国内市场或国际市场的机会，并为配置物质资源创造了有利条件。

在过去的 15 年中，中国的年均 GDP 增长率比全球平均水平高出 2—3 倍。这足以表明，在过去 5 年中，按可比价格计算的 GDP 的增长幅度在 7%—8%。在全球经济风险增加的条件下，这是一个非常高的发展指标。毫无疑问，这种经济发展直接关系到一个事实，即该国的投资流量很大，并且基于生产性投资正在迅速增加。我们已经提到，中国政府逐年加强国家经济发展的财政基础。因此，中国国民生产总值的总量比世界平均水平高出 2 倍。其经济总投资的年均增长率比国内生产总值的增长率高出 2 倍。有趣的是，预算在分配给国家经济的投资基金中的作用往往会增加。这一趋势在世界金融市场危机后加剧。据了解，预算支出是政府在经济发展过程中调控政策的最重要机制之一，预算在确定和执行经济发展方向中的存在反映了政府的利益，增加了总需求。因此，流通中的货币供应量增加，投资活动和生产基础设施的发展机会也在扩大。

中国经济的快速、动态发展无疑需要客观地评估国家在经济中的作用。简言之，我们想通过参照中国和其他国家的经验来表达我们的一些想法。

一般而言，政府干预经济的最佳水平应该是多少？公有部门与私营机构的比例应如何？如何改变这个比例？所有经济都能集中在私营部门吗？这在目前是，在过去是，在未来也将是争端与调查所围绕的热点问题。

从 20 世纪下半叶开始，国家在经济中的作用和角色问题，始终是世界上最有影响力的组织、国家元首、经济学家和政治家们关注的焦点。纵观 20 世纪的发展历程，我们得知，在不同的发展阶段，国家在经济中所起到的作用在一些西方国家，包括美国，都是不同的。有人提出了关于在一定时期内以市场关系为基础加强国家对经济的影响和经济管理的概念。今天，我们应提醒那些激进者们，美国前总统罗斯福和约翰逊关于在美国组建一个大社区的想法已经实现，因为这能够为国家的经济创造一个强大的影响机制，而美国也正是借此摆脱了危机。

政府的参与和领导，直接解决了控制通货膨胀、增加就业、建设社会保障制度等问题。

值得注意的是，在世界经济文献中，关于国家在经济发展和整个社会中的作用问题有不同的看法。当然，对这些观点再做详尽的调查已不太可能。然而，应当承认，国家对经济的干预问题取决于每个国家的具体国情、历史发展、社会经济发展水平和国内政治局势。在这个问题上想让所有国家采取一成不变的做法是不正确的。

中国专家表示，由于不存在意识形态的内容，市场是中性的、普遍的、世俗的，且并不意味着中国的转型不会选择一个新的社会发展道路，或绝不会使用任何外国模式。如果中国政府从某个国家学习并借鉴了什么，不意味着这个国家更文明、更民主，而是代表了中国从该国引进来的东西更符合中国的国家利益。

一般而言，在发达国家和包括中国在内的发展中国家，国家对经济的干预问题在近期乃至长期都将是一个非常重要的问题。我们必须不断地关注这个进程，分析它们，并在关乎国家利益方面对它们加以利用。

中国政府专注于货币政策以使国家摆脱危机，货币管制，加强改革的法律框架，为保护其他形式的所有制以及国家财产创造条件，逐步形成健康的竞争环境，保护国内市场，准备计划以帮助增加就业，所有这些都取得了积极的结果。

政府认为，确定消费和收获间的有效定额、调整工业和农产品交换、加强对财政资金的使用的控制、增加财政部的现金流量等，是经济发展重要的先决条件。

历史上人民面临过的一个重要问题是供粮问题。

在改革进程中，中国政府引导其人民走向正确的方向，制定正确的政策，用一切手段来确保粮食的充足，解决这个重大问题。

世界农产品的生产和国际贸易中有一个有趣的明显的趋势。这一事实是，尽管世界农产品产量增加，但其在世界贸易中的作用却有所下降。过去40年来，食品和农产品的份额大幅下降，这是解决中国这个超过13亿人的大国的粮食问题的主要原因之一。

中国应用了世界农业经验中行之有效的方法和管理技术，对其在当地条件下的应用机会进行了调查，并取得了积极的结果。我们要重申，做好一个超过13亿人的国家的粮食供应确实是一项具有全球性意义的人类成就。

引人注意的一个关键性问题是，在这里，让一个村民更感兴趣的是生产力的问题，而不是种植面积的扩大问题。

中国政府特别重视缩小地区间、城市和乡村间居民收入水平的差异。当然，完全性的调节是非常困难的。然而，值得注意的是，在约40年的时间里，中国政府为缩小城市人口人均收入与农村地区相应指标之间的差距做了许多重要工作。

中国政府采取了增加小城镇和定居点的经济活动的措施，这使它们能够有效地利用劳动力，消除一些区域、村庄的发展差异，创造区域市场，并在总体上优化区域和国民经济的地域结构。

　　农业产业发展战略的重要方向之一是技术进步，提高农村人口的文化水平，培养现代技术的人才。服务于农业部门发展的各项举措再次表明，国家领导人实施经济改革的制度和逻辑顺序来自经济政策的主线，这一主线是提高耕地总量的建模水平，动态、定性地发展经济，有效地消除其地域结构的差异。

　　最令人惊叹的是，当今世界粮食安全正面临严峻挑战，而中国这个巨大的国家已经成功地解决了这些问题。

　　笔者进行的长期研究表明，在全球紧张形势的今天，中国显现出的高水平发展，是国家政策符合国家利益的合乎逻辑的结果。[1]

　　另外我还要提到的是，欧洲—高加索—亚洲运输走廊的启动在很久以前就已成为焦点，但当时其实施的客观条件很有限。在苏联时期，这个想法是不可能实现的，因为当时苏联只有一条单一的运输系统。货物通过俄罗斯和哈萨克斯坦从欧洲运往中国以及其他邻国，这也被认为是一条重要的战略性通道。在这种情况下，苏联政府不会同意开放一个通过高加索、中亚各共和国过境的新的运输走廊。苏联解体，各新的独立国家的成立，为实现这一运输走廊创造了客观条件。欧盟促进启动了欧洲—高加索—亚洲走廊的项目，并将它提

---

　　① 阿塞拜疆国家议会经济政策与工商企业委员会主席、院士兹亚德·萨梅德扎德出版过三本关于中国经济的书——《中国的经济奇迹》、《全球世界经济中的中国》的俄语版和阿塞拜疆语版。2001年4月，在巴库举行了题为"从计划经济向市场经济和经济发展模式过渡"的国际科学理论会议，取得了巨大成功。阿塞拜疆的经济学家联盟、中华人民共和国大使馆和人民外交学会是该会议的组织者。这次会议得到了媒体的广泛报道，并引起专家的极大兴趣。

升至一个全球性的议题，以加强各新独立国家的独立性。在21世纪十年后，中国政府也提出了大规模的倡议。

在每个国家的历史上，都有这样的事件，对它正确的评估和解决方式成为其永恒发展的一个强大因素。欧洲—高加索—亚洲运输走廊的"一管一路"项目^①（One Pipeline One Road）的实现正是这样一个事件。由于阿塞拜疆位于这条运输走廊的中心，是连接两大洲的点，这条交通走廊的经济政治潜力是如此广泛，它对于阿塞拜疆共和国来说意味着恒定的资本、稳定的政治地位、持续稳定的发展，以及在国际经济关系中的永久的积极参与。

因此，我认为这次巴库峰会是阿塞拜疆外交和阿塞拜疆外交政策中最重要的成就之一，是近年来举行的国际大会中最重要的一场峰会。

中国领导人强调，"一带一路"倡议不仅对中国，而且对世界都很重要。我要高兴地说，在中华人民共和国主席习近平与阿塞拜疆共和国总统伊利哈姆·阿利耶夫的会晤中，更是强调"一带一路"项目的实现扩大了两国之间的有益的合作机会。

中国共产党十九大就国家的进一步发展提出了很多根本性的任务，我以下提及的是其中的一部分。这些任务首先是要确保社会主义最大的胜利，以新时代的中国规范为主要特征，实施新的发展观，建立现代化的经济体制，深化结构改革，促进实体产业更快、更好地发展，加快构建创新型国家，

---

① 特指欧盟启动的项目。

实施增长战略，平衡协调区域战略，迅速完善社会主义市场经济体制，抓住机遇有效、系统地贯彻实施"一带一路"倡议，提高人民的生活质量。我很高兴地指出，我有信心中阿关系将在所有领域都有长足发展。两国元首之间的友好关系、阿塞拜疆古丝绸之路的重建、为发展"一带一路"倡议相关合作所采取的措施，包括巴库海港的启用，阿塞拜疆连接亚欧的巴库—第比利斯—卡尔斯铁路，在里海巴库沿岸建立 Alat 经济区，这些都将进一步加强中国和阿塞拜疆之间的经济关系，并将有助于我们两国的经济和社会进步。

政府调控养老金体系的
跨国比较研究[*]

拉斯米娅·阿卜杜拉耶夫亚[**]

一 假设

自由主义会对养老金体系产生怎样的影响？能否衡量政府调控养老金体系的程度？

近年来，大部分国家的经济体系里都存在着自由主义的倾向。阿塞拜疆国家科学院经济研究所一系列最新的研究证实，大部分情况下，自由主义对社会经济的发展都有积极作用。然而，经济自由主义这种助益的潜力并不持久。原因在于，首先，到达某一阶段后，经济自由主义注定将走向终结；其次，自由主义发展到某种程度（并非最终程度）后，它的固有缺陷（市场的欺骗性）就可能显露出来，给自由市场带来毁灭性的后果。

这解释了为什么经济学的主要（也是非常困难的）责任

---

[*] 本译文依据作者英文原文翻译，作者文责自负。

[**] 拉斯米娅·阿卜杜拉耶夫亚，阿塞拜疆国家科学院经济研究所副教授。

之一，就在于确定自由主义（及对应的政府调控）对特定国家和特定时期的适用范围。对阿塞拜疆而言，弄清这一点十分迫切。阿塞拜疆国家科学院经济研究所近来的研究表明，该国经济的自由主义程度距离产生积极作用的门槛还有差距。若要在短期内加速该国的经济发展，增强人民的社会保障，自由主义将是不可或缺的条件之一，尽管这种情况并不令人满意。① 而通过养老金体系的自由化及建立非国有养老金的保障制度，我们可以满足这一时期的主要需求，即减轻政府的社会负担、巩固社会保障体系。

养老基金与其他社会保障体系的一大不同在于，该体系可以自由化。政府的政治经济意识形态，无论是经济政治上的左倾还是右倾，都会影响养老金体系的结构，以及国有和非国有养老基金的比例。谈到政治和经济的意识形态，我们首先就要涉及经济自由主义和国家干预主义的概念。前者指的是减少政府对经济的影响，后者则相反，指的是增加政府对经济的影响。倾向于干预主义的左倾方和倾向于自由主义的右倾方会出台最新的公共福利改善计划。按照左倾方的观点，最有可能实现目标的"捷径"就是让政府采取管制措施，而右倾方的方案则是"放手"让经济自由发展。两大阵营的竞争，是现代世界政治和经济发展的主要推动力量。②

---

① Müzəffərli, N. , *Iqtisadi inkişaf və ictimai rifah.* – AMEA Iqtisadiyyat Institutu, 2016 [http://economics.com.az/index.php/tedbirler/t-dbirl-r/item/694 – zhoerkaemli-alim-azhil-aeliyevin-90-illik-yubileyi-kidzhirilmishdir.html; son baxılma-yanvar 2017].

② Müzəffərli, N. , *Iqtisadiyyatın sosialyönlüyü sağçı və solçu sistemlərdə.* – Bakı, "Şərq-Qərb" Nəşriyyat Evi, 2014 [http://economics.com.az/images/fotos/sag-solluq/N. Muzaffarli_Iqtisadiyyatin_ Salliqi (Sollugu). pdf; son baxılma-fevral 2017].

一般而言，养老金体系会受到政治、经济、人口和社会因素的影响。无论政治和经济意识形态如何，各个政府在养老金体系改革时都必须考虑现有的经济发展水平、人口状况、人民的心理状态（经济心理学的本质）和政府增强社会保障的能力，此外，还需要对上述每一项在不久以后的情况进行预测。因此，就养老金体系的构建而言，进行跨国比较研究，比弄清政府究竟是要采用自由主义还是干预主义更加重要。

二　研究方法

从各种分类研究来看，对养老金体系进行定量评估是优化养老金制度的必要条件。就此而论，养老金体系的自由化程度，即政府干预的程度，对该体系而言至关重要。

一些论文的作者认为，养老金投入不足的情况在贫穷国家十分普遍，而富有的国家在养老金上的投入更多。[①] 实际上，这种观点是错误的。尽管许多经济上高度发达的国家的公共养老金成本很低，但它们的整体养老金储备、养老金替代率和养老金收入都很高。原因在于这些国家的私人养老金体系非常发达。一个国家的养老金成本取决于政府介入国家养老金体系的程度，而不是国家的富有程度。经验表明，政府对

---

① Pallares-Miralles, M. , C. Romero and E. Whitehouse, *International Patterns of Pension Provision II: A Worldwide Overview of Facts and Figures.* – World Bank Discussion Paper No. 1211, June 2012 [http://documents.worldbank.org/curated/en//1436114681685606687/International-patterns-of-pension-provision-II-a-worldwide-overview-of-facts-and-figures; son baxılma-yanvar 2017]; OECD, *Pension Markets in Focus*, 2016. – OECD Annual Report, 2016 [http://www.oecd.org/daf/fin/private-pensions/pensionmarketsinfocus.htm; son baxılma-dekabr 2016].

养老金体系的非直接干预（通过刺激私人养老金体系的建立与发展）可以增强养老金领取者享有的社会保障。这是一种普遍的模式，可以被看作社会福利的一种。Müzəffərli，N. 证实，那些形式上"不""以社会为导向"的做法，即右倾的经济政策，可能比所谓的"以社会为导向"的经济政策更有利于社会，而大部分情况下都是如此。[①]

我们通过研究发现，世界上还没有一种衡量政府干预养老金体系程度的指数。为此，阿塞拜疆国家科学院经济研究所首次推出了养老金体系自由度指数（Pension System Liberalization Index，PSLI），可用于测算政府对养老金体系的干预程度。最初在缺乏必要数据时，该指数的计算只基于一个指标——通过各种金融工具募集的私人养老基金的估值与 GDP 的比值。

不过在未来的计算中，以下指标也会纳入考量范围：私人养老金体系与公共养老金体系的比值、私人养老金资产与GDP 的比值、私人养老金资产和公共养老金资产在管理上的限制、社会保险税率等。

PSLI 的计算方式与阿塞拜疆国家科学院经济研究所每年发布的左倾（右倾）经济指数 [IL（R）E，2015 年] 一致，它的计算基于通过各种金融工具募集的私人养老基金的估值与 GDP 的比值。其目标在于衡量政府对养老金体系的干预程度。PSLI 的区间是 0—1，0 表示养老金体系"绝对右倾"

①　Müzəffərli，N.，*Iqtisadiyyatın sosialyönlüyü sağçı və solçu sistemlərdə*. – Bakı，"Şərq-Qərb" Nəşriyyat Evi，2014 ［http://economics.com.az/images/fotos/sag-solluq/N. Muzaffarli_Iqtisadiyyatin_ Salliqi（Sollugu）. pdf；son baxılma-fevral 2017］.

（政府完全不干预养老金体系），1 表示"绝对左倾"（政府完全管制养老金体系）。

私人养老基金的投资价值与 GDP 的比值按照公式（V_i − V_{min}）／（V_{max} − V_{min}）进行计算。

在计算过私人养老基金的投资估值与 GDP 比值的国家中，丹麦名列第一（205.9%），而阿塞拜疆位列最后（0）。因此 V_{max} 和 V_{min} 分别以 250 和 0 来代替。数据来源于经济合作与发展组织（Organization for Economic Cooperation and Development，OECD）2015 年的数据库（OECD，2016 年）。

最早一批参与 PSLI 计算的国家共有 54 个。

三　结果与意义

图 1 与图 2 列出了通过各种金融工具募集的私人养老基金的投资估值与 GDP 的比值，以及据此计算的 PSLI 值与经济左倾（右倾）状况的对比。各国按照养老基金与 GDP 的比值从大到小的顺序进行了排列。

PSLI 指数显示，最右倾的国家是丹麦（0.176）和荷兰（0.286）。而根据 IL（R）E 的数据，丹麦（0.190）和荷兰（0.317）也同样是右倾国家。IL（R）E 认为经济上最左倾的国家是法国（0.416），PSLI 同样认为它左倾（0.965）。

一些国家（德国、法国、土耳其等）在 IL（R）E 和 PSLI 的评判体系中都属于左倾国家。

PSLI 的结果详见图 3。该指数的相对中位数（0.850）比图表的几何中心值（0.500）要更高。这意味着在这些受到研

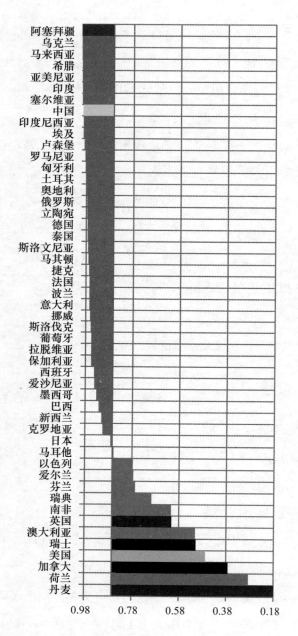

图 1   养老金体系自由度指数（PSLI）

资料来源：计算结果基于 2016 年的 OECD 数据和 2015 年的 IL（R）E 数据。

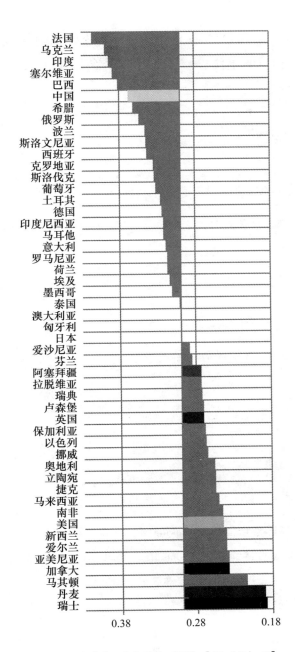

图2　经济左倾（右倾）指数［IL（R）E］

资料来源：计算结果基于2016年的OECD数据和2015年的IL（R）E数据。

究的国家中，养老金体系普遍左倾。阿塞拜疆则是极端左倾。
得出的结果与一些国际机构的指数类似（见图4）。

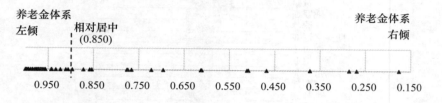

养老金体系
左倾

相对居中
(0.850)

养老金体系
右倾

0.950 0.850 0.750 0.650 0.550 0.450 0.350 0.250 0.150

图 3 养老金体系自由度指数（PSLI）（2015 年，54 个国家）

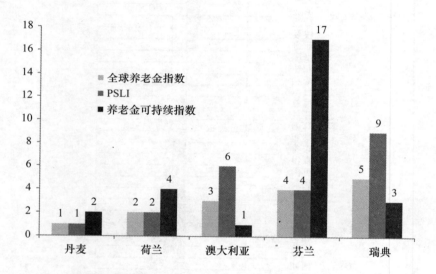

图 4 全球养老金指数（Ranking of Global Pension Index）、PSLI 和
养老金可持续指数（Global Sustainability Index）的排名
（2015 年，5 个国家）

资料来源：墨尔本美世全球养老金指数（2016 年）、养老金可持续指数（2016 年）。

丹麦（81.7）和荷兰（80.5）在 2015 年全球养老金指
数（GPI）涉及的 25 个国家中名列前二。GPI 根据三大指标
评级：养老金充裕程度（40%）、可持续性（35%）和整合

度（25%）。各国被分为六级（A 是最高级，E 是最低级）。在 2015 年的报告中，获得 A 评级的是丹麦和荷兰，B + 评级的是澳大利亚，B 评级的是智利、英国、加拿大、芬兰、瑞士和瑞典。公共养老金水平最高的法国（57.4）获得了 C 级。日本（44.1）和中国（48.0）则是 D 级。① 根据 PSLI 和 GPI 报告，丹麦的养老金体系是全球最自由（右倾）的（两套评价体系下均是如此，仅限于被调查的国家）。在 IL（R）E 的图表中，丹麦几乎位于最右。荷兰、加拿大、美国、澳大利亚的养老金体系都很自由，位于 PSLI 图标的右端。我们或许可以据此总结出一个规律：政府对经济干预较少的国家，养老金体系也更加自由。

联合国从 2011 年起发布养老金可持续指数（PSI），评估养老金体系长期的财务可持续性，以及在此基础上各国进行养老金改革的需求。这项指数对 54 个国家进行了评分，满分为 10，代表该国的改革需求最小，最低分为 1，表示该国政府迫切需要改革。2016 年得分前五的国家分别是澳大利亚（8.08）、丹麦（7.93）、瑞典（7.81）、荷兰（7.75）和挪威（7.59）。美国（7.23）、智利（7.23）和英国（7.20）分列第十名至第十二名。显然，在 PSLI 指数中排名靠前的国家，在 PSI 上也名列前茅。

全球年龄观察指数（Global Age Watch Index，GAWI）会根据四项指标（财务状况、健康水平、个人潜力和有利条件）评估养老金领取者的经济和健康状况。按照 GAWI 的报

---

① Melbourne Mercer Global Pension Index（2016）[http：//www. globalpensionin-dex. com；son baxılma-oktyabr 2016].

告，排名前十的国家分别是瑞士、挪威、瑞典、德国、加拿大、荷兰、冰岛、日本、美国和英国。① 进入 GAWI 指数前十甚至前五的，既包含经济左倾国，也包含经济右倾国。排名第一的瑞士，私人养老金体系的份额占比达到了 71%。

PSLI 与其他指数有许多不同之处。GPI 评估的是退休后的收入水平、养老金体系的可持续性和私人养老金对养老金收入的贡献；PSI 评估的是养老金体系的财务可持续性；GAWI 评估的是养老金领取者的财务状况。而 PSLI 则旨在计算养老金体系的自由主义程度，评估各国社会经济发展在养老金体系中扮演的角色。

四　自由化的决定因素

当然，养老金体系的形成与发展不单单由自由—干预主义的程度决定，还会受到人口、经济和社会因素等其他许多方面的影响（见表1）。

表1　　　　　　　　　自由化的决定因素

人口因素	经济因素	社会因素
人口老龄化 人口自然增长下降 预期寿命增长 移民进程等	经济增长 资本积累 投资潜力 股市活动 税收自由化 保险体系 ……	养老金领取者的收入 总养老金替代率 健康程度 贫困程度 ……

---

① Global Age Watch Index, 2015.

五　人口因素

在本项研究中，人口因素指的是人口老龄化、自然增长下降、预期寿命增长和移民进程等。按照联合国专家的分类，如果某国或地区 65 岁及以上人口的比例只有 4% 或更少，则该国为年轻型社会，4%—7% 的为成年型社会，7% 及以上的为老年型社会。① 全球大部分国家的人口年龄构成都会在 21 世纪发生巨大的变化。联合国的数据显示，2015 年，全球老年人（65 岁及以上）占总人口的比例为 12.2%。按照预测，到 2050 年，这一比例将提高到 16.0%，到 2100 年，将提高到 22.7%。2015 年，劳动年龄人口占总人口比例最高的国家是摩尔多瓦（74.3%）和中国（73.2%）。到 2100 年，相应的比例都会下滑，例如，摩尔多瓦和中国的数据会变为 57.9% 和 52.8%。2100 年劳动年龄人口占总人口比例最低的国家将是新加坡（49.0%）。②

人口结构的改变会在退休年龄人口与劳动年龄人口的比值上有所体现。图 5 的数据是截至 2100 年，针对退休年龄人口与劳动年龄人口比值的预测。这些预测让我们意识到：养老金体系在未来将出现严重问题。正如图 5 所示，到 2100 年，全球大部分国家退休年龄人口与劳动年龄人口的比值都

---

① Muradov, Ş. M. , *Müasir dünyada və Azərbaycanda gedən demoqrafik dəyişikliklər: əsas meyillər və problemlər.* – Müasir mərhələdə Azərbaycanda demoqrafik inkişafın, məşğulluq və işsizliyin sosial-iqtisadi problemləri, Elmi-praktik konfransın materialları. – Bakı, 2003, s. 6 – 13.

② UN World Population Prospects, 2015.

将上升。最高的三个国家将是新加坡（82.3%）、阿尔巴尼亚（72.6%）和韩国（71.5%）。

按照全球年龄观察指数的预测，60 岁及以上人口的比例到 2030 年将提高至 16.5%，到 2050 年将提高至 21.5%。[①]而在 2015 年，这一比例还只有 12.3%。从 2015 年到 2050 年，发达国家中 65 岁及以上人口与劳动年龄人口的比值将出现飙升，德国将从 32.2% 提高至 58.5%，日本将从 43.4% 提高至 70.0%，美国将从 21.4% 提高至 36.5%。但这一趋势不仅限于发达国家，正如前文所述，全球大部分国家的政府都将面临类似情况。例如，同期格鲁吉亚的比值也从 20.4% 提高至 42.8%，阿塞拜疆的比值则从 7.8% 提高至 26.3%（见图 5）。

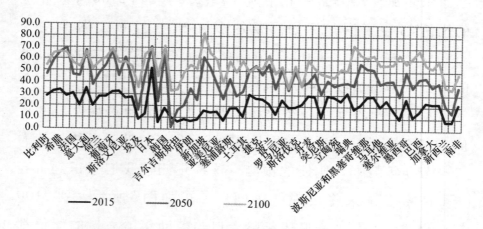

图 5　65 岁及以上人口与劳动年龄人口（15—64 岁）的比值

（2015 年，62 个国家，%）

资料来源：联合国世界人口展望，2015 年。

---

① Global Age Watch Index, 2015.

按照联合国的分类，阿塞拜疆属于成年型社会，2015 年
65 岁及以上人口的比例为 5.6% 。然而不久以后，该国就将
进入老年型社会的大名单。预计到 2020 年，相应比例就会提
高至 7.35% ，到 2050 年提高至 16.95% ，到 2100 年提高至
23.9% 。此外，劳动年龄人口的占比也逐渐萎缩，从 2015 年
的 72.5% 下降到 2100 年的 60% 。这些数据都表明政府的社
会负担将日益加重。①

　　当然，这是一个十分严重的变化。未来每个老年人对应
的劳动人口数量减少，意味着社会负担会进一步加重。为了
应对这一趋势，政府需要削减养老金成本，或被迫延迟退休
年龄。② 因此，发达国家和发展中国家需要特别关注养老金政
策制定和发展的要素。我们观察到阿塞拜疆出现了类似的趋
势，因此养老金体系的自由化改革势在必行。

六　经济因素

　　在本文中，影响养老金体系的经济因素包括：经济增长、
资本积累、投资潜力、股市活动、税收自由化和保险体系等。
　　在其他条件（如退休年龄）不变的情况下，要满足养老
金的供给，政府要么增加社会保险的缴纳额，要么减少养老
金发放额。这两种手段，尤其是减少养老金发放，在政治上

①　UN World Population Prospects, 2015.
②　Bonoli, G., *The Politics of Pension Reform*: *Institutions and Policy Change in Western Europe*, Cambridge University Press, 2000 [http://assets.cambridge.org//97805217/72327/sample/9780521772327ws.pdf; son baxılma-mart 2017].

很不受欢迎，所有政府都会试图避免。有时候"社会税"，即强制缴纳的社会保险，会因为商业的发展而有所增加，但这起不到太大效果，经济发展也可能因此受到拖累。

在这种情况下，所有社会团体可以接受的解决方案就是在国有养老金体系之外，再建立非政府的养老金体系。此外，雇主和员工也可以自愿投资私人养老基金，这会让养老基金获得更多募资机会，并间接让企业家获益。发达国家的经验表明，非政府养老金体系的构建（建立私人养老基金）对投资环境的复苏乃至整体经济的发展起到了重要作用。实际上，在一些国家，私人养老基金的资产甚至超过了 GDP。非政府养老金保障对促进国家经济发展、减轻政府社会负担、进一步增加投保员工数量、阻止高端人才离开大型企业有着重要的作用。

尽管早在 1875 年，美国就诞生了第一份非政府的养老金计划，但这类基金直到第二次世界大战之后才开始在西欧国家蓬勃发展。目前，根据全球（政府和私人）养老基金的水平，13 个国家和地区（澳大利亚、巴西、加拿大、法国、德国、中国香港、爱尔兰、日本、荷兰、南非、瑞士、英国、美国）被确定为最大的养老金市场，它们有时被称为"P13"。在一些报告中，这些国家里尤为突出的 7 个（澳大利亚、加拿大、日本、荷兰、瑞士、英国、美国）又被称为"P7"。

在全球金融市场中，养老基金（尤其是私人养老基金）也扮演了特殊的角色。2015 年，P7 国家对私人养老基金的总投资超过了 31.32 万亿美元，其中投资最多的是美国

（23.85 万亿美元）。一旦国家为私人养老基金营造了适宜的
环境，资本就会闻风而动。2005—2015 年，美国、荷兰和英
国的私人养老基金投资数额分别增加了 1.6 倍、1.8 倍和
1.6 倍。

如前文所述，在那些养老金体系比较自由的国家，非政
府养老基金的投资数额很高，在一些国家（美国、澳大利亚、
荷兰、加拿大和瑞士）甚至超过了 GDP。下面的图 6 显示了
P7 国家的 PSLI 在 2005 年、2010 年和 2015 年的变化。由于
缺乏私人养老基金投资数额的统计数据，我们没有计算日本
的情况，表中也不包含日本的信息。

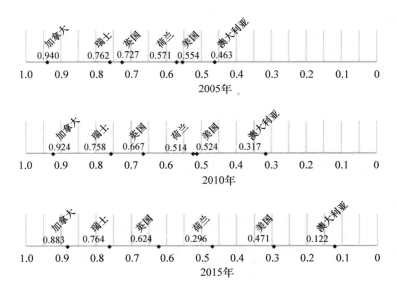

图 6　PSLI 指数（P7 国家，2005 年、2010 年和 2015 年）
资料来源：根据 2016 年 OECD 数据进行计算的结果。

从图 6 中我们可以发现，2005—2015 年，P7 国家的养老

金体系在不断自由化。2005 年，澳大利亚的 PSLI 是 0.463，在 2015 年已经降到了 0.122。同期美国从 0.554 降到了 0.471，英国从 0.727 降到了 0.624，加拿大从 0.940 降到了 0.883，只有瑞士从 0.762 上升至 0.764。不过，瑞士的左倾并不持久，我们观察发现从 2011—2012 年开始，瑞士又开始了右倾。

如前文所述，私人养老基金的投资在国家的经济发展中起到了重要的作用。图 7 展示了美国 GDP 和私人养老基金投资的关系。

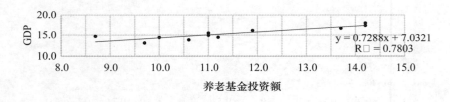

图 7　美国 GDP 和私人养老基金投资的关系

（2005—2015 年，十亿美元）

从图 7 中我们可以发现，美国的 GDP 和私人养老基金投资的关系很大（r = 0.8833）。

有趣的是，拥有养老基金资产的那些国家都是进行了右倾（自由化）改革的国家。我们可以将此解读为：政府对养老金体系的干预越少，养老金机构的发展就越好。养老基金更多的那些国家拥有更多私人机构。例如，2011 年，私人机构在英国的份额为 89%，在澳大利亚的份额为 86%，在美国的份额为 72%，在瑞士的份额为 71%，在荷兰的份额为 70%。

　　在美国和英国，2015 年非政府养老基金投资与 GDP 的比值相应为 79.4% 和 97.4%。在德国（6.6%）、法国（0.6%）等政府养老基金占据统治地位的国家，养老资产与 GDP 的比值都不足 10%（见图 8）。

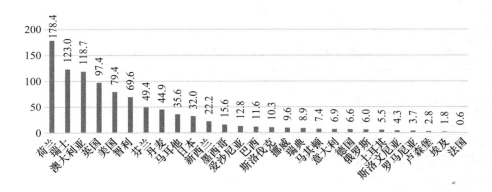

图 8　私人养老基金投资与 GDP 的比值

（2015 年，27 个国家，%）

资料来源：根据 2016 年 OECD 数据进行计算的结果。

　　如前文所述，除了私人养老基金之外，还有一些通过各种金融工具募集的养老基金。与私人养老基金一起，它们能够提供更多资金。例如，通过多种金融工具募集的私人养老基金投资与 GDP 的比值在丹麦是 205.9%，在荷兰是 178.4%，在冰岛是 157.2%，在加拿大是 156.9%，在美国是 132.9%。

七　社会因素

　　养老金体系自由化的社会因素包括养老金领取者的收入、健康程度、贫困程度等。

　　为了描绘养老金领取者的社会地位，我们会使用一系列
指标。通常这些指标包括养老金领取者劳动期间积累的平均
养老金财富，以及养老金的水平（包括相对表现），这与养
老金领取者的贫困程度相关。表 2 列出了养老金领取者在劳
动期间积累的平均养老金财富。

表 2　　　　平均养老金财富（2015 年，25 个国家，千美元）

国家	男性	女性
澳大利亚	802	856
奥地利	539	598
比利时	401	462
加拿大	357	400
智利	100	101
捷克	128	148
丹麦	943	1054
爱沙尼亚	120	152
芬兰	520	618
法国	435	522
德国	467	544
希腊	249	281
匈牙利	131	154
冰岛	601	668
爱尔兰	336	379
以色列	398	427
意大利	454	518
日本	371	426
韩国	253	296
卢森堡	1015	1170
墨西哥	42	44

国家	男性	女性
荷兰	1083	1248
新西兰	428	483
挪威	863	1000
波兰	88	104

资料来源：OECD——养老金概览（2015 年）。

　　在那些数字很大的国家（荷兰、卢森堡和丹麦），养老金体系的自由化程度都更高。平均养老金财富较多的国家，员工和雇主的社会保险费率都很低。丹麦为员工 2.7%，雇主 0；卢森堡为员工和雇主 11.0%；荷兰为员工 13.9%，雇主 9.7%。养老金体系较为自由的其他一些国家的社会保险费率也较低，例如，美国为员工 5.1%，雇主 8.9%；澳大利亚为 0 和 5.6%；爱尔兰为 0.4% 和 7.2%；智利为 7.0% 和 0；瑞士均为 5.9%；新西兰均为 0。相反，公共养老金占比很高的国家，社会保险费率也都很高。法国为 9.5% 和 30.6%，德国为 17.3% 和 16.4%，意大利为 7.2% 和 24.3%。[①]

　　描绘养老金领取者的社会地位的核心指标之一，就是总养老金替代率（养老金和每月平均工资的比值）。

　　2014 年各国的总养老金替代率如下：荷兰为 90.5%，丹麦为 67.8%，加拿大为 36.7%，美国为 35.2%，日本为 35.1%，而总养老金替代率最高的国家为印度（96.5%）。

---

　　① OECD, *Taxing Wages* – 2011 – 2012. – OECD, 2013 ［http：//www.keepeek.com//Digital-Asset-Management/oecd/taxation/taxing-wages – 2013_ tax_ wages – 2013 – en# page18；son baxılma – sentyabr 2016］.

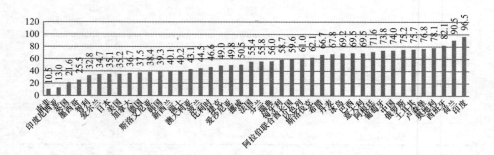

图 9　总养老金替代率（养老金和每月平均工资的比值）

（2014 年，42 个国家，男性，%）

资料来源：2014 年 OECD 数据。

　　显然，养老金的相对水平（尤其是替代率这个指标）和养老金体系的自由程度之间关联性不强。换句话说，养老金的相对水平在养老金体系自由化很高的国家也可以很低，在公共养老金占比很高的国家也可以很高。

　　养老金领取者社会地位的另一个指标是贫困程度。图 10 展现了一些国家养老金领取者的贫困程度。

　　在这些国家中，2014 年养老金领取者贫困率最高的是韩国（48.8%）。这项指标在以色列是 22.6%，澳大利亚是 25.7%，美国是 21.0%，日本是 19.0%，智利是 15.0%，英国是 13.5%，德国是 8.5%，加拿大是 6.2%，挪威是 4.3%，法国是 3.5%，荷兰是 2.2%。正如前文所述，养老金领取者的贫困率与养老金体系的自由化程度关联不大：无论一国的养老金体系是左倾还是右倾，都不太能够影响养老金领取者的贫困程度。不过，养老金领取者贫困率最低的国家是荷兰，那里的养老金体系自由化程度更高。

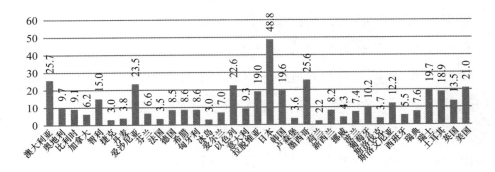

图 10   65 岁及以上（退休年龄）人口的贫困程度

（2014 年，35 个国家，%）

资料来源：OECD 收入分布数据库。

同样的情况在养老金收入与总收入的比例上也有体现。例如，在 65 岁及以上老年人的收入结构中，养老金的占比可能很高或很低，与养老金体系主要是国有或私人（也就是养老金体系左倾或右倾）关系不大。2015 年，这个比例在法国是 100.0%，在美国是 92.1%，在加拿大是 91.6%，在荷兰是 87.3%，在德国是 86.9%。

多种因素导致阿塞拜疆的养老金体系亟须自由化，其中人口老龄化、国家的社会负担加重和养老金领取者的生活水平较低是最重要的几大原因。有趣的一点在于，阿塞拜疆的邻国（吉尔吉斯斯坦、格鲁吉亚、亚美尼亚）经济更弱，却拥有非国有养老金体系。

八　结论

全球范围内，人口老龄化的进程正在持续，老年人的养老金需求有所增加，每位养老金领取者对应的劳动人口数量有所减少，国家的社会负担十分沉重。基于上述原因，有必要进行养老金体系的自由化改革。阿塞拜疆的人口也有老龄化的趋势，不久之后，这一趋势还会逐渐加速。

政府可以通过直接或间接方法（如鼓励私人养老金体系的构建）调控养老金体系，也可以通过这种方式增强养老金领取者享有的社会保障。

多种因素导致阿塞拜疆的养老金体系亟须自由化，其中人口老龄化、国家的社会负担加重和养老金领取者的生活水平较低是最重要的几大原因。

因此，行政改革（延迟退休年龄、增加社保缴纳）无法满足政府或人民（尤其是养老金领取者）的需求。在阿塞拜疆，养老金保障完全由政府承担（完全左倾的体系），它需要部分自由化（右倾）。PSLI 的初步结果也支持这一结论。

"一带一路"建设与中国—阿塞拜疆经贸合作

裴长洪[*]

中阿关系自建立外交关系后发展平稳，双方高层访问不断，政治互信不断加强，经贸合作稳步推进。目前，中国已成为阿塞拜疆第 5 大贸易伙伴和第 3 大进口来源国。合作领域从单纯进出口贸易扩大到油气开发、建材生产、信息通信、农业养殖等领域。阿政府和舆论普遍认为，中国"一带一路"倡议的提出，为阿塞拜疆等沿线传统能源国家经济转型提供了难得的历史机遇，阿方积极响应并参与。因此，深入研究在"一带一路"合作框架下发展中阿经济贸易合作关系，具有互利共赢的积极意义。

一 世界直接投资的变化与中国
对外直接投资的增长

2007 年是世界直接投资流入量的最高年份，达到 1.97

---

* 裴长洪，中国社会科学院经济研究所研究员。

万亿美元，国际金融危机发生后，处于下降阶段，2011 年有所回升后又处于下滑期，2015 年回升到 1.8 万亿美元左右，2016 年又略有下降，2017 年略有回升。

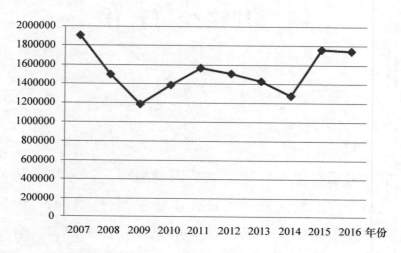

图 1　国际金融危机后世界对外直接投资额（流入量，百万美元）

联合国贸易和发展组织（以下简称"贸发组织"）2017 年 6 月 15 日发布的 2017 年《世界投资报告》（以下简称《报告》）称，全球外国直接投资（FDI）2016 年小幅下降 2%，至 1.75 万亿美元；2017 年将呈现温和复苏的势头，预计全球 FDI 流量增长 5%，达 1.8 万亿美元。2018 年将进一步增加到 1.85 万亿美元。

2000 年，中国政府提出了企业"走出去"战略，鼓励中国企业到海外投资。进入"十二五"期间，中国企业对外投资发展很快。2010 年中国对外直接投资为 688.1 亿美元，2013 年增加到 1078.4 亿美元（全行业），首次突破千亿美远大关。联合国贸易和发展会议《2017 年世界投资报告：投资和数字经济》称，2016 年亚洲发展中国家的外国直接投资流入量下降 15%，但中国以 1830 亿美元的对外直接投资总额首次成为全球第二大投资国。

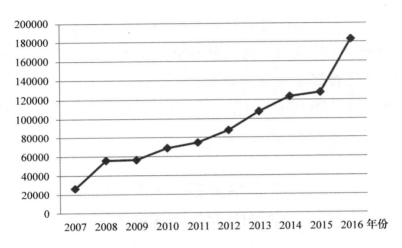

图 2　中国对外直接投资额（流出量，百万美元）

据商务部和外汇局统计，2016 年中国企业对外直接投资 1832 亿美元，连续第二年位列世界第二，其中非金融类对外直接投资 1701 亿美元。中国对外投资的快速发展不仅惠及中国企业，带动了中国相关产品、装备、技术、服务走出去，推动了国内经济转型升级，也惠及世界，有力促进了世界经济和东道国的经济增长，实现了互利共赢、共同发展。据统计，2016 年，中国境外企业销售额 1.5 万亿美元，向所在国缴纳税费 400 亿美元，雇用外方员工 150 万人。2017 年上半年中国企业对外投资更趋理性。针对一些企业的非理性投资，政府有关部门开展了真实性、合规性审核，指导对外投资的企业增强风险防范意识，促进对外投资健康规范发展。因此，

上半年对外直接投资 3311 亿元（约合 509 亿美元），下降了
42.9%，非理性对外投资得到有效遏制。从对外投资的国别
看，中国企业对"一带一路"沿线国家投资下降比较少，总
的对外投资下降 42.9%，但对"一带一路"沿线国家仅下降
了 3.6%，低于总体对外投资的降幅。从投资结构上看，企
业更加重视实体投资，对境外制造业投资降幅要小于对房地
产、文化体育娱乐产业的投资。一批并购项目顺利实施，特
别是大的并购项目还是比较顺利的。此外，中国对外承包工
程完成营业额 4622 亿元，增长了 7.2%。

二 中国企业在"一带一路"建设中对外投资情况

现阶段中国企业在"一带一路"沿线的投资中，国企、
央企是投资的主力军和领头羊，"开拓产品和业务的国际市
场、占领当地市场、提高全球市场份额、增加盈利能力"等
市场因素是企业"一带一路"沿线投资的第一大动因，政府
政策位居其次。随着"一带一路"倡议的落实，越来越多的
国内企业参与到"一带一路"沿线国家的投资当中，由于
"一带一路"沿线相关国家投资企业以国企为主，企业来源
地也主要集中在国内一线大城市。①

"一带一路"沿线各区域经济发展程度和社会文化具有多
样性，与中国在空间距离和国际关系方面也不尽相同，这些

---

① 国内对外直接投资额前 10 个省份为广东、北京、上海、山东、江苏、浙江、辽
宁、天津、湖南、云南。

直接影响到了中国对沿线国家投资的区位选择。根据商务部相关数据显示，2016 年，中国企业共对"一带一路"沿线的 53 个国家进行非金融类直接投资 145.3 亿美元，同比下降 2%；在"一带一路"沿线 61 个国家新签对外承包工程项目合同 8158 份，新签合同额 1260.3 亿美元，同比增长 36%；完成营业额 759.7 亿美元，同比增长 9.7%。

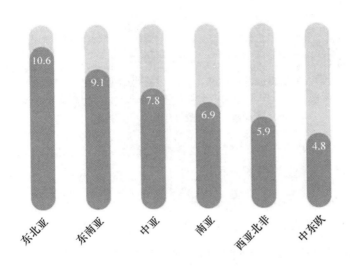

图 3　中国企业与"一带一路"各区域投资
合作指标平均得分情况（满分为 12 分）

资料来源：公开资料整理。

"一带一路"相关国家要素禀赋存在较大差异，与中国经济互补程度不同，中国对沿线国家直接投资的产业领域也呈现异质性。能源是中国对"一带一路"相关国家直接投资规模最大、最为重要的产业领域；交通运输也具有重要地位，其投资规模仅次于能源类投资；此外，作为信息基础设施建设的一部分，电信等技术类投资也是中国对"一带一路"相关国家直接投资较为重要的产业领域之一。

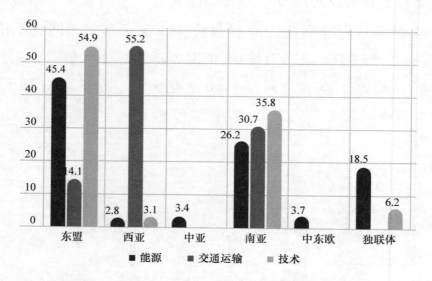

图 4　中国对"一带一路"沿线各类直接投资的区位结构分析（%）

资料来源：公开资料整理。

　　在中国企业"走出去"取得成功的同时，中国企业遭遇
到的阻碍也在大幅增加。自 2016 年 1 月至 2017 年 3 月，针
对中国企业或可能对中国企业产生影响的贸易救济调查达
215 起，包括反倾销、反补贴、双反、反规避、保障措施。
从争议解决看，有 31% 的被访者提及企业在"走出去"过程
中曾遭遇程序诉讼或处罚，其中以遭遇民事诉讼和仲裁的企
业较多。纠纷所涉领域主要为采购合同、销售合同纠纷。涉
案最大标的在 500 万元以下以及 1 亿元以上区间的最多。诉
讼费用在 10 万—50 万元的最多。诉讼和仲裁的结果以和解、
调解居多。此外值得关注的是，由于"一带一路"沿线国家
多为发展中国家，发展阶段差异巨大，国情复杂多样，在为

中国投资者提供广阔空间的同时，也加大了中国企业在海外投资、运营过程中的潜在风险。相关调查结果显示，近四成受访者认为投资过程中遇到的主要困难是政治不稳定、恐怖主义、战争、内乱、军事冲突等。

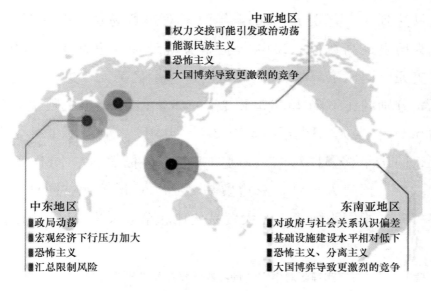

图5　2017年中国企业在"一带一路"

相关地区需关注的风险

资料来源：公开资料整理。

随着"一带一路"建设的深入推进，中国企业也将更多地参与到国际规则的运用中。相关配套措施，包括区域投资争端解决机制的设立、投资争端解决规则及程序的指引、双边投资保护协定的完善等将成为政府及相关机构的重点工作之一。

三 中国与阿塞拜疆经济贸易关系发展回顾

2000 年中阿两国双边贸易额接近 1 亿美元，2003 年两国贸易额达到 2 亿多美元。联合国贸发会议统计，2010 年两国贸易达到 8.3 亿美元。2014 年两国双边贸易达到 9 亿美元，成为历史最高数值。2014 年据中方统计，双边贸易额达 9.4 亿美元，同比下降 16%。中国出口 6.4 亿美元、进口 3 亿美元，分别同比下降 25.8% 和增长 3.9%；2015 年中阿贸易额达 6.66 亿美元，同比下降 29.3%。其中，对阿出口 4.4 亿美元，同比下降 31.7%。自阿进口 2.26 亿美元，同比下降 24.2%。据阿方统计，双边贸易额达 7.6 亿美元，同比下降 14.3%，中国为阿第十三大贸易伙伴和第五大进口来源国。

表 1   阿塞拜疆对中国和世界的货物贸易进出口总量

单位：千美元

年份	阿塞拜疆向中国出口	阿塞拜疆总出口	阿塞拜疆向中国进口	阿塞拜疆总进口
2010	252314.3	26476026	587618.7	6596797
2011	135397.4	34494900	628250.2	9732869
2012	243954.8	32634038	631856.1	9641724
2013	188286	31702945	568160.1	10763392
2014	206322.3	28259629	697079.6	9178588
2015	148678.8	15586052	512505.3	9211126
2016	51995.14	10900000	468875.5	8670511

资料来源：UNCTAD 数据库。

　　据阿塞拜疆海关统计，阿塞拜疆对华出口商品主要有矿物燃料、塑料及其制品、化学产品、铜及其制品、皮革、矿砂等，自华进口商品主要有机械器具及零件、服装及衣着附件、电气和音像设备、家具、灯具、车辆及其零附件等。据联合国贸发会议统计的贸易结构主要见表2和表3。

表2　　　　　　　　　阿塞拜疆对中国货物贸易出口结构　　　　单位：千美元

年份	初级产品	化学产品	机械和交通装备	其他工业产品
2010	240175	11836	162	141
2011	100416	34162	573	246
2012	219355	23886	599	115
2013	142677	43730	1100	780
2014	133719	67034	59	5511
2015	112356	34764	70	1489
2016	32596	18192	182	1024

　　资料来源：UNCTAD 数据库。

表3　　　　　　　　　中国对阿塞拜疆货物贸易出口结构　　　　单位：千美元

年份	初级产品	化学产品	机械和交通装备	其他工业产品
2010	10379	5995	228490	601291
2011	11874	7059	298463	575155
2012	13405	17695	514185	524543
2013	18186	21832	353505	475046
2014	17755	16774	297180	312216
2015	10728	13441	165607	250095
2016	8001	7969	149518	185898

　　资料来源：UNCTAD 数据库。

据阿塞拜疆经济部统计，2016 年阿中双边贸易大幅度增长了 73%，达到 9.7 亿美元，其中阿从中国进口 7.39 亿美元，增长 38%；阿对中国出口 2.7 亿美元，增长 4 倍，主要还是石油和天然气。2017 年上半年中阿进出口贸易达到 6.7 亿美元，其中从中国进口 3.35 亿美元，对中国出口 3.4 亿美元，贸易差额显著改善。阿塞拜疆对华出口商品主要有矿物燃料、塑料及其制品、化学产品、皮革、饮料及酒类等；自华进口商品主要有机械器具及零件、服装及衣着附件、电器和音像设备、车辆及其零附件、家具、灯具等。

2001 年中国石油企业开始与阿进行能源开发合作，截至 2016 年年底中国对阿非金融类直接投资累计 7.12 亿美元。其中 6.15 亿美元集中在油气、工程承包等领域，主要有中石油、中国建材、中材建设、四川机械、沈阳远大幕墙等公司承建的 K&K 油田开采、水泥厂、电解铝厂、巴库新月宫幕墙等项目。

表 4   中国对世界及阿塞拜疆直接投资流量（2007—2015）

单位：百万美元

国家或地区	2007	2008	2009	2010	2011	2012	2013	2014	2015
总计	26506	55907	56529	68811	74654	87804	107844	123120	145667
阿塞拜疆	-1.15	-0.66	1.73	0.37	17.68	0.34	-4.43	16.83	1.36

资料来源：2015 年度中国对外直接投资统计公报。

根据联合国贸发会议统计，2011 年至 2016 年 6 年间，阿塞拜疆每年吸收的外国直接投资分别为：14.65 亿美元，

20.05 亿美元，26.32 亿美元，44.30 亿美元，40.48 亿美元，45 亿美元。当然也主要集中在油气产业领域。中国的非油气企业的投资也有很成功的案例，如华为公司作为中国国内国产品牌，很多年的努力之后，在阿塞拜疆国内的电信市场中占据着很大的份额。

表5　　　　阿塞拜疆吸收外资和对外投资流量（2011—2016）

单位：百万美元

Region/ economy	FDI inflow						FDI outflow					
	2011	2012	2013	2014	2015	2016	2011	2012	2013	2014	2015	2016
阿塞拜疆	1465	2005	2632	4430	4048	4500	533	1192	1490	3230	3260	2574

资料来源：《世界投资报告2017》。

从阿塞拜疆国内的经济战略来看，经过国际金融危机后，世界经济对油气需求下降，阿塞拜疆油气出口锐减，经济增长下降，贸易赤字带来国际收支问题，本币贬值，人民生活水平没有提高。2013 年子承父业的新总统提出了发展非石油工业，转变经济结构的雄心勃勃的计划，但几年来成效甚少，外国投资在这方面也难有大的作为。因此亟希望"一带一路"建设项目能够帮助该国实现经济结构转型的经济战略目标。

2015 年 4 月，阿塞拜疆成为亚投行创始成员国，7 月成为上海合作组织对话伙伴国。2015 年 12 月，伊利哈姆·阿利耶夫总统成功访华，与习近平主席共同见证签署两国共建"一带一路"合作备忘录，为双边关系发展开辟了新的广阔前景。在"一带一路"建设中，阿塞拜疆积极促进本国 2020 年发展战略与"一带一路"建设的对接，希望能在基础设施互联互通方面加强合作。主要包括：（1）加强信息互联互通。阿塞拜疆早在 2012 年提出要建设欧亚大陆信息联通公路，这个建议引起欧盟和联合国的重视。（2）加强运输联通。阿塞拜疆希望发挥欧亚大陆桥的作用，将正在建设的巴库—第比利斯—卡尔斯铁路与欧洲和亚洲连通起来。2015 年 8 月 3 日，国际跨里海运输路线上的"中国—阿克套（哈萨克斯坦）—阿拉特"集装箱列车在巴库国际海港上行驶。巴库将充分提高里海的过货能力，成为连接欧亚大陆的枢纽地区。阿方希望中方能帮助巴库港进行现代化的改造，投资兴建港口的基础设施建设和联通欧亚大陆的铁路。（3）加强农业、旅游合作。阿塞拜疆国内耸立着著名的山脉高加索山，从山下到顶峰，分布着各个气候带，因此，农业和旅游资源非常丰富。阿方希望引进中国的农产品种类和农产品加工机械以及用于农业生产的高科技。高加索和里海旅游资源尚待深入开发，未来均具有良好的合作空间。发展农业和旅游业同时可提高非石油经济领域在国民经济中的占比。（4）发挥巴库港的地缘战略优势和地理空间优势，将巴库港打造为国际五星级的交通枢纽，正在建设的巴库国际海上贸易港口位于卡拉达赫区阿拉特镇。2016 年贸易港口吞吐量为 27000 个集装箱，或 600 万吨国际 TEU 当量。2020 年建成后，贸易港的吞吐量将达到 2500 万吨。阿方希望中国帮助在巴库新港建立自贸区，辐射周边国家，未来建立像深圳那样的工业区和自贸区；成为出口加工区，重要的过境点，并提高产品的附加值，进行产品再加工生产。（5）加强两国工业区的合作。访阿期间，代表团赴卡拉达赫区参观，它是首都巴库市的 12 个行政区之一，占首都领土面积的 51.3%，属于国家直属区。区域面积为 1080 平方千米，里海滨海沿线长度为 106 千米。卡拉达赫区也是阿塞拜疆的主要工业中心。该地区有 90 多个工业企业，其中大型工业企业 22 家。该地区工业企业的主要活动是石油和天然气生产，建筑材料，包括石材的建设和生产。2016 年 3 月 17 日，阿塞拜疆共和国总统签署了一项行政命令，建立一个自由贸易区和特别行政经济区，并将其授予卡拉达赫区管辖。自贸区将覆盖 40 平方千米土地面积，包括上述巴库国际海港的一部分。目前这个工业区首要任务是招商引资，同时希望建成中白工业园区那样的园区。

四　阿塞拜疆在"一带一路"建设中的战略意义与战略构想

（一）战略意义

首先，从地理位置上看，阿塞拜疆处于连接欧亚大陆南线（北线为目前中欧班列经过的哈萨克斯坦和俄罗斯至欧洲的路线）的中心地位，是中国制造业产品深耕国际市场的潜在基地。该国北连俄罗斯，隔里海与哈萨克斯坦、土库曼各港口衔接，西接格鲁吉亚通黑海港口，南接伊朗通土耳其和中东各国，是欧亚大陆南线交通通道的重要枢纽点。2015 年 8 月 3 日来自中国的第一列试运行集装箱列车到达巴库国际商业海港；随后，阿塞拜疆、哈萨克斯坦、格鲁吉亚和乌克兰四国签署了货物运输优惠价格协议；2016 年 6 月 1 日起，里海国际运输路线还实行了新的竞争性关税。

其次，阿塞拜疆油气资源极为丰富，可以成为中国油气进口的来源地之一。目前已探明石油储量约 20 亿吨，地质储量约 40 亿吨，且石油埋藏浅，杂质少，易于开采和后期综合利用。天然气资源探明储量 2.55 万亿立方米，远景储量达到 6 万亿立方米，是外高加索三国中资源禀赋最为优越的国家。除了油气资源，阿塞拜疆毗邻里海，渔业和农业资源也较为丰富。

再次，中阿在"一带一路"建设中的利益公约数愈大，愈有利于中国在世界经济政治外交上的主动。由于资源丰富，阿塞拜疆长期以来被视为欧洲解决被俄罗斯能源反制困境的关键国家，也正因为如此，俄罗斯、美国对阿塞拜疆的争夺十分激烈。阿塞拜疆与亚美尼亚的"纳卡"问题久拖不决，其实质就是俄美两国有意制造的可控混乱。阿塞拜疆尽管奉行平衡外交，但由于其在纳卡地区的惨痛教训，以及保持经济、政治独立的意愿，阿塞拜疆与西方的联系始终处于不断加强之中。为了避免俄罗斯对自身石油资源的控制，阿塞拜疆与土耳其、格鲁吉亚、哈萨克斯坦等国合作修建了绕开俄罗斯的巴库—第比利斯—杰汉伊（BTC）石油管道，从根本上打破了俄罗斯对中亚石油资源的垄断。让阿塞拜疆在"一带一路"建设项目中得到经济上的实惠，弱化其向西靠拢的经济预期，并缓解俄罗斯对其西向发展的不满，这对于保持该地区和平稳定发展，增强中国在该地区的影响力，具有重要作用和示范效应。

最后，密切中阿关系有利于建立国际统一战线，遏制和打击中国新疆"东突"分裂势力。阿塞拜疆是伊斯兰教国家，阿语属于突厥语系，与土耳其和整个伊斯兰教世界都有密切关系，同时其世俗化程度又很高，更便于建立经济贸易和文化交流关系。中国新疆维吾尔族在土耳其有20万左右的移民，在阿塞拜疆也有少量移民，这是国内"东突"分裂势力在国外藏身和培植的土壤。密切中阿经济贸易关系，不仅有利于与阿塞拜疆建立反恐和反分裂的国际联系，而且还可以通过阿国的影响与其他国家建立相同的联系，彻底切断"东突"分裂势力的国际渠道。

（二）基本战略构想

第一，使中国成为阿塞拜疆重要油气出口市场，实现其出口市场多元化目标，弱化俄、欧两方对其油气出口的争夺。

自2006年巴库—第比利斯—杰汉伊（BTC）石油管线开通以来，阿塞拜疆逐渐以此通道向欧洲出口石油，年出口量已经达到5000万吨以上，使得巴库—新罗西斯克这条经俄罗斯出口的管道形同虚设。在2011年，欧盟为了解决俄罗斯的天然气限制措施，进一步强化了与阿塞拜疆的合作，提出了南方天然气走廊计划。希望通过建设从土耳其—保加利亚—罗马尼亚—匈牙利—奥地利的纳布科天然气管道、希腊—阿尔巴尼亚—意大利的TAP跨亚德里亚海天然气管道、格鲁吉亚—乌克兰的白溪管道、土耳其—希腊—意大利的ITGI管道。该计划一旦实施，将对俄罗斯的能源霸权构成毁灭性的打击，也引起了俄罗斯的强烈反应，并耗费巨资、针锋相对地提出了南流计划。从目前的状况来看，南方天然气走廊管线体系已经初步形成，俄罗斯在外高加索地区能源竞争中将逐步处于被边缘化的状态。也正因为此，俄罗斯将会以何种方式惩罚阿塞拜疆，已经成为令人关注的问题。尽管，阿塞拜疆政府在近期通过参与莫斯科阅兵等方式频繁对俄罗斯示好，但从长远来看，阿塞拜疆在油、气、电上倒向西方已经不可避免。有观点认为，阿塞拜疆或迟或早将完全依赖于西方的军事保护，甚至成为北约的一员。因此，其石油、天然气出口的根本利益已成为其政治倾向的经济基础。

中国从阿塞拜疆进口石油天然气是有增长潜力的，要实现中国成为阿国重要出口市场的目标，未来中国进口阿国油气及其产品应占阿出口贸易总额的10％左右，这样才能夯实中阿经贸关系的基础。

第二，促进中国企业在阿投资非油气产业，既实现中国制造业产品深耕国际市场的目标，又助力阿经济结构转型。

中国已在白俄罗斯与白方共建中白工业园区，中方利益目标之一就是拓展中国产品进入欧洲和欧亚联盟的市场通道。作为丝绸之路南线的阿塞拜疆，其国内市场化程度高于白俄罗斯，劳动力价格也低于白俄罗斯，其1000千米的市场辐射范围覆盖东欧、中东和独联体许多国家。如果这里能够成为中国产品的加工和再加工基地，也同样有利于中国制造业产品的市场开发。因此应当促进中国企业对阿投资，特别是帮助阿塞拜疆兴建出口加工区和自由贸易区，利用阿方的要素禀赋优势和邻近中东、欧洲的地理区位，开拓国际市场，同时推进阿经济结构转型，发展非石油产业。

五　在"一带一路"框架下加强中阿经贸合作的战略措施

第一，从完善基础设施入手。与阿塞拜疆隔里海相望的哈萨克斯坦和土库曼，都有通往中国的油气管线，目前阿正在规划巴库新港口建设，中国企业可以通过参与新港口建设，增强阿港口石油天然气的存储容量和船舶公司的运输能力，与哈萨克斯坦和土库曼港口的铁路运输或油气管线对接，向中国输送石油天然气，形成阿国多元化国际能源营销格局。因此，应把巴库的新港口建设作为中国实现在阿塞拜疆"一带一路"建设的战略构想的首要项目。同时，把巴库作为中欧班列的重要站点。目前，义新欧班列已经有开行德黑兰的记录，开往巴库已经没有技术问题；郑欧班列也已经积累了大量的开行记录经验，开辟巴库站点也不存在技术困难，因此开行巴库班列的条件已经基本成熟，这就为运输物流的扩大创造了条件，也为贸易和生产扩大创造了条件。

第二，共商、共建中阿自由贸易区（实际是海关特殊监管的出口加工区）。目前，阿已经成立了由副总理牵头的阿拉特自由贸易区的筹划机构，规划工作已经进行。在距离巴库以南 70 千米左右的新区建设新港口和自由贸易区。阿迫切期待中国企业能够作为一级开发商介入开发并负责招商引资。中方应在详细可行性研究基础上回应阿方要求，积极介入该项目建设。由一些大型企业承担园区一级开发，实现"七通一平"，并采取更为优惠的措施吸引中国企业到阿塞拜疆投资，一方面实行进口替代的工业发展模式，阿塞拜疆每年要进口 100 亿美元以上的商品，主要进口商品是：机械和电子电气设备，汽车及配件，黑色金属和粮食，建筑材料，陶瓷产品等，逐步培育有竞争力的非石油工业产品，再逐步扩大出口；另一方面，在对比中欧班列更具有成本优势的条件下，鼓励中国出口欧洲产品的企业，在阿建立生产线和加工组装线，扩大对周边市场的出口。

第三，引进中国太阳能发电技术和投资。阿塞拜疆光照充足，气候干旱，有利于太阳能发电，中国太阳能发电设备和发电技术成熟，阿塞拜疆可以引进设备和技术进行太阳能发电，发展清洁能源，促进阿塞拜疆走能源利用多样化的发展路径。

第四，引进中国农业技术，开发节水农业。阿塞拜疆地处温带，人口密度小，可耕地资源相对丰富，人民也有长期耕作的传统。在此进行种植和畜牧业方面的投资，投资单位成本和风险都比较小。中阿两国应促进农业合作和技术交流，中国政府除每年在阿塞拜疆招收农业主管官员和技术专家进行交流考察外，还可以鼓励中国粮食生产和流通企业到阿进行农业投资。

第五，发展旅游服务贸易和基础设施。阿塞拜疆有独特的旅游资源和民俗文化，以及独特的气候条件，一方面可以鼓励旅游，另一方面还可以发展与旅游相结合的医疗康复等健康产业项目。应鼓励中国企业投资于酒店业、运输业以及健康产业等基础设施。

第六，建设中阿空中丝绸之路。空中丝绸之路是"一带一路"建设中基础设施联通的重要内容。中国与阿塞拜疆相隔几千公里，需要依靠空中丝绸之路拉近两国的距离，因此要多开辟两国城市间的空中航线，目前只有北京和乌鲁木齐有直飞巴库的航班，应至少增加到 5 个城市，同时要鼓励中国的航空公司安排飞往巴库的航班。

第七，加强两国学术与人文交流。鼓励两国自然科学和社会科学的交流合作、教育合作，除了在阿塞拜疆举办孔子学院外，中国也应有些高校举办中阿学院，以学习阿语和从事中阿经贸实务为主，两国互派留学生，互相交换访问学者应当纳入政府计划。

第八，共建中阿"一带一路"研究中心。在"一带一路"机遇中寻找两国合作发展的路径成为共同愿望，如何实现这个愿望，如何实现"共商、共建、共享"，应成为两国学者共同研究的课题，因此有必要成立由两国科学研究机构共同建立的研究中心，把"一带一路"框架下中阿经济贸易合作作为长期研究任务不断深入进行下去。

"十三五"期间中国经济发展的
主要趋势分析

常 欣*

"十三五"期间,中国经济发展的主要趋势包括两个大的方面:一是从经济增长率变化的趋势看,将继续沿着高速增长向中高速增长转换的路径发展。基于劳动供给、资本供给、资源环境约束和总和要素生产率变化所带来的供给面潜在增长率下降,并基于人口结构变化和居民资产再配置效应所带来的房地产市场变化和相应的有效需求不足及可能的负产出缺口,"十三五"期间的年均增长率将下降到6.5%左右。二是从经济结构调整的趋势看,在需求结构方面,针对内外需结构失衡以及内需中消费与投资比例关系失调的问题,将继续促进经济增长由主要依靠投资、出口拉动向依靠消费、投资、出口协调拉动转变;在产业结构方面,针对农业基础薄弱、工业大而不强、服务业发展滞后以及三大产业之间比例不合理的问题,将继续促进经济增长由主要依靠第二产业

---

* 常欣,中国社会科学院经济研究所研究员。

带动向依靠三大产业协同带动转变；在要素投入结构方面，针对全要素生产率增长对经济增长贡献较低的问题，将继续促进经济增长由主要依靠要素投入向主要依靠技术进步转变。

一　经济增长总体格局：从高速转向中高速

国际金融危机以来，中国经济增长速度总体上呈现持续放缓的态势，季度 GDP 增长率从 2007 年第二季度的 14.2%大幅下降至 2016 年第三季度的 6.7%（2016 年第四季度以来有所企稳）；年度 GDP 增长率也从 2007 年 14.2%的高位明显放缓至 2016 年的 6.7%（见图 1）。中国经济由过去的两位数高速增长转向低于 7%—8%的中高速增长，是长期增长趋势性因素和短期周期波动性因素相互叠加的结果，是供给面潜在增长率下降和需求面负的产出缺口（实际增长率低于潜

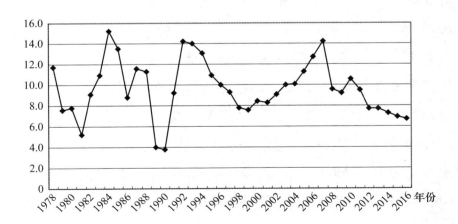

图 1　中国年度 GDP 增长率（%）

资料来源：国家统计局。

在增长率）相互交织的产物。预计整个"十三五"时期，这一态势仍可能持续。

（一）长期增长趋势性因素分析

从供给面潜在增长率下降层面看，与要素供给格局的阶段性改变密切相关。主要体现在以下几个方面。

1. 劳动力要素供给的变化

在过去若干年的时间里，由于快速的人口转变，劳动力绝对量持续大规模增长的势头出现调整。首先是新增劳动年龄人口数量经历急剧的下降，由 2006 年的 1491 万下降到 2007 年的 894 万，并由此开始呈现单调下降的趋势。"十二五"中期以来，劳动年龄人口的总量又出现拐点。2012 年 15—59 岁的劳动年龄人口比 2011 年减少 345 万，占总人口的比重为 69.2%，比 2011 年年末下降 0.6 个百分点。这是劳动年龄人口数量在相当长时期里第一次出现绝对下降。2013 年，16—59 岁劳动年龄人口[①]又较上年减少 244 万人，占总人口的比例为 67.6%，继续呈现双下降趋势。之后几年，劳动年龄人口净减少的趋势持续存在（见图 2）。

中国人口的结构性变化也使人口抚养比的走势出现扭转。2012 年开始，无论是总抚养比，还是少儿抚养比和老年抚养比，均停止不断下降的趋势，初步呈现出止跌向上的迹象（见图 3）。预计"十三五"期间，"人口红利"的衰减趋势

---

① 为了更好地与《劳动法》衔接，2013 年的《国民经济和社会发展统计公报》调整了人口年龄分组标准，其中，劳动年龄人口分组标准由原来的 15—59 岁修改为 16—59 岁。

仍可能持续，劳动力要素供给对经济增长的积极效应可能继续呈现减弱态势。

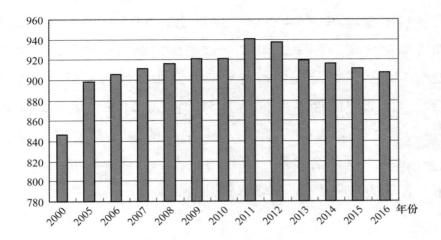

图 2　中国劳动年龄人口规模的变动（百万人）

资料来源：国家统计局。

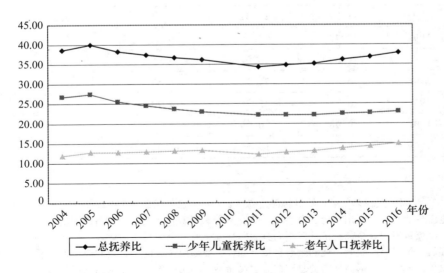

图 3　中国人口抚养比的变化情况（％）

资料来源：国家统计局。

2. 资本要素供给的变化

一直以来，中国都是一个高储蓄的国家。表 1 反映了 1992—2015 年中国的国民储蓄率和居民、企业和政府三大部门各自的储蓄率。① 从表中可以看出，2007—2011 年，国民储蓄率持续高于 50%，2012 年以来国内部门总储蓄率也大体处于 47.0%—49.5% 的较高水平（其中，政府部门、企业部门、居民部门的储蓄率分别为 5% 左右、20% 左右、25% 左右），远高于多数国家通常 20% 左右的国民储蓄率（见图 4），也高于以"高储蓄"著称的日本、韩国等东亚经济体的水平，成为世界上储蓄率最高的国家之一。

表 1　　　　　　　中国国民储蓄率与部门储蓄率：1992—2015　　　　　单位:%

年份	国民储蓄率	居民储蓄率	企业储蓄率	政府储蓄率
1992	40.29	21.08	13.33	5.89
1993	41.72	19.32	16.15	6.24
1994	42.73	21.49	16.02	5.22
1995	41.62	20.04	16.7	4.88
1996	40.32	21.32	13.57	5.43
1997	40.76	20.75	14.73	5.65
1998	39.98	20.39	14.33	5.27
1999	38.61	18.55	14.31	5.75

---

① 中国自 1992 年开始编制资金流量表，迄今已经编制出 1992—2015 年共 21 张资金流量表。这里利用资金流量表（实物交易）来计算国民储蓄率和各部门的储蓄率。在资金流量表中，全部经济部门被划分为非金融企业、金融机构、政府、居民和国外五个部门。可以将非金融企业和金融机构合并为企业部门。居民、企业和政府共同构成了国内部门。国内三部门储蓄的总和即为国民储蓄。国民储蓄与整个国内部门的可支配收入之比就是国民储蓄率。将各部门的储蓄与整个国民可支配收入相比，可以得出该部门的储蓄率。三大部门的储蓄率相加，即为国民储蓄率，即：国民储蓄率 = 居民储蓄率 + 企业储蓄率 + 政府储蓄率。

续表

年份	国民储蓄率	居民储蓄率	企业储蓄率	政府储蓄率
2000	37.6	21	17.9	-1.4
2001	38.5	20.6	18.9	-1.1
2002	40.2	20.3	19.3	0.6
2003	43.1	21.7	19.9	1.4
2004	45.7	20.6	22.5	2.6
2005	46.5	21.5	21.6	3.3
2006	48.2	22.4	21.5	4.2
2007	50.9	23.1	22.1	5.7
2008	51.9	23.3	22.7	5.9
2009	50.6	24.4	21.2	4.9
2010	51.8	25.4	21.2	5.2
2011	50.6	24.8	20	5.8
2012	49.5	25.2	18.5	5.8
2013	48.3	23.6	19.8	5
2014	49.1	23	20.5	5.6
2015	47.2	22.8	19.8	4.5

资料来源：根据相关年份《中国统计年鉴》有关数据计算得到。

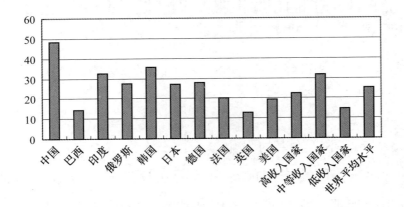

图4　国民储蓄率的国际比较（2015，%）

注：其中低收入国家为2014年数据。

资料来源：世界银行世界发展指标数据库。

　　尽管高储蓄模式在短期内不会有大的改变，但中国的老龄化问题在加重，65 岁及以上老年人口比重，新中国成立以来基本上呈稳步上升态势，近几年则有加速上升的趋势（见图 5）。随着人口年龄结构的变化，高储蓄的水平也出现下行趋势。预计"十三五"期间这一趋势仍可能持续。储蓄率降低将导致资本形成率相应下降，资本积累对经济增长的贡献率亦趋于减弱。

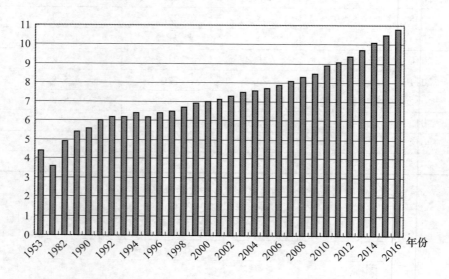

图 5　中国 65 岁及以上老年人口比重的变动情况（%）

资料来源：国家统计局。

3. 资源环境约束的强化

　　近年来，随着中国能源消费的快速增长，导致能源消耗强度不断增加。这里重点从国际比较的视角考察单位 GDP 能耗水平。以每千美元 GDP（购买力平价法 2011 年不变价）的能源使用量（单位为千克石油当量）作为衡量指标，2014

年中国为 175.3，高收入国家为 113.1，中等收入国家为
138.0，世界平均水平为 126.7。中国单位 GDP 能耗水平是
高收入国家的 1.5 倍，中等收入国家的 1.3 倍，世界平均水
平的 1.4 倍。从国别看，美国为 134.2，德国为 87.0，日本
为 93.0，巴西为 96.6，印度为 118.3，俄罗斯为 195.6。中
国单位 GDP 能耗水平明显高于发达国家和除俄罗斯外的其他
新兴经济体（见图 6）。

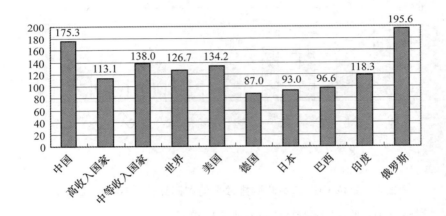

图 6　单位 GDP 能耗的国际比较（2014，千克石油当量）
资料来源：世界银行世界发展指标数据库。

在资源约束增强的同时，中国的环境压力也在不断增大，
近年来主要的污染物排放处于较高水平。这里重点也从国际
比较的视角观察一下单位 GDP 主要污染物排放水平。以每美
元 GDP（购买力平价法 2011 年不变价）二氧化碳排放量
（单位为公斤）作为衡量指标，2014 年中国为 0.59，高收入
国家为 0.26，中等收入国家为 0.39，世界平均水平为 0.34。
中国单位 GDP 二氧化碳排放量是高收入国家的 2.3 倍，中等

收入国家的 1.5 倍，世界平均水平的 1.7 倍。从国别看，美国为 0.32，德国为 0.20，日本为 0.26；巴西为 0.17，印度为 0.32，俄罗斯为 0.47。中国单位 GDP 二氧化碳排放量不仅明显高于发达国家，也高于其他新兴经济体（见图 7）。预计"十三五"期间，中国的资源约束和环境压力仍可能持续，这无疑会对过度依赖要素投入的增长模式构成约束。

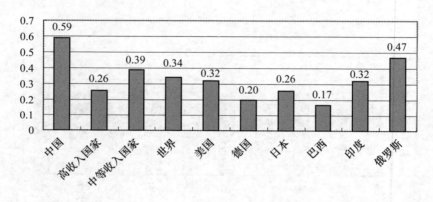

图 7   单位 GDP 二氧化碳排放量的国际比较（2014，公斤）

资料来源：世界银行世界发展指标数据库。

在上述要素投入的驱动作用下降的同时，全要素生产率的驱动作用并没有及时补位，甚至有所弱化，主要体现在：第一，由于服务业的资本边际产出率和劳动生产率总体上低于制造业，因此制造业向服务业转型将带来生产率增速的变化；第二，中国与发达国家技术水平的差距逐步缩小，通过引进技术"干中学"的溢出效应下降，原有依靠模仿创新的技术进步动能趋于衰减。这也是造成潜在增长率下降的重要原因。

(二) 短期周期波动性因素分析

从需求面负的产出缺口层面看，与有效需求不足密切相关。21 世纪以来的扩张周期，主要由投资和出口驱动。国际金融危机以来，出口驱动因素持续疲弱。而担当稳增长重任的投资驱动因素，愈来愈面临可持续性问题的困扰。

1. 出口需求持续疲弱

2008 年以来，中国经常项目顺差与 GDP 之比总体呈现较为明显的下降趋势，从高峰时期 2007 年的 10% 大幅下降至最近几年的 2% 左右 (2016 年为 1.7%)，已逐步降至国际公认的合理区间。① 其中，货物和服务贸易差额与 GDP 之比从高峰时期的 8.7% 下降至最近几年的 2.5% 左右 (2016 年为 2.2%) (见图 8)。这既在一定程度上体现了矫正外部失衡的努力，同时也有国际国内经济金融形势变化的因素。

从国际因素看，国际金融危机后，世界经济结束了一个"大稳定"的长周期，进入一个低速增长的新常态。无论是发达经济体还是发展中经济体，其潜在增长率 (或趋势增长率) 都有所下降。发达经济体的潜在增长率大约下降了 0.5—1 个百分点，而发展较快的发展中经济体，其增速大约

---

① 过去，理论界对于经常项目顺差多少为宜没有统一标准。进入 21 世纪以来，随着国际社会对全球经济失衡愈演愈烈的状况日益担忧，才开始关注经常项目顺差问题。2007 年，国际货币基金组织通过《对成员国汇率政策监督的决定》，要求成员国避免引发外部不稳定，包括过大的经常项目顺差。2010 年底的二十集团首尔峰会上，美国等国家曾经动议，在"均衡、强劲、可持续增长"政策框架下，各国承诺将经常项目差额控制在 GDP 的 ±4% 以内。后由于各方分歧较大，会上没有达成一致，而被一揽子参考性指南所取代，且未设统一的量化标准。欧盟 2011 年 12 月出台了旨在提高经济财政一体化程度的"六项规则"，其中一项预警指标是经常项目逆差与 GDP 之比不应超过 4%，顺差占比不应超过 6% (参见《2011 年中国国际收支报告》)。

下降了 1. 5—2 个百分点。国际货币基金组织总裁拉加德多次
提到全球经济增长可能在更长时间内陷入疲弱的"新的平庸
状态（new mediocre）"。目前来看，发达经济体正在遭遇
"生产力危机"。无论是劳动生产率的增长率还是综合要素生
产率的增长率，在金融危机之后都呈现下降的趋势，对长期
经济增长构成威胁。美国前财政部长萨默斯甚至发出了"长
期停滞（secular stagnation）"的警告。在此背景下，将难以
为中国经济提供强大的外部需求。这样一种态势可能还会维
持一段时间。

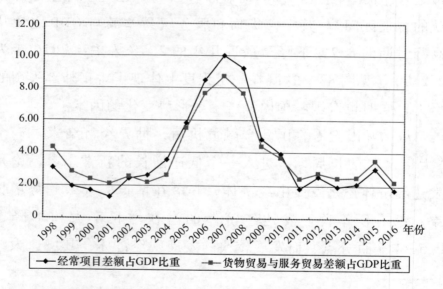

图 8　中国经常项目差额、货物与服务贸易差额与 GDP 之比（%）
资料来源：国家外汇管理局，国家统计局。

从国内因素看，随着劳动力资源从无限供给发展到供求
趋于平衡再到出现结构性的短缺，导致工资成本的相应提升。
特别是国际金融危机发生以来，中国名义劳动力成本呈现出

持续上涨的态势。图9显示，外出农民工月收入水平的增长率2010年和2011年连创新高，分别达到了19.3%和21.2%。2012年之后在GDP增速降到8%以下的情况下，农民工工资仍保持了较高的增长速度。这无疑在中国依托低劳动力成本优势与相关国家进行出口竞争的格局中增添了掣肘性因素。

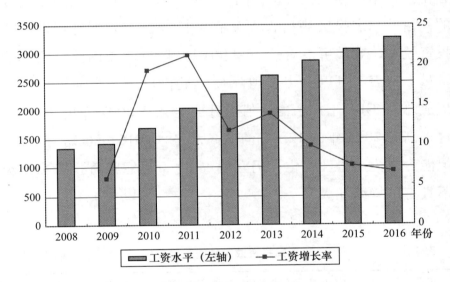

图9　中国外出农民工人均月收入和增长率（元，%）

资料来源：历年《全国农民工监测调查报告》及作者计算。

2. 投资需求的可持续性面临挑战

过去若干年，伴随着投资规模的不断提高，中国经济出现了某种程度的过度投资的倾向，导致投资效率不断恶化。从"资本—产出比率"的变动情况看，该指标自20世纪90年代中期特别是进入21世纪以来就呈现上升之势，从不足3的水平上升到3以上的水平，表明为获得单位产出所需要投入的资本存量在增加，也就意味着资本的产出效率在降低。再从"边际资本产出比率"（Incremental Capital-Output Ratio, ICOR）［也就是资本存量变动（投资流量）与产出增量比率］的变动情况看，该指标从 20 世纪 90 年代中期以来也呈上升态势，从 3 左右的水平上升至 5 左右的水平（国际平均水平一般为 2），意味着资本边际效率或者资本边际生产率在不断恶化。根据国际经验，ICOR 保持在 3 左右时资本利用是高效的，由此判定投资高增长不具有可持续性。为更直观地考察投资效率，我们可以看一下单位 GDP 增量所需的固定资产投资量。从表 2 可以看出，国际金融危机以来，当期固定资本形成总额/GDP 增加值的数值上升明显，从 2007 年的 2.77 大幅提高到 2015 年的 12.47 的畸高水平（2016 年虽略有下降，但能否成为趋势性变化，仍有待观察），也意味着投资高增长不具有可持续性。

表 2　　　　　　　　　中国投资效率的变化情况　　　　　　　单位：亿元

年份	当年全社会固定资产投资	当年 GDP 增量	固定资产投资/GDP 增量
2007	137323.9	49495.9	2.77
2008	172828.4	48235.1	3.58
2009	224598.8	26857.4	8.36
2010	251683.8	60610.0	4.15
2011	311485.1	71591.2	4.35
2012	374694.7	45838.1	8.17
2013	446294.1	49375.1	9.04
2014	512760.7	48119.9	10.66

年份	当年全社会固定资产投资	当年 GDP 增量	固定资产投资/GDP 增量
2015	561999.8	45078.1	12.47
2016	606465.7	55075.1	11.01

注：固定资产投资的统计口径在此期间进行了一次调整，即：自 2011 年起，除房地产投资、农村个人投资外，固定资产投资的统计起点由 50 万元提高到 500 万元。

资料来源：根据国家统计局数据整理计算得到。

影响投资需求可持续性的另一个重要因素是房地产投资需求的变化。从房地产市场的中长期走势看，有两大结构性变化因素需要重视。

一是人口结构变化的因素。地产周期与人口结构存有重要关联。而人口结构的一个重大变化是购房适龄人口在达到最大值后将趋于减少，特别是作为刚性需求即住房新增需求主要来源的适婚年龄人口将会达到顶峰。这与 20 世纪 80 年代的婴儿潮消退之后人口出生率及自然增长率不断走低（见图 10）密切相关。这可能导致住房市场需求的萎缩，房价的一支重要支撑力量将在一定程度上被削弱。

二是居民资产再配置的因素。从目前中国居民资产配置的情况来看，房地产依然是最重要的资产项目，其在总资产和非金融资产中的占比分别保持在近 60% 和 90% 的水平。相对而言，包括银行理财、股票、基金、信托、保险等在内的金融资产在总资产中的比重相对较低，大约占1/3。但随着房价回调预期的形成，作为房地产双重属性之一的投资品属性趋于弱化，再加上金融资产收益率的提升，居民的财富配置正逐步从房地产转向金融资产。如果从宏观层面的金融结构看，一国金融资产与实物资产的比率（称为金融相关比）在趋于稳定之前也会经历一段上升的时期。这种财富再配置效应也是影响房地产市场中长期走势的重要因素。

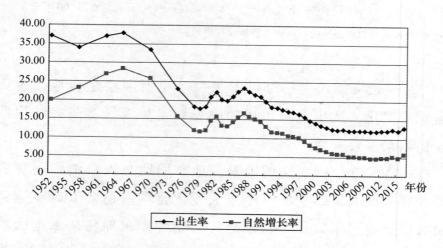

图10　中国人口出生率与自然增长率的变化情况（‰）
资料来源：国家统计局。

　　基于此，住房市场或正由总量供不应求进入结构性过剩阶段。特别是多数三、四线城市市场，前期积累了较高的库存水平，由于缺乏大量且可持续的人口净流入规模，需求相对疲弱，市场供过于求问题更加突出。

　　面对上述局面，"十三五"期间乃至未来更长一个时期，要使中国经济导入可持续的增长路径，本质上还需要经济结构重构和增长动力重塑的过程。就需求层面的增长动力转换而言，主要是解决投资比重过高、消费比重过低的问题。特别是如何进一步扩大国内消费需求，以此获取稳定、持续的需求侧经济增长动力。就供给层面即要素投入层面的增长动力转换而言，主要是解决技术进步或全要素生产率（TFP）增长对经济增长的贡献比较低的问题。这就需要进一步发挥技术创新的作用，通过对旧生产方式的改进以及通过对新生产方式的引入，以边际累进的方式，使整个经济体向生产可能性边界推进，或者推动生产可能性边界外移。

二　产业结构调整：从主要依托第二产业向更多依托第三产业转变

进入 21 世纪以来，随着重化工业化进程的加快，中国制造业的资本密集程度和资本劳动比趋于上升。特别是 2008 年以来，随着资本深化的加速，资本替代劳动的特征进一步显现。在制造业吸纳劳动就业能力相对下降的同时，服务业吸纳劳动就业的能力却没有显著跟进；尽管服务业吸纳劳动就业的比重在不断上升，分别于 1994 年和 2011 年先后超过了第二产业和第一产业，成为吸纳就业的主力军（见图 11），但从发达国家和与中国发展程度相当国家的标准来看，中国服务业对劳动就业的贡献率还是偏低。表 3 显示，高收入国家服务业劳动就业的比重占到了 74%，中高收入国家为 50%，世界平均水平 2010 年就达到 47.5%，而中国 2016 年只有 42.4%。如何进一步发展就业弹性较高的服务业仍是"十三五"时期产业结构调整的努力方向。

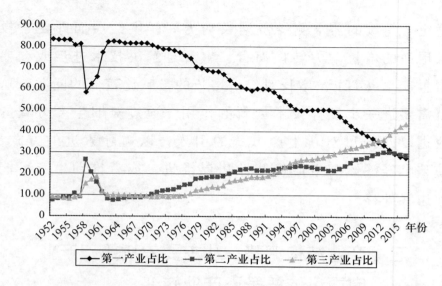

图11　中国就业人员的产业分布（%）

资料来源：国家统计局。

表3　　　　　　　服务业增加值占比和就业占比的国际比较　　　　单位：%

	服务业增加值占比	服务业就业占比
中国	51.6	42.4
巴西	73.3	77.3
德国	68.9	70.9
印度	53.8	26.6
日本	70.0	69.3
俄罗斯	62.8	66.1
美国	78.9	79.9
高收入国家	74.2	74.0
中高收入国家	59.2	50.0
世界平均水平	69.0	47.5

注：服务业增加值占比数据中，日本、美国、高收入国家和世界平均水平为2015年数据，其余为2016年数据；服务业就业占比数据中，印度和世界平均水平为2010年数据，其余为2015年数据。

资料来源：世界银行世界发展指标数据库。

　　客观而论，近年来服务业发展有所提速。2013 年，第三产业增加值占比首次超过了第二产业（见图 12），但通过比较中国与相关国家的产业结构，可以看出，不管是发展水平比中国高的国家，抑或与中国发展水平相近的国家，服务业增加值占比都远高于中国。中国的水平要比高收入国家、中高收入国家和世界平均水平分别低 22.6 个、7.6 个和 17.4 个百分点（见表 3）。中国服务业发展滞后，主要是生产性服务业的发展与发达国家或者同等发达程度的国家相比，有着很大的差距，对就业的拉动作用也相对有限。据估计，中国生产性服务业占全部服务业的比重大约为 50%，占国内生产总值的比重大约为 25%。而发达国家生产性服务业占全部服务业的比重普遍超过 50%，甚至达到 60%—70%，占 GDP 的

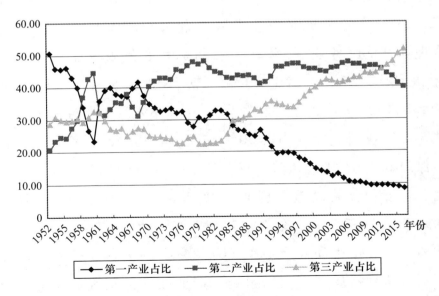

图 12　中国国内生产总值的产业构成（%）

资料来源：国家统计局。

比重也大都在30%—40%或者更高的水平。这就意味着，中国生产性服务业的发展与世界先进水平尚有一定距离。

进一步分析，服务业不发达特别是生产性服务业发展滞后，与多个因素有关，突出是与经济体制的制约有很大关系，其中尤与行业垄断密切相关。目前除批发零售贸易餐饮业、部分交通运输业和社会服务业等传统产业市场化程度比较高外，在一些服务业部门，市场化程度还不足，至今仍在价格方面由政府实行管制，同时进入壁垒还较严重，市场准入环境远未宽松，特别是在位企业与新进入企业处于不对等竞争的状态。在民间资本难以进入的背景下，仍然是国有经济一统天下或居垄断地位。从2016年全社会（不含农户）服务业投资看，国有控股投资达49.4%。14个大类行业中，除批发和零售业（11.2%），住宿和餐饮业（14.3%），房地产业（28.8%），科学研究和技术服务业（31.3%），居民服务、修理和其他服务业（35.2%），租赁和商务服务业（37%），金融业（42%），信息传输、软件和信息技术服务业（44.8%），文化、体育和娱乐业（47.8%）9个行业外，其他5个行业国有投资均占50%或以上。其中，公共管理、社会保障和社会组织（81.2%）的国有投资占80%以上；水利、环境和公共设施管理业（78.1%），交通运输、仓储和邮政业（76.7%），教育（74.4%）等行业的国有投资占70%以上；卫生和社会工作（61.2%）的国有投资也占60%以上。这种格局的存在，影响了产业效率的提高和产业整体的发展。从一定意义上说，缺少竞争已经成为阻碍服务业发展的唯一重要原因。基于此，要彻底改变服务业发展滞后的现状，将其就业潜力充分发挥出来，"十三五"期间，就必须继续深入推进服务业领域的改革：打破部门垄断，放宽产业准入限制，使非公资本更多地参与服务业的发展和市场竞争。

三　需求结构调整：从主要依托投资需求向更多依托消费需求转变

进入 21 世纪之后，尽管中国的消费需求在平稳增长，但由于消费的增长远远落后于投资的扩张，导致最终消费率逐年下降，投资率不断上升，投资与消费比例关系不协调的问题逐渐突出。特别是为了应对 2008 年国际金融危机，在推出政府刺激计划、扩张公共投资的过程中，投资与消费之间比例关系失调的矛盾进一步加剧。

从最终消费率看，改革开放之后曾长期波动在 60%—70%，但进入 21 世纪后呈现明显的逐年下降趋势，从 2000 年的 63.7% 持续下降到 2010 年的 49.1%，降低了 14.6 个百分点，为改革开放以来的最低点。2011 年之后虽有所回升（见图 13），但与国际比较，中国的最终消费率比世界平均水平要低 20—30 个百分点。而同样为东亚国家的日本和韩国，历史上消费率最低的时候，也在 60%—70%。从消费需求的组成看，最终消费率偏低主要表现为居民消费率过低，从 2000 年的 47% 持续下降到 2010 年的 35.9%，下降了 11.1 个百分点。2011 年之后虽有所回升，但 2016 年也只有 39%。而美国的这一比例接近 70%，多数欧洲国家为 55%—65%，

多数发展中国家则为 65% —70% 。即使是其他奉行节俭的亚
洲国家，也在 50% —60% （见表 4 ）。

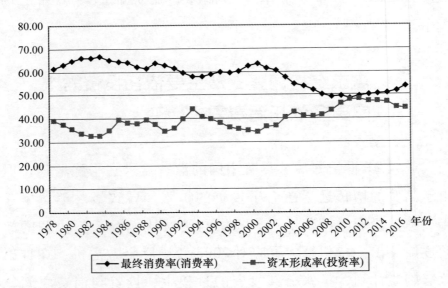

图 13　改革开放以来中国的投资率和消费率 （％）

资料来源：国家统计局。

表 4		消费率与投资率的国际比较 （2015）	单位:%
	消费率	其中: 居民消费率	投资率
中国	51. 1	37. 1	45. 4
巴西	83. 6	63. 8	17. 6
德国	73. 2	53. 9	19. 2
法国	79. 1	55. 4	22. 2
英国	84. 4	65. 0	17. 2
印度	69. 4	59. 1	32. 9
日本	76. 4	56. 6	23. 9
韩国	64. 1	49. 1	28. 9
俄罗斯	69. 6	52. 1	22. 4

续表

	消费率	其中：居民消费率	投资率
美国	82.5	68.1	20.3
高收入国家	—	59.6	21.4
中等收入国家	—	54.0	31.1
低收入国家	—	77.9	26.8
世界平均水平	—	58.0	24.2

资料来源：世界发展指标数据库（WDI）。

　　与最终消费率的持续下降相对应，投资率（资本形成率）总体上呈现上升态势，由 2000 年的 33.9% 上升到 2011 年的 47.3%，提高了 13.4 个百分点，达到改革开放以来的最高点。由图 13 可以看出，投资率从 2003 年开始超过 40% 的水平，高于 40% 的投资率已经持续长达 14 年之久。特别是 2009 年大规模扩张投资计划使投资率从连续六年维持在 45% 以上的高位。与国际比较，中国的投资率比世界平均水平要高近一倍（见表 4）。① 从经济发展历史上看，高投资率主要

---

　　① 当然，考虑到国民经济核算体系和统计方法的差异，无论是对消费率还是对投资率进行国际比较，都需要小心对待。比如消费率可能被低估的问题。目前 GDP 中的消费包括实物消费和服务消费两个方面。实物消费以社会消费品零售额中实物部分为基础，在统计时一般采用联网直报的方式（特别是限额以上部分），因此数据真实性较高。而服务消费核算中估算的成分较大，因此存在低估的可能。特别是服务消费中的居住消费被低估的可能性较大。一般来说，居民住房服务消费包括租房和自有住房两种形式。租房服务消费是房屋承租者消费的由出租者提供的住房服务，按承租者支付的租金计算。自有住房服务消费指自有住房者消费了自己提供的住房服务，按虚拟租金计算。理论上，自有住房的虚拟租金应该等于住在自有房屋中的居民要在租赁市场上租住类似的房子需要支付的租金，即应使用市场租金法，国际上不少国家就采用了这种方法。但中国实践中自有住房服务消费是按成本法计算，即按建筑成本乘以一个固定的折旧率（2%—4%）计算。近年来，随着房屋市场价格的较快上升，房屋租金也随之上涨。在这种情况下，用成本法计算的自有住房消费可能会比按市场租金计算的自有住房消费有一定程度的低估。再考虑到中国自有住房的比重较高（根据国家统计局的数据，自有住房比例超过 80%）的实际，数据失真的可能性确实需要关注。

发生在东亚的新兴工业化国家，在工业化大推进阶段大都经历过高投资率，特别是日本和韩国的投资率曾经连续几十年保持在较高的水平：1946—2003 年，日本年均投资率为30.7%，1965—1973 年是日本经济发展最快的时期，年均投资率曾达到36.2%；韩国的投资率比日本略高一些，在经济发展高峰时期曾接近40%。但无论是日本还是韩国，投资率连续 14 年超过 40% 的情形还是相当罕见的。

从制约居民消费进一步快速增长的最直接因素看，与收入分配体制密切相关。近年来，宏观收入分配结构向非居民部门倾斜的趋势未得到明显改观，居民部门在国民收入分配中的地位相对下降的态势仍未显著改变。

从要素收入分配看，劳动者报酬在收入法国内生产总值中的比重过去十多年总体上呈现下降趋势，从 1998 年的53.1% 下降到 2016 年的 47.5%，下降了 5.6 个百分点；而同一时期，生产税净额和企业营业盈余则分别从 13.4% 和19.0% 上升到 14.2% 和 24.6%，各自上升了 0.8 个和 5.6 个百分点（见图 14）。从国际上看，在成熟市场经济体中，初次分配后劳动者报酬占 GDP 的比重一般在 50%—60%。尽管劳动者报酬占比下降，有统计制度调整的因素（2004 年国民经济核算体系的调整，将"自雇者营业收入"由原来归属"劳动者报酬"调整为归属"企业营业盈余"），但一个基本的判断是：中国居民部门在功能性分配中相对于政府部门和企业部门而言总体处于不利地位。

从《中国统计年鉴》中资金流量表所反映的国民收入在三大部门之间的分配看，过去二十多年里，居民部门无论是在

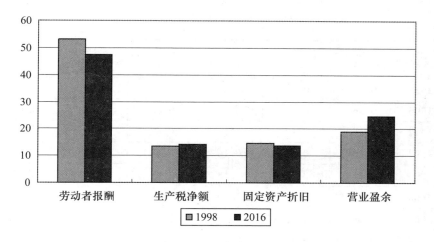

图 14　中国按收入法计算的要素收入分配情况（%）

资料来源：根据相关年份《中国统计年鉴》省际收入法 GDP 数据计算所得。

初次分配收入比重中还是在可支配收入比重中总体上都趋于
下降。表 5 显示，1995—2015 年，住户部门的初次分配收入
份额和再分配收入份额分别从 65% 和 67% 下降到 61% 和
62%，各自下降了 4 个和 5 个百分点。同一时期，政府部门
的再分配收入份额从 17% 提高到 19%，上升了 2 个百分点
（初次分配收入份额基本保持未变）；而企业部门的初次分配
收入份额和再分配收入份额分别从 20% 和 16% 上升到 24%
和 20%，均提高了 4 个百分点。

表 5　　　　　　　中国国民收入在三大部门之间的分配情况

年份	住户部门：初次分配	政府部门：初次分配	企业部门：初次分配	住户部门：再分配	政府部门：再分配	企业部门：再分配
1992	0.66	0.17	0.17	0.68	0.20	0.12
1993	0.63	0.17	0.20	0.65	0.20	0.16
1994	0.65	0.17	0.18	0.67	0.19	0.15

续表

年份	住户部门：初次分配	政府部门：初次分配	企业部门：初次分配	住户部门：再分配	政府部门：再分配	企业部门：再分配
1995	0.65	0.15	0.20	0.67	0.17	0.16
1996	0.66	0.17	0.17	0.68	0.18	0.14
1997	0.66	0.17	0.17	0.69	0.18	0.13
1998	0.66	0.18	0.16	0.68	0.18	0.13
1999	0.65	0.17	0.18	0.67	0.18	0.15
2000	0.67	0.13	0.20	0.68	0.15	0.18
2001	0.66	0.13	0.21	0.66	0.15	0.19
2002	0.64	0.14	0.22	0.64	0.16	0.19
2003	0.64	0.14	0.22	0.64	0.16	0.20
2004	0.61	0.14	0.25	0.61	0.16	0.23
2005	0.61	0.14	0.25	0.61	0.18	0.22
2006	0.61	0.15	0.25	0.60	0.18	0.22
2007	0.60	0.15	0.26	0.59	0.19	0.22
2008	0.59	0.15	0.27	0.58	0.19	0.23
2009	0.61	0.15	0.25	0.61	0.18	0.21
2010	0.61	0.15	0.25	0.60	0.18	0.21
2011	0.61	0.15	0.24	0.61	0.19	0.20
2012	0.62	0.16	0.23	0.62	0.20	0.18
2013	0.61	0.15	0.24	0.61	0.19	0.20
2014	0.60	0.15	0.25	0.61	0.19	0.20
2015	0.61	0.15	0.24	0.62	0.19	0.20

资料来源：根据相关年份《中国统计年鉴》有关数据计算所得。

考察居民部门收入比重相对下降的趋势，还可以将城乡居民收入的增速与 GDP 增速进行对比。图 15 显示，1978—2015 年，GDP 扩大了 29.3 倍，年均增长速度达到 9.7%；而同一时期，城镇居民家庭人均可支配收入和农村居民家庭人

均纯收入则分别扩大 13 倍和 14.1 倍，年均增长速度分别为
7.4% 和 7.6%。由此可见，城乡居民收入增速明显低于 GDP
增速。"国富"与"民富"之间的这一缺口，亦在某种程度
上表明了居民部门在国民收入分配格局中地位的相对下降
趋势。

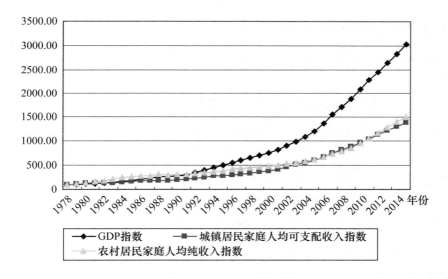

图 15　改革开放以来中国经济增长与居民收入增长的对比

注：GDP 指数和居民收入指数均以 1978 年为 100。

资料来源：国家统计局。

　　进一步分析可以看出，居民部门在国民收入分配格局中
的相对地位下降，与要素报酬决定机制、公共收入再分配机
制多个因素有密切的关系。"十三五"期间，要进一步提高
居民的可支配收入，进而扩张消费需求，需要从以下几个方
面着手，逐步理顺收入分配体制，加大国民收入分配向居民
部门倾斜的力度。一是增强劳动者在工资和福利谈判中的话

语权，确保劳动要素的贡献与报酬相匹配，以此提高劳动报酬在要素分配中的比重。二是确保农民的土地权益，特别是应开放农村集体经营性建设用地进入建设用地市场，并允许农民以多种合法方式参与开发经营，进而从土地增值中获得收益。三是加强国民收入再分配的调节力度。加快完善个人所得税（改革以个人为单位、分项征收的方式）以及公共产权收入再分配制度（进一步完善国有资本经营预算制度；进一步实施国有股减持、划转国有资本充实社会保障基金）。

四　长期增长动力结构：从主要依托要素投入向更多依托全要素生产率提升转变

一般来说，影响长期经济增长的因素可归结为两个方面：一是土地、劳动、资本等生产要素的规模；二是生产要素之间的组合关系或全要素生产率。单纯依靠要素投入增加在短期内会实现经济的高速增长，但这种增长方式面临着要素供给能力不足和边际报酬递减的双重制约，因此，构建在要素密集投入基础上的经济增长通常是难以持续的，而要素间的交互作用或者说全要素生产率（TFP）提升是长期经济增长的真正源泉。

从中国全要素生产率（TFP）增长率的变动情况看，在过去近 20 年间，处于持续下降的过程中，2015 年仅为 -1.3%。相对而言，美国和欧洲在经历了下降的过程后都处于弱势恢复的阶段；印度则是处于持续上升的过程（见

表 6)。

表 6　　　　　世界及部分经济体全要素生产率增长率的对比　　　　单位:%

年份	世界	美国	欧洲	日本	印度	中国
1999—2006	0.9	0.5	0.4	0.1	0.1	2.3
2007—2013	0.1	-0.2	-0.6	0.1	0.6	1.3
2013	0	-0.5	-0.2	0.7	0.9	0.2
2014	0	0.1	-0.1	-0.8	1.6	0.1
2015	-0.3	0.1	0.3	-0.1	1.9	-1.3

资料来源:世界大型企业联合会 (The Conference Board) 宏观经济数据库。

　　如果对经济增长的贡献率进行分解,可以发现:近几年在中国经济增长的动力源泉中,相较于劳动数量、劳动质量和资本要素的贡献,全要素生产率 (TFP) 增长率的贡献处于相对弱势的低位 (见图 16)。事实上,之前已经有不少经济学研究成果在保罗·克鲁格曼早期关于东亚经济增长模式反思的基础上,基于经济增长核算的研究框架,尝试用全要素生产率的方法分析中国经济增长的来源,认为过去 30 多年中国经济增长主要由大量资本、能源和原材料以及劳动力投入推动,而技术进步或全要素生产率增长对经济增长的贡献比较低,以此判断中国现有经济增长模式是不可持续的。[①]

　　如果从中国劳动生产率增长率的变动情况看,国际金融危机以来,也处于持续下降的过程中,从 2007 年的峰值

---

　　① Krugman, P., "The Myth of Asia's Miracle", *Foreign Affairs*, November/December, 1994, pp. 62 – 78; Young, A., *Gold into Base Metals: Productivity Growth in the Peoples Republic of China during the Reform Period*, NBER Working Paper W7856, National Bureau of Economic Research, Cambridge, 2000.

13.1%大幅下降至2015年的6.6%，八年间累计下降了6.5个百分点，年均下降0.8个百分点（见图17）。

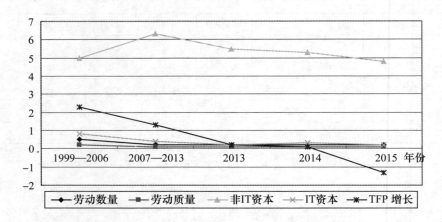

图16   中国经济增长率的贡献来源（%）

资料来源：世界大型企业联合会（The Conference Board）宏观经济数据库。

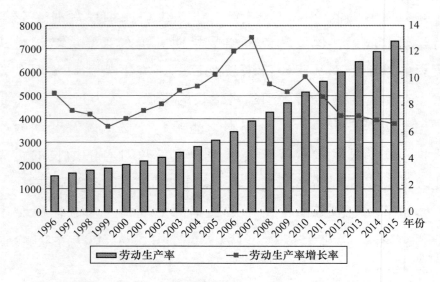

图17   中国劳动生产率及增长率变动（美元/人,%）

资料来源：国际劳工组织。

目前来看，中国的单位劳动产出仍然较低。2015 年只有 7318 美元，明显低于世界平均水平 18487 美元；与美国的 98990 美元相比，差距更大（见表 7）。

表 7　世界及部分经济体单位劳动产出（2005 年不变价）　单位：美元/人

年份	世界	美国	日本	欧元区	印度	中国
1996	14453	73880	65648	54768	1340	1535
1997	14792	75782	66174	56470	1372	1652
1998	14946	77219	65019	57809	1425	1772
1999	15180	79411	65700	59144	1524	1885
2000	15606	81720	67568	60767	1555	2018
2001	15601	82459	67759	61469	1574	2172
2002	15707	84392	68897	62105	1599	2347
2003	15864	86318	70124	62885	1669	2561
2004	16241	88776	71556	64444	1751	2801
2005	16497	90072	72209	64992	1872	3088
2006	16906	90542	73183	66391	2039	3459
2007	17310	91773	74157	68007	2218	3912
2008	17359	91242	73637	67745	2314	4290
2009	16963	92560	70477	64946	2503	4674
2010	17449	95069	73631	66586	2731	5146
2011	17711	95724	74108	67559	2909	5586
2012	17883	96062	75510	67083	3024	5990
2013	18107	97748	75958	67164	3189	6423
2014	18285	98116	75376	67867	3370	6866
2015	18487	98990	76068	68631	3559	7318

注：欧元区数据为 19 个成员国平均值。

资料来源：国际劳工组织。

　　"十三五"期间，中国能否实现可持续经济增长，最终取决于是否可以完成从"外生增长"模式向"内生增长"模式的转变。要实现这样的转变，创新驱动是根本途径。而要使科技创新成为持续发展的根本推动力，从体制保障的视角看，主要是要解决两个问题：一是"校准激励"（getting incentives right）；二是"校准价格"（getting prices right）。

先看校准激励。目前总的看，创新激励机制明显不足，主要表现在两个方面。

一是知识产权制度的激励作用未能充分发挥。知识产权制度是保护企业技术创新的重要手段，在缺乏知识产权保护的情况下，企业技术创新的溢出效应不能得到应有的收益补偿，导致普遍的"搭便车"问题，从而抑制企业的创新行为，造成模仿和复制盛行。中国20世纪80年代中期以后虽加大了对知识产权的保护，但目前来看保护还不完全到位，导致这项政策的激励作用还未充分发挥。

二是对人力资本的薪酬和产权激励机制尚不健全。在技术创新中，企业家和科技人员等人力资本所有者承担的风险和责任重大，付出的创造性劳动巨大，薪酬和产权分配应体现对其价值的充分认可。但目前中国对技术进步中人力资本的价值重视不够，分配中基本没有考虑到劳动的复杂程度和对企业的贡献程度，从而挫伤了人力资本所有者不断创新、承担风险的积极性，这已成为许多企业进行技术创新的重大障碍。

为完善创新激励机制，应进一步完善知识产权保护制度，加大惩戒力度，提高违法成本，形成可置信的威慑力量。同时，构建人才创新活动的科学评价和有效激励机制。比如，可推行技术入股和技术期权制度，推进"技术资本化"，使技术人员获得强大创新动力。

再看校准价格。在市场经济条件下，价格具有重要的信号传递作用，在资源配置的调节过程中发挥着重要的利益导向作用。日本、韩国、中国台湾地区的发展实践表明，在正常的市场机制作用下，由于经济增长中各种生产要素相对价格的变动，经济增长方式自身会逐步地从粗放转向集约。但目前在要素市场上，政府对要素配置和价格形成直接干预依然过多，价格不能真实反映要素的稀缺性和供求关系以及环境损害程度，从而在一定意义上导致了要素价格的扭曲。在土地、资本等要素价格存在不同程度的低估倾向时，直接刺激了市场主体密集使用相对廉价的有形要素，而较少有动力和压力投资于自主创新。

纠正这一局面的关键是要把价格信号搞对，通过持续推进要素市场的发育和完善，以此形成要素的有效定价机制，使要素价格能够"逼近"供求决定的真实均衡水平。在此基础上，让微观企业能按市场信号进行理性决策。通过正确的价格信号引导各经济主体预期和调整微观主体行为，建立起持续创新的机制。

除了上述两大关键性制度保障外，政府在创新中的作用也有必要厘清。一方面应承认，在创新过程中，一些外部效应没有办法被市场完全考虑。比如企业创新升级会为其他企业提供公共知识，基础设施建设会降低企业的交易成本和提高投资回报率。由于这些外部效应无法完全通过市场途径解决，需要政府在产业升级和技术创新方面发挥应有作用。另一方面也应强调，政府在产业选择、技术选择方面，不能过度干预。近年来政府在推动战略性新兴产业过程中，通常以自身对市场供需状况的判断以及对未来供需形势变化的预测来判断某个行业是否具备发展前景，并以政府的判断和预测为依据制定相应的行业发展规划。但事实上，由于存在不确定性和政府的有限理性，政府可能无法对经济形势做出较为准确的判断。这实际上是以政府的判断和控制来代替市场的协调机制，具有一定的计划经济色彩。近期以光伏产业为代表的一些新兴产业所经历的巨幅震荡，就与政府主导背景下押注错误的技术方向，以及大规模重复投资不无关系。我们认为，在有必要实行产业政策的情形下，为克服政府失灵，有必要区分选择性产业政策和功能性产业政策、直接干预型产业政策和间接诱导型产业政策。[①] 这里的核心要义是，产业政策应是作为矫正市场失效的工具，而不是替代市场的工具。也就是说，政府在实施产业政策的过程中，不应设法取代市场，而应设法强化市场信号和私人活动。

---

① Lall, S. , " Industrial Policy: The Role of Government in Promoting Industrial and Technological Development", *UNCTAD Review*, 1994, pp. 65 – 90.

中国居民收入分配与社会保障制度

王　震[*]

中国自 20 世纪 70 年代末期改革开放以来，经济快速增长，GDP 总量在 2010 年超过日本，成为世界第二大经济体，到 2013 年中国的 GDP 已达美国 53.58%（见图 1）。从人均 GDP 的角度，中国总体上已经进入上中等收入经济体行列，一些大城市和东部沿海地区已进入高收入经济体行列（见图 2）。在经济快速增长的同时，中国居民的收入分配状况却呈现不断恶化的趋势，城乡差距、地区差距和行业间收入差距不断扩大。这是中国当前必须面对和解决的重大经济问题，也是重大的社会问题。

为应对收入差距的扩大，建立和完善社会保障制度是重要的手段。改革开放以来，为适应社会主义市场经济，中国构建了新的以社会保险为主体的社会保障制度。中国社会保障制度建设的基本原则是保基本、广覆盖、多层次。截止到 2011 年，中国已实现了社会保险的制度全覆盖，到 2013 年实

---

* 王震，中国社会科学院经济研究所研究员。

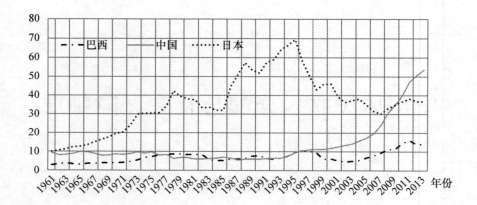

图 1　中国、日本、巴西对美国的赶超指数（Catch-up Index，%）

注：赶超指数等于该国 GDP 总量占当年美国 GDP 总量的比重。当年价格；美元。

资料来源：World Bank Database。

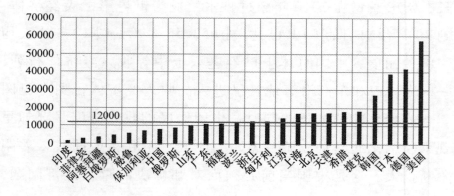

图 2　2015 年部分国家及中国部分城市和地区的人均 GDP（美元）

注：当年价格。

资料来源：World Bank Database，中国国家统计局。

现了社会保险的人口全覆盖。当然，中国的社会保障制度仍
然存在一些问题，亟须进一步的改革和完善。

　　本部分的内容将中国居民收入分配状况的介绍作为开端，
对中国社会保障制度的建立、演变及主要特征进行分析，并

对中国社会保障制度进一步的改革与完善进行分析。

一　中国改革开放以来居民收入分配状况

（一）居民收入分配状况的变动趋势

　　基尼系数是衡量居民之间收入分配结构的综合性指标。当每个人的收入都一样时，处于绝对公平，基尼系数为 0；当所有的收入集中在一个人手中时，处于绝对不公平，基尼系数为 1。这两类是极端情况，在实际经济社会中，基尼系数处于 0—1，基尼系数越大，则居民收入差距越大，越不公平。一般认为，基尼系数小于 0.2 时，居民收入绝对平均；在 0.2—0.3 时，居民收入比较平均；0.3—0.4 则比较合理；在 0.4—0.5 时，居民收入差距过大；超过 0.5 时，则认为收入差距悬殊。

　　基尼系数反映的是总体收入的差距。基尼系数的变化取决于所有居民的相对收入的变化，是一个综合性指标。基尼系数的变化可能与一个群体相对于另一个群体的变化并不一致。例如，总体上低收入群体的收入提高，高收入群体的收入得到有效调节，中等收入群体扩大，这将使收入分配结构更加公平，基尼系数降低。然而，与此同时，有一部分群体因病致贫，他们的收入相对于原来相当收入水平来说则处于恶化的状态。总体的基尼系数并不能反映这一情况，除非针对其做特殊群体的计算。另外，基尼系数虽然能够衡量收入差距，并根据通用的标准来判断收入分配的状况，但是基尼系数并不能反映收入差距过大的来源及群体之间的特征，因此大量研究对基尼系数进行分解，来讨论不同群体之间的收入差距，并与总体的收入差距进行比较，从而判断收入差距来自哪些群体。

根据世界银行的估算，改革开放初期，中国 1981 年的基尼系数仅为 0.2911，1984 年则降至 0.2764，处于比较平均的情况。虽然此时处于比较公平的水平，但是中国当时的经济发展水平比较落后，是低收入的发展中国家。尽管每个人之间收入水平比较平均，但是每个人的收入都非常低。经济产品也不够丰富，城镇居民的生活用品依然实施配给制，需要凭票购买。在共同富裕的理念下，一部分有条件的地区和一部分人先发展了起来，一部分地区则发展比较慢。这样就带来了收入差距的持续扩大。1987 年恢复至 1981 年的水平，达到 0.2985，1990 年的基尼系数是 0.3243，进入收入分配比较合理的阶段。此后一路上升，1999 年达到 0.3923，仍然在比较合理的区间，只是接近于国际警戒线。2002 年则已经超过了公认的国际警戒线，高达 0.4259。国家统计局发布的 2003 年的基尼系数为 0.4790。由此可见，1984—2002 年，中国的基尼系数持续上升，先后经历了比较平等、比较合理和收入差距过大三个阶段。

2013 年国家统计局公布了 2003 年以来的基尼系数，此后基尼系数成为各年经济和社会发展统计公报中的一项常规指标。尽管这一指标与其他社会调查的基尼系数的结果存在一定差异，但是国家统计局公布的数据具有较高的权威性。一是因为国家统计局的数据覆盖范围最广。基于人力、财力的限制，学术群体进行的社会调查只能是抽样调查，且抽样数量远小于国家统计局的数量。二是因为统计的数据是逐年公布的。学术群体的调查同样基于上述原因，大多是具有时间跨度的，难以实现每年都调查，数据的连续性比较差。鉴于此，我们依据 2013 年国家统计局公布的数据分析 2003—2014 年的基尼系数趋势。国家统计局公布的 2003 年的基尼系数为 0.479，延续了世界银行公布的基尼系数的增长趋势。尽管两组数据在统计数据和统计标准上存在差异，但是数据的结构都显示出中国的基尼系数偏高，超过了国际警戒线 0.4 的水平。2003—2008 年，基尼系数仍然在不断地小幅上升，2008 年最高，达到 0.491。这与收入悬殊的判断标准 0.5 仅差一步之遥。基尼系数从 2009 年开始呈现出下降趋势，持续 7 年不断地降低，尽管幅度比较小，2015 年降至 0.462。在可比的数据范围内，2015 年的基尼系数已经低于 2003 年的水平。

基尼系数的持续下降说明总体收入水平表现出的收入差距出现了下降。尽管 2009 年基尼系数刚出现下降时，对于下降趋势的判断并不明了，但是持续 7 年的下降，总体上可以说明这段时间内的下降趋势。从另一个方面来说，2009 年以来基尼系数没有进一步提高，收入差距没有进一步的恶化是一个普遍认可的事实。

然而，值得注意的是，基尼系数依然比较高，2015 年还在国际警戒线之上。从基尼系数的判断标准来看，中国仍是一个收入差距过大的国家。从国际比较来看，中国的基尼系数同样偏高。2016 年世界发展指标数据显示，2010 年基尼系数超过中国的国家只有 20 个，其中除了格鲁吉亚、以色列和越南以外，其他国家均为非洲或拉丁美洲国家，这说明中国的收入差距在国际上也处于较高水平。

（二）居民收入分配差距扩大的原因分析

市场化水平逐渐提高，要素配置和收入分配更多由市场决定，突出了个体之间的差异。改革开放以后，劳动力市场和要素市场的市场化程度逐步提高，特别是国有企业改革之后，非公有制经济、民营经济、外资经济等获得了较快的发展，进一步推动了要素市场市场化程度的提高。劳动报酬是居民主要的收入来源。在市场化提高的情况下，劳动的边际产出决定劳动的报酬，边际产出越高则劳动报酬越高。边际产出在很大程度上是由劳动者自身的人力资本决定的。由此可见，个体之间人力资本的差异，导致其边际生产力不同，进而带来劳动报酬差异。在打破大锅饭、要素市场化的过程中，由个体特征导致的收入差异逐渐被显现，进而带来了收入差距的扩大。

要素流动受阻，加大了不同群体之间的收入差距。虽然要素配置和收入分配过程的市场化程度不断提高，但是要素自由流动依然受到限制，没有形成统一的要素市场。相对于资本而言，劳动力的自由流动则更加困难。劳动力在城乡之间、地区之间、行业之间的流动都存在进入壁垒。劳动力在乡城之间的流动囿于户籍制度的限制，长期受到歧视。1989—1991年控制农村居民的盲目流动，1992年之后鼓励农村劳动力流动，但是国有企业改革之后，1995—2000年，对下岗职工实施的再就业使部分省市出台了各种限制农村劳动力进城及外来劳动力务工的规定和政策。即使在 2003 年农民工工资大幅增长之后，农民工在进入公有制部门时依然存在较强的歧视。资本的流动性强于劳动，而且各地为了招商引资纷纷给出优惠条件，但是资本的流动也存在一定的障碍。资本市场的政府管制和垄断使资本要素价格难以完全由市场决定，致使资本要素容易获得超过其边际产出的价格或收益。[①] 资源报偿方面，由于相关制度的不健全，资源报偿分配方面表现出的不平等、不公正则更加突出。鄂尔多斯地区，仅亿万富翁就有 7 千人。他们主要是靠卖资源致富的，如靠卖煤致富。这主要是钻了政策的空子，甚至是违法、违规，可能与贿赂腐败联系在一起。[②]

　　要素分配结构向资本倾斜。改革开放以来，中国借助劳动力方面的比较优势获得了快速的发展。然而，在发展过程中，资本相对于劳动严重稀缺，由此导致资本收益率高。高投资率和高收益率成为经济快速发展过程中的主要特征。在劳资关系中，资本处于主导地位，掌握话语权，劳动处于弱势地位，资本获得了较高的报酬，用于劳动报酬分配的份额较低。资本垄断又导致资本收益集中在少数人的手中。在劳动分配份额较少和资本收益集中的双重作用下，拉大了居民之间的收入差距。

　　法律制度不健全，不合理收入和非法收入的存在，扩大

---

　　① 张车伟、赵文：《中国劳动报酬份额问题——基于雇员经济与自雇经济的测算与分析》，《中国社会科学》2015 年第 12 期。

　　② 李强：《社会分层与社会空间领域的公平、公正》，《中国人民大学学报》2012 年第 1 期。

了收入差距。在经济快速发展的同时，分配制度也在不断地调整。与此同时，关于收入管理方面的法律制度也不断出台，但是依然存在错位和缺位的问题。这就使得部分人能够凭借不合理甚至不合法的手段获得收入。如前所述，资源税费的缺位与不健全，使部分人将出卖资源获得的收入据为己有。另外，近些年来隐性收入的规模不断扩大，这也增加了收入差距。当考虑隐性收入时，以"城镇居民家庭总收入"为标准计算的基尼系数从原始数据中的 0.31—0.34 上升到了 0.45—0.51，测算出收入瞒报所导致的"隐性收入"规模约占中国 2002—2009 年相应各年 GDP 的 19% 至 25%。[①]

再分配调节力度有限，初次分配格局基本决定了再分配之后的可支配收入格局。一是税收调节是再分配调节的重要手段，但是中国个人所得税表现为税额累进但税率累退，高收入群体的纳税额高但是税率却偏低。以 2009 年为例，如果不存在不公平，个人所得税将使城镇居民税前收入基尼系数降低 0.018，但实际上仅仅降低了 0.0129。[②] 也就是说，个人所得税的这种累退性降低了税收的调节功效。二是社会保障制度分割，难以发挥再分配的功效。社会保障制度是一项重要的再分配手段，以社会共济的方式缩小收入差距。然而，中国社会保障制度中存在的城乡分割、部门分割等问题，使本应被扶持的弱势群体难以通过社会保障获得扶持，甚至存在"逆向调节"。

---

　　① 白重恩、唐燕华、张琼：《中国隐性收入规模估计——基于扩展消费支出模型及数据的解读》，《经济研究》2015 年第 6 期。
　　② 徐静、岳希明：《税收不公正如何影响收入分配效应》，《经济学动态》2014 年第 6 期。

例如，在城市工作的农民工，他们很难获得社会保障。即使制度允许之后，农民工参保的比例依然非常低，这主要是因为转续衔接等问题使农民工难以达到领取社会保障的要求。非缴费型的社会保障（如最低生活保障）主要是针对城市本地居民，农民工则难以获得。

城市化滞后于工业化，减弱了工业化进程对收入差距缩小的能力。伴随着工业化的快速发展，大量农村剩余劳动力从农村迁移至城镇，就业从农业转向工业，进而生活也从农村转向城市，从而推动城市化的进程。然而，囿于户籍制度的限制，中国的城市化进程被分为两个阶段，农民成为农民工，农民工成为市民。户籍制度背后的基本公共服务成为使农民工转变为市民的障碍。换句话说，虽然农民工在城市就业，但是其享受的基本公共服务依然是农村的标准。基于中国农村和城市之间基本公共服务方面的巨大差异，这则降低了工业化缩小收入差距的能力。随着工业的不断发展，农民工规模不断提高，2015 年农民工的规模达到了 27747 万人，占全部就业人口的 35.8%。[①] 农民工规模扩大则进一步减弱了工业化缩小收入差距的能力。

二　覆盖全民的社会保障制度

中国适应社会主义市场经济体制的社会保障制度包括社会保险、社会救济、社会福利、优抚安置和社会互助、个人

---

① 数据来源：2015 年国民经济和社会发展统计公报，http://www.gov.cn/xinwen/2016 – 02/29/content_ 5047274. htm。

储蓄积累保障等内容。①

（一）计划经济时期的社会保障

中国当前的社会保障体系直接来源于计划经济时代的社会保障制度安排。计划经济通过政府的指令性计划对整个社会的经济活动进行调配与控制。而要实现行政性指令性计划对经济活动的调配与控制，需要背后一整套的制度支持。在重工业优先发展的计划目标下，为了将资源集中到工业部门，逐步形成了以户籍制度为主体的城乡二元分割体制。② 与城乡二元分割体制相对应的，计划经济时代中国社会保障体系的主要特征也体现为城乡二元分割：农村居民主要以家庭自我保障及集体经济组织提供的保障为主，政府对农村社会保障并无财政支付责任；城镇居民则又根据就业身份区分为不同的社会保障类型。

在农村，20 世纪 50 年代中期之后，随着农村合作化的完成，形成了人民公社制度以及村级集体经济组织。与这一制度相对应，农村也形成了以"五保"供养及农村合作医疗为代表的社会保障项目。农村"五保"供养规定了农村村级集体经济组织对丧失劳动能力的成员提供的基本生活保障。这一保障形式实际上通过集体成员之间的互济，在集体经济组织内部建立了一种非缴费型的救助制度。农村合作医疗制度

---

① 十四届三中全会报告：《中共中央关于建立社会主义市场经济体制若干问题的决定》，1994 年。

② 林毅夫、蔡昉、李周：《中国的奇迹：发展战略与经济改革》，格致出版社、上海三联书店、上海人民出版社 1999 年版。

也是在当时农村主要的社会保障项目。与"五保"制度不同，合作医疗要求成员缴纳一定的费用，并用这些费用获得医生的服务及药品。与"五保"制度相同的是，合作医疗也是内嵌到农村集体经济组织之内的。合作社的农村赤脚医生同时也是社员，其医疗服务也纳入到合作社的工分系统中。

　　在城镇地区，城镇居民根据职业的不同，分别纳入到不同的社会保障项目中。第一类是机关事业单位就业人员，他们实行的财政直接支付的公费医疗及退休制度；第二类是国有企业及集体企业职工，他们实行的是基于企业与职工缴费的劳动保险制度；第三类是非就业城镇居民，他们没有单独的社会保障项目，但可以依据机关事业单位及企业职工的家属身份获得部分保障，例如医疗费用的报销等。

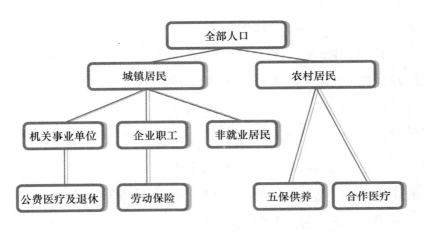

图3　计划经济下中国人群分割与社会保障体系

　　图3给出了计划经济时代基于人群分割的社会保障的制度安排框架。实际上，在计划经济下，这一框架逐渐演变成为不同单位的职工福利制度，失去了社会共济的职能。在农

村，"五保"供养及合作医疗本就依托村级集体经济组织；在城镇，企业职工的劳动保险在文化大革命时期演变成了企业的职工福利，机关事业单位的社会保障待遇也与本单位的财政支付能力相关。

（二）　改革开放初期至 20 世纪 90 年代中期的社会保障制度改革探索

计划经济时期的社会保障在农村依托于人民公社制度及集体经济，在城镇则演变为依托单位或企业的职工福利。这两个基础在 20 世纪 70 年代末期开始的改革开放中被打破：首先在农村，人民公社制度解体，家庭联产承包责任制瓦解了集体经济组织；其次在城镇地区，国有企业也开始了放权让利、承包制、股份制等改革探索。这样，原有的社会保障体系失去了依托，趋于瓦解。

在农村，随着人民公社制度的解体，以及家庭联产承包责任制的推行，农村集体经济组织弱化，已失去了承担为其成员提供保障的能力。在这样的情况下，首先农村的合作医疗制度逐步瓦解，覆盖率从 20 世纪 70 年代中期最高峰的 90% 左右急剧下降到 5% 左右（1983 年）。[①] 直到 2003 年中国重建新型农村合作医疗，农村的医疗保障基本上处于空白。

不同于合作医疗，"五保"供养制度对集体经济的依赖更甚，因为"五保"供养的资金直接来源于合作社。而随着集体经济组织的弱化，"五保"供养的资金来源接近枯竭。为

---

① 王禄生、张里程：《我国农村合作医疗制度发展历史及其经验教训》，《中国卫生经济》1996 年第 8 期，第 12—15 页。

解决这一问题，中央提出农村"五保"供养的资金来源应从农民直接收费解决，并将其纳入到村提留和乡统筹的范畴中，管理层次也逐步上移至乡镇政府。①

在 20 世纪 80 年代及 90 年代初期，随着国有企业改革的推进，以及一些企业出现的破产等问题，城镇待岗、失业人群开始大量出现，城镇贫困人口急剧增加，亟须在城镇地区建立针对失业、待岗职工及城镇贫困人口的救助措施。② 在这样的情况下，上海市在 1993 年建立了非缴费型的城镇居民最低生活保障制度，初步在城镇建立了一道社会"安全网"，并成为未来中国最低生活保障制度的雏形。

同时，在原有企业劳动保险制度的基础上，各地也在探索重建企业职工社会保险的社会统筹。在中央层面，1986 年国务院在《国营企业实行劳动合同制暂行规定》中专门对企业劳动合同制工人的动保险统筹进行规定，并提出："劳动合同制工人退休养老实行社会保险制度。退休养老基金的来源，由企业和劳动合同制工人缴纳。"1991 年国务院将统筹的社会保险制度扩展到全部国有企业工人。③

这一时期的社会保障制度改革，其主要目的还是为国有企业改革提供环境，使国有企业能够摆脱原先承担的承重的

---

① 1985 年中共中央国务院《关于制止向农民乱派款、乱收费的通知》规定，"供养五保户等事业的费用，原则上应当以税收或其他法定的收费来解决。在这一制度建立之前，实行收取公共事业统筹费的办法"。1991 年国务院《农民承担费用和劳务管理条例》规定，"村提留包括公积金、公益金和管理费"，其中"公益金，用于五保户供养、特别困难户补助、合作医疗保健以及其他集体福利事业"，"乡统筹费可以用于五保户供养"。

② 杨立雄：《中国城镇居民最低生活保障制度的回顾、问题及政策选择》，《中国人口科学》2004 年第 3 期。

③ 《国务院关于企业职工养老保险制度改革的决定》，1991 年。

职工福利，成为合格的市场竞争主体。因此，在不面临市场竞争、无须成为市场主体的政府及事业单位中，原有的政府直接支付的公费医疗及退休制度就没有实行改革，仍保留了原来的制度安排及资金来源。

（三）适应社会主义市场经济体制的社会保障制度建设

党的十四大提出了中国经济体制改革的目标模式是建立社会主义市场经济体制；党的十四届三中全会则对社会主义市场经济体制的制度框架进行了规定，在其中，明确提出了社会保障改革的功能、地位及目标模式。

首先，党的十四届三中全会提出了中国社会保障体系建设的目标模式是"建立多层次的社会保障体系"，其主要内容包括社会保险、社会救济、社会福利、优抚安置和社会互助、个人储蓄积累保障。

其次，在改革重点方面，将城镇职工养老保险和医疗保险作为重点，并提出了二者在筹资上实行"社会统筹 + 个人账户"制度。在农村社会保障体系建设上，仍强调"农民养老以家庭保障为主，与社区扶持相结合"。

最后，确定了社会保险基金保值增值的主要渠道是"用于购买国债"。党的十四届三中全会对社会保障的功能定位为国有企业改革进行配套，强调其在"深化企业和事业单位改革"中的重大意义。党的十四届三中全会确定的社会保障建设的基本模式及一些基本原则构成了当前中国社会保障体系制度安排框架的主体。从 20 世纪 90 年代中期直至 2000 年，中国依次建立了城镇职工基本养老保险制度、城镇职工基本医疗保险制度、工伤保险制度、失业保险制度以及生育保险制度；在非缴费型的社会救助方面，建立了城镇居民最低生活保障制度。

（四）覆盖全民的社会保障制度

从改革开放直至 21 世纪初，农村社会保障制度大部分时间处于空白状态。党的十五大确立的中国社会保障建设的基本原则，仍强调城镇社会保障建设，并强调其作为国有企业改革配套的重要性，并未认识到社会保障自身的意义。自党的十六大以来，中国新的社会保障建设的目标及原则也在逐渐发生改变。在党的十六大报告中，提出了农村社会保障建设的政策取向，即"有条件的地方，探索建立农村养老、医疗保险和最低生活保障制度"。2003 年的"非典"冲击，也使中国政府认识到建立一个覆盖全面的社会保障制度的重要性。

此后的十年间，中国社会保障建设进入全面覆盖的新阶段。在 2003 年年底中央开始推动新型农村合作医疗制度。新型农村合作医疗制度首次明确了政府对农村社会保障的财政责任。新农合的筹资结构设计为"政府补贴、集体补助、个人缴费"，政府按照一定比例为新农合提供财政支持。此后，2009 年开始建立的新型农村养老保险也秉承了这一筹资结构，明确了政府对农村居民养老保险的财政支持责任。政府对农村社会保障的财政支持责任还体现在新的农村五保供养上。2006 年新的《农村五保供养工作条例》规定，"农村五保供养资金，在地方人民政府预算中安排"，正式确定了农村五保供养作为政府非缴费型社会救助项目的地位。

在非缴费型社会救助项目方面，这一时期还正式建立了城镇与农村的最低生活保障制度以及城镇与农村的医疗救助制度。在城镇非就业居民方面，除了非缴费型的社会救助项目外，还分别在 2007 年及 2011 年建立了城镇居民的医疗保险制度及城镇居民养老保险制度，将城镇非就业纳入到社会保障体系中。

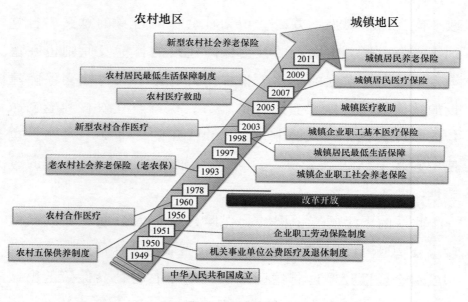

图 4   中国社会保障体系的建立

随着城镇居民养老保险制度的建立，中国在社会保障体系建设上实现了全部人群的制度全覆盖。在农村地区，农村居民的社会保障体系，既有非缴费型的社会救助项目，"五保供养"、农村居民最低生活保障及医疗救助制度，也有社会保险性质的新型农村合作医疗及新型农村养老保险；城镇居民社会保障的主体是城镇职工社会保险制度，包括养老保险、医疗保险、失业保险、工伤保险及生育保险，也包括覆盖城镇居民的非缴费型的城镇居民最低生活保障及医疗救助制度。此外，城镇非就业居民也建立了城镇居民养老保险及医疗保险制度。

三　中国社会保障制度面临的挑战及问题

中国社会保障实现制度全覆盖意味着所有人群都可以被至少一种社会保障项目所覆盖，这是中国社会主义现代化建设取得的伟大成就。但是，由于中国社会保障体系的建设脱胎于计划经济体制，在改革过程中又担负了为国有企业改革提供配套的职能，因此形成了一些特征。这些特征在新形势、新情况下，产生了诸多问题，面临着巨大的挑战。

在中国社会保障体系存在的诸多问题中，基本都可以归结到中国社会保障体系的两个主要特征：一是制度分割，社会保障项目之间的"碎片化"；二是隐性负债沉重，可持续性堪忧。

（一）中国社会保障体系的"碎片化"

中国社会保障体系的一个基本特征是"碎片化"，一是制度分割，二是地区分割。这两个层面的分割相互缠绕在一起，形成了中国社会保障体系的极度"碎片化"的特征：不同的"碎片"之间，不仅待遇差距明显，显失公平；转移接续困难，缺乏便携性，不适应流动性。

1. 制度分割及地区分割：社会保障公平性不足

在当前中国的社会保障体系下，不同的人群适用不同的社会保障项目。首先是城乡居民之间，城镇居民和农村居民实行不同的社会保障项目；即使实行具有相同制度安排框架的社会保障项目，其间也存在明显的差异。在非缴费型的社会救助项目方面，城镇居民和农村居民都实行了居民最低生活保障制度，且制度安排相类似，但实际待遇水平却有较大差距。农村平均的低保标准及实际的平均补助水平都仅相当于城镇水平的一半左右。在缴费型社会保险方面，居民养老保险的年养老金支付水平仅相当于城镇职工养老保险平均养老金水平的 4% 左右；在医疗保险方面，新型农村合作医疗的人均筹资额在 2012 年只有 308.5 元，低于城镇居民基本养老保险的人均筹资额，更远低于城镇职工基本医疗保险的人均筹资额。

中国社会保障体系不仅存在制度之间的分割，而且还存在严重的地区之间的分割。在社会保险方面，中国社会保险项目基本统筹区域为县级（县级市、市辖区）统筹，不同的统筹区域之间，缴费率有差异，缴费基数不同，保障水平差距明显。以养老保险为例，虽然中央政府制定了养老保险的指导缴费率，但是各地的缴费基数却与本地的平均职工工资相挂钩，缴费上下限与本地的最低工资标准挂钩，导致实际缴费水平存在较大差异。在养老金待遇方面，更是存在明显的地区差距。以企业职工基本养老保险为例，2012 年平均的养老金水平，最高的省份是最低省份的 2.15 倍，次高省份是次低省份的 1.78 倍。

在非缴费型的社会救助方面，也存在地区差异。以城镇和农村最低生活保障为例，2012 年城镇最低生活保障的平均标准及实际补助水平最高省份为最低省份的 2.27 倍、2.45倍，次高省份为次低省份的 2.06、2.27 倍；农村居民最低生活保障制度的差距更加明显，平均低保标准及实际补助水平，最高省份为最低省份的 3.75 倍、3.96 倍，次高省份为次低省份的 3.72 倍及 2.79 倍。

社会保障水平要与地区经济社会发展相适应，是社会保障建设的一个重要原则；但是，社会保障作为调节收入再分配的重要手段，若不能在不同地区之间实现收入的再平衡，那么社会保障就失去了其本来的含义。而从社会保障分散社会风险的角度，统筹范围过低意味着风险分散的范围过低，其抵御社会风险的能力必然下降。制度分割与地区分割导致的社会保障待遇差异，不仅阻碍了社会保障收入再分配功能的发挥，而且其本身的不公平性也已成为引发社会冲突的一个焦点。

2. 社会保障便携性不足、不能适应流动性

"碎片化"的社会保障除了导致不公平外，还存在一个问题，即不同"碎片"之间的转移困难，便携性不足。这种"碎片化"的状态比较适应人口流动较少的社会。在计划经济时代，由于人口流动被严格控制，因此不同人群之间的不同制度安排以及由此引致的便携性不足，还不至成为一个重要的社会问题。但是，随着改革开放以及快速工业化、城镇化，中国出现了大规模的乡—城流动人口（农民工）。外出就业的

农民工①规模从 2006 年 1. 32 亿增长到 2016 年的 1. 67 亿，占城镇总就业人员的比重也一直维持在 40% 以上。也就是说，在城镇就业人口中，有接近一半为进入城镇就业与生活的农民工。农民工已成为中国"产业工人的重要组成部分"②。

　农民工进入城镇地区主要从事非农就业，其面对的社会风险性质主要是工业化的社会风险。从保障模式与社会风险匹配的理论上讲，他们应该在被覆盖在城镇社会保障体系中。从中国社会保障的制度设计及具体实施细则上，在城镇正规就业的农民工可以参加城镇企业职工社会保险。但是，已有的调查显示，农民工参加就业所在地城镇职工社会保险的意愿低，实际覆盖率低。统计数据显示，2016 年农民工养老、医疗、工伤、失业保险的参保率只有 35. 1%、28. 5%、44. 3%、22. 1%，远低于同期城镇企业职工社会保险的全部覆盖率。这其中的一个重要原因就是中国社会保障体系的地区分割及制度分割。

表 1　　外出就业农民工参加城镇企业职工基本社会保险情况

单位：百万人，%

		2011	2012	2013	2014	2015	2016
外出就业农民工总量		158. 63	163. 36	166. 1	168. 21	168. 84	169. 34
工伤保险	总量	68. 28	71. 79	72. 63	73. 62	74. 89	75. 1
	比例	43. 0	43. 9	43. 7	43. 8	44. 4	44. 3

---

　① 根据国家统计局的解释，外出就业的农民工定义为在本乡外从事非农就业的农民工；全部农民工包括外出就业农民工及在本乡（镇）内就业的农民工。
　② 《国务院关于解决农民工问题的若干意见》，2006 年。

续表

		2011	2012	2013	2014	2015	2016
养老保险	总量	41.4	45.43	48.95	54.72	55.85	59.4
	比例	26.1	27.8	29.5	32.5	33.1	35.1
医疗保险	总量	46.41	49.96	50.18	52.29	51.66	48.25
	比例	29.3	30.6	30.2	31.1	30.6	28.5
失业保险	总量	23.91	27.02	37.4	40.71	42.19	37.4
	比例	15.1	16.5	22.5	24.2	25.0	22.1

注：农民工定义为外出就业农民工。

资料来源：人力资源和社会保障部相关年份"人力资源和社会保障事业发展统计公报"。

（二）　中国社会保障的隐性负债沉重，影响社会保障的可持续性

中国社会保障体系的另一个特征是隐性债务负担沉重，影响社会保障的可持续性。隐性债务也可称之为潜在负债，其含义为虽未体现在账面上，但需要在未来加以偿还的债务。中国社会保障体系的隐性债务主要体现在社会保险项目上。

制度转轨导致的历史债务主要体现在城镇职工基本养老保险方面。中国在 20 世纪 90 年代开始建立与社会主义市场经济体制相适应的社会保障体系。当时设计的制度模式是社会统筹加个人账户制度。对于新制度建立之后进入制度的职工，不存在历史债务问题；对于新制度建立时已经退休的职工，其养老金由原渠道解决，也不构成历史债务问题。但是，对于那些新制度建立时已参加工作，还未退休的"中人"，则在制度建立后，其原就业时间的统筹缴费及个人账户缴费

形成了历史债务。

　　按照当时的设计，历史债务主要由政府财政负担。但在当时的情况下，由于一些地方财政困难，无力补充社会保险基金，因此一些地方开始从个人账户余额中划拨资金支付统筹基金支付的养老金。这就导致了所谓的个人账户的"空账运行"问题。在之后的改革过程中，虽然规定不能使用个人账户补充统筹基金，但一些地方仍然将个人账户资金划拨到统筹基金中进行支付。当前对城镇企业职工社会养老保险的个人账户"空账规模"，不同的估计差别很大，规模在 0.5 万亿元到 1.4 万亿元。[①]

四　中国社会保障体系的改革与完善

　　如前所述，中国社会保障体系存在的主要问题一是"碎片化"，制度分割、地区分割、管理分割，导致不同社保"碎片"之间公平性差、便携性差，不能适应流动性，无法发挥社会保障的整体功能；二是隐性负债沉重，可持续状况堪忧。针对上述问题，社会保障体系改革的基本原则一是实现社会保障的公平性，二是保证社会保障体系的可持续性。

（一）全覆盖、保基本与多层次

　　改革开放之后，中国社会保障体系的改革与建设沿袭了

---

　　① 盖根路：《企业基本养老保险个人账户究竟有多少空账》，《中国社会保障》2012 年第 6 期；张映芹、校飞：《中国养老保险个人账户空账问题研究》，《宁夏社会科学》2011 年第 3 期。

计划经济时期分不同人群实行不同制度的特征。这也是导致后来中国社会保障出现制度分割及地区分割的历史原因。在制度分割的情况下，出现了一部分人群保障福利化与另一部分人群保障缺失并存的状态。在城镇地区，机关事业单位人员以及部分国有企业单位职工，享受了过高的福利化待遇，形成了保障福利化的趋势；而在广大农村地区，则缺乏最基本的保障，大多数农村居民只能依靠家庭及个人保障。进入21世纪以来，虽然中国社会保障已经实现了制度全覆盖，但实际覆盖率仍较低，一些生活困难的居民仍然难以获得基本的保障。而实现全部居民"人人享有基本保障"不仅是社会保障的应有之义，也是全面小康社会的重要内容。

与实现全覆盖原则相对应，社会保障的保障水平要保基本。这一方面是因为社会保障不是普遍性的社会福利，而是社会对脆弱群体提供的一种社会保护（Social Protection）。另一方面，保基本也有利于激发社会活力。从欧洲一些福利国家产生的弊病来看，养"懒人"是高福利下产生的不可避免的弊端。从现实角度，保基本也适应了中国当前的经济社会发展水平。对中国这样一个人口规模巨大的发展中国家而言，超过经济发展水平的社会保障，不仅给政府财政带来不可承担的负担，而且直接影响劳动市场效率。特别是社会保险项目，其资金来源主要是雇主和雇员缴费，而雇主的缴费实际上也是从雇员劳动报酬中扣除。在现收现付制下，提高保障待遇实际上是提高实际缴费率，提高年轻在职职工对退休职工的代际转移支付。

在基本保障之上，居民可以根据自身情况通过其他途径获得不同水平的保障。这就要求建设一个保基本之上的多层次的社会保障体系。多层次的社会保障体系与国际社会积极倡导的社会保障"多支柱"模式相呼应，适应了不同层次居民的社会保障需求。多层次的社会保障体系，第一个层次是非缴费型的社会救助，第二个层次是强制性缴费型社会保险，第三个层次就是自愿的，或通过企业年金，或通过商业保险，或通过社会慈善事业等方式提供的多种方式的保障。

（二）增强社会保障公平性

中国社会保障存在的制度分割及地区分割所导致的不公平，不仅严重损害了社会保障的功能发挥，而且在很大程度上已经成为社会冲突的重要原因。从现实情况看，能力较高、收入较好的群体，例如，机关事业职工以及部分国有企业职工，他们的社会保障水平反而越高，而能力较差、收入较低的群体，例如，落后地区的农村居民、部分农民工以及城镇失业人员，他们的社会保障水平反而较低。这种状况严重违背社会保障收入再分配的功能。而制度之间的攀比，则有直接导致不同群体的利益冲突，成为社会不稳定的诱发因素。

在党的十八届三中全会中，对提升社会保障的公平性提出了相关的政策建议，首先是不同制度之间的并轨，包括城乡居民社会保险制度的合并以及整合城乡居民最低生活保障制度，以消弭城乡居民之间的社会保障差别；机关事业单位养老保险及医疗保险制度改革，以消弭机关事业单位职工与企业职工之间的社会保障差别。其次是提升统筹层次，以消弭地区之间的社会保障差异。

（三）　提高社会保障的便携性，适应流动性

与增强社会保障公平性相关的是提高社会保障的便携性，以适应人口的大规模流动。制度分割及地区分割带来的社会保障关系转移接续困难，已经成为流动人口参保的主要障碍。从政策途径及国际经验分析，提高社会保障关系的便携性，主要有两个途径：一是提高统筹层次，在更大范围内实现社会保障资金的统筹；二是建立顺畅合理的社会保障关系在不同制度之间、不同地区之间的转移通道。

具体而言，一是要推进基本养老金全国统筹，二是要实现城乡居民养老保险、医疗保险的制度合并，三是要完善社会保险关系的转移继续政策。

（四）　社会保障的可持续性

中国社会保障体系面临的另一个大问题是隐性负债沉重，可持续性存在问题。特别是中国正进入一个老龄化加速发展的时期，再加上历史负债以及制度安排导致的负债，中国社会保障体系面临巨大的隐性负债。虽然《社会保险法》从法律上规定了政府财政对社会保险的兜底责任，但这一做法只是将社会保险的负债转移，并没有从根本上解决问题。实际上，社会保障体系的隐性负债问题也是多数实行现收现付制社会保险体系国家面临的问题。

首先，"划拨部分国有资本充实社会保障基金"。这一部分对应的是中国社会保障的历史负债问题。如前所述，在20世纪90年代中后期进行建立的城镇职工基本养老与医疗保险

制度，实际上对当时已参加工作及已退休的职工有一个历史
负债问题。这些人在改革之前，特别是计划经济时期，实行
的"低工资、高福利"制度，其中隐含着政府对他们老年之
后的负债。而这笔负债，从理论上讲形成了国有企业的积累。
因此，划拨国有资本充实社会保障基金，具有应对历史负债
的含义。

其次，坚持和完善个人账户制度，健全多缴多得的激励
机制。在养老保险制度中，个人账户制度的筹资实行的是基
金积累制，待遇确定实行的是缴费确定制。相比于现收现付
制，个人账户制度不存在代际转移，也就不存在隐性负债
问题。

再次，在待遇确定方面，提出要"坚持精算平衡原则"，
"建立健全合理兼顾各类人员的社会保障待遇确定和正常调整
机制"。这是从基金"支出"的角度提高社会保障基金的可
持续性。按照一般的社会保险原理，社会保险基金要实现自
我平衡，而自我平衡要求基金的支出根据精算平衡原则进行
调整。

最后，提高可持续性的另一个重要举措是提高社会保障
基金的回报率。社会保障基金，特别是社会养老保障基金，
具有未来支付的特征，需要一定的积累。这部分积累的投资
收益也成为社会保障基金的重要收入来源。

中国的医疗保险制度及其与
劳动力市场的关系

姚　宇[*]

一　引言

　　中国进入了新的经济发展时期，经济社会政策正在被赋予新的理论解释，作为经济发展中心位置的劳动力市场发展理论再次被给予新的关注。在这个领域，曾经被西方学者担忧的问题主要是：（1）中国庞大的人口规模产生的就业需求难以解决；（2）就业质量难题提升。在过去十多年的时间里，关于中国就业问题的国际对话会议一直围绕着类似的话题，开展了喋喋不休的争论。但不容否认的是：中国政府在扩大就业规模与提升就业质量两方面的实践，都取得了巨大的成就。虽然宏观经济政策道路的选择，对于劳动力市场的健康发展具有决定性的影响，但我们也需要看到，一些社会政策在促进劳动力市场发展方面也发挥了重要作用。今天，

　姚宇，中国社会科学院经济研究所研究员。

我们选择从医疗保险制度变迁的视角来分析中国社会政策在经济发展过程中的是如何发挥积极有为的配角作用的。

从实践发展的历史中做好理论的总结，才能让我们看清下一步发展的方向。同时，研究这个题目，也是当前劳动力市场的现实需要，劳动力市场中新进入人口对于健康的需求已经不同于以往，既往已经进入的人口，甚至已经退出的人口因为年龄增长的因素也对健康政策有了更高的期盼，人们的健康意识逐渐觉醒，对自己的健康状况有了更多的关注，对健康政策也抱以更高的期待。作为医疗政策的核心——医疗保险制度需要理性地给予政策回应，需要策略性地给予宣传引导，才能促进劳动力市场政策继续平稳地适应新的经济发展形势。

本文将以历史发展为叙事的逻辑框架，对医疗保险制度和劳动力市场变革发展过程中相互联系、相互影响的作用机制进行探讨。

二　文献综述

一般来说，医疗保险制度和劳动力市场的关系研究中，大多数的研究关注医疗保险制度的变动对劳动力的市场需求、工资率、劳动力的市场流动等方面产生的影响，也有的研究综合研究了这些影响的后果。

（一）医疗保险对工资和劳动力需求的影响

医疗保险制度看似直接影响着参保者的就医行为，它更影响着劳动者的市场行为，同时也会对劳动需求方的行为产生影响。这是因为，以医疗保险为代表的社会保障提高了企业的用工成本。特别是以"城镇职工医疗保险"制度为代表的医疗保险开支，对用人单位提出了较高要求，法律规定企业必须为职工提供相应的医疗保障，并按照职工工资总额的一定比例（用人单位承担职工工资总额的6％左右，职工缴费率一般承担本人工资收入的2％）进行缴费。在这个方面，大多数的未能参加医疗保险的就业者大多从事的是非正规就业，我们很难准确测量这些就业者的规模，因此关于这个问题研究的计量文献非常少见。关于这个问题的讨论，大量的学者开展的是如何为非正规就业者提供社会保护研究，研究者记录了企业主与员工之间共谋并且逃避缴参保费的事实，同时描述了企业主难以背负包括医疗保险在内的社会保险的历史事实。

（二）医疗保险对劳动力流动的影响

大量的文献记载了东南沿海城市到了每年的春节前后，城市社保中心被流动人口排队围得水泄不通的场景。一些准备春节后不再返回这个城市的就业者，会选择在离开城市之前，注销个人的社会保险账户，并且提取个人账户中的费用。这样的情况，在2009年金融危机之前，是很普遍的。[1] 不同城市，不同行业企业，对于是否给职工上保险，表现的形态

---

[1]　郑飞北：《正规就业流动人口参加职工医保的现状与对策》，《中国医疗保险》2015年第1期；樊士德等：《长三角地区流动人口医疗保险政策研究》，《人口学刊》2016年第38期。

是不一样的。当医疗保险存在时，劳动者改变其就业状态或转换雇主，常常会考虑医疗保障因素的影响，特别是对于高年资的工人，更会考虑这个因素，这在客观上构成了对劳动力流动的限制。① 医疗保险作为社会福利保障的一部分，一般具有很强的地域性和不可携带性。因此，当一个地区所拥有的社会医疗保障资源较为充足时，该地区对自由劳动力的吸引就更为显著，就会促使更多劳动力向该地流动。② 同时，由于医疗保险在报销上对参保人就医地域的种种限制，它往往成为阻碍人口向低保障的欠发达地区流动的原因之一。③ 我国的区域经济发展不平衡，不同地区基本医疗保险和补充医疗保险报销目录和水平存在巨大差异。在农村地区实行的新型农村合作医疗制度由于其在异地参与和就诊方面的限制和歧视政策，使其对中国农村劳动力的跨城乡迁移产生了显著的负面影响。

对于中国的劳动力市场来说，医疗保险的广泛普及也可能会影响劳动者在正式与非正式部门的就业流动。刘国恩等人认为，对于正规部门来说，"五险一金"所包含的医疗保险往往需要用人单位负担一部分的保险费用，从而提高了企业的经营成本，也在一定程度上抑制了正规企业对劳动力的需求。同时由于非正规部门的社会保障不完善，这将促使更

---

① 李红娟等：《流动人口城镇职工医疗保险水平的区域差异研究》，《人口与社会》，2017 年。

② 吴传俭等：《社会医疗保险可持续发展机制研究》，经济科学出版社 2014 年 11 月版。

③ 秦雪征、刘国恩：《医疗保险对劳动力市场影响研究评述》，《经济学动态》2011 年第 12 期。

多的劳动力从非正规部门流向正规部门，造成两个分割的部门之间劳动力供求的矛盾，使正规部门的劳动力市场出现过剩现象，而非正规部门的劳动力市场呈现短缺现象。[①] 但是也有学者表达了不同的观点，认为医疗保险的普及，特别是中国制度环境下的针对不同人口推出的医疗保险制度，导致非正规经济部门的运行成本增加幅度有限，推出强制性的医疗保险制度后，反而能够吸引更多的劳动力。

（三）医疗保险对就业与退休倾向的影响

中国实行法定退休年龄制度，劳动者一旦到达退休年龄即退出工作岗位并享受养老待遇，而且对能够提前退休的特殊情况也有详细规定。在这种制度下劳动者对退休年龄的选择余地较小，不能对医疗及养老保险制度做出充分自由的反应。2007 年城居保制度的出台使未达到退休年龄的劳动者也可以参加社会医疗保险，这种制度对退休决策也产生了影响。这是因为，中国目前广泛存在着"内退""假病退"等非正式退休现象[②]，因为医疗保险制度出现的创新形式，以及医疗保险制度快速的推进速度，让一部分劳动者对于自己的劳动力市场参与意愿发生了变化，特别是在正规就业部门，过去也客观存在着对提前退休的需求，一部分人认为这是必须把握的历史机遇，迅速地办理退休手续，虽然这种普惠制的制

---

① 秦雪征、刘国恩：《医疗保险对劳动力市场影响研究评述》，《经济学动态》2011 年第 12 期。

② 封进、胡岩：《中国城镇劳动力提前退休行为的研究》，《中国人口科学》2009 年第 4 期。

度安排使得中老年劳动力具有更自由的退休选择，但它直接影响了我国劳动力市场在年龄和质量上的优化配置。[①]

总结起来说，中国学术界对于医疗保险问题的研究主要集中在保险制度本身的研究成果较多，缺少比较坚实的关于医疗保险制度演化的分析，也缺乏紧密联系劳动力市场变化的分析视角。虽然也有一些研究发现，医疗保险与劳动就业的结合研究，能够对劳动力的横向与纵向流动、劳动者的退休和就业决策起到显著的干扰作用；但是，对于两者之间相互促进的共生关系缺乏较为深入的讨论。[②]

三　不同历史阶段的劳动力市场情况及其对应的医疗保险制度

为了深入讨论本文的主题，我们把中国改革开放以来划分为三个时期进行讨论：（1）1980—1992 年，有计划的商品经济时期；（2）1992—2002 年，从计划经济向社会主义市场经济体制转型期；（3）2002 年以来的社会主义市场经济时期。

（一）1980—1992 年的劳动力市场及医疗保险制度改革

1. 计划经济体制下的劳动制度延续

20 世纪 80 年代的劳动力市场有以下特点：（1）计划经

---

①　王军、王广州：《中国城镇劳动力延迟退休意愿及其影响因素研究》，《中国人口科学》2016 年第 3 期。

②　秦雪征、刘国恩：《医疗保险对劳动力市场影响研究评述》，《经济学动态》2011 年第 12 期。

济条件下的劳动力主要是按照政府的计划方式组织培训、调配、所有劳动者获取工作的唯一途径是政府的安排。（2）因为资本的概念在社会上处于较弱的一面，社会生产的资源要素中离不开人，人成为比资本更重要的资源。（3）随着城市国有企业改革的进步，企业在一定程度上焕发了生机，企业为了扩大经营规模，需要不断增加、补充或更新劳动力，而这种需求日益难以满足。（4）因"文化大革命"期间下乡的市民返乡后的就业需求与企业发展的劳动力需求之间存在摩擦，无技能、低技能人员成为政府难以解决的治理问题，政府开始尝试使用市场手段来解决这一难题。具体来说，这一时期又存在如下几个发展阶段：

1984 年开始试行劳动合同制，并推行"优化劳动组合"。这是中国劳动制度改革的初步尝试，其意义主要是打破了传统的固定用工制度，在一定程度上开始实行择优上岗和合同化管理，一部分技能较低的员工则逐渐下岗，成为企业"富余劳动力"，这一次可以看成是建立劳动力市场的萌芽。

1986 年开始实行劳动合同制度。1986 年 7 月 12 日，国务院颁布《国营企业实行劳动合同制暂行规定》，要求企业与在国家计划指标内招收的常年性工人一律签订劳动合同。随后，劳动合同制度逐渐扩大到企业干部群体，并最终实现企业全员劳动合同制。这一改革否定了在国营企业实施了几十年的固定用工制度，通过企业与工人签订劳动合同，将企业的用工制度逐步纳入市场轨道，使得国营企业中的劳动者和管理者开始演变为市场经济条件下的"雇佣者"与"被雇佣者"，这次改革可以看作是建立劳动力市场的进一步尝试。

2. 计划经济体制下的医疗保险制度难以为继

改革开放后，随着经济体制转向商品经济的改革不断深化，覆盖城镇职工的劳保制度和公费医疗制度面临着一系列的挑战。一方面原有的医疗保障制度中，个人基本不负担医疗费用，能够享受这项福利的人，存在把医疗资源和医疗服务过度使用的现象，响应的政府部门很难控制医疗费用开支的迅速增长；另一方面原有的医疗保障制度是将企业员工、机关事业人员、农民分割在不同的制度中封闭运行，制度本身缺乏社会统筹的风险分散机制，在一个体制内还存在着巨大的福利差异，形成的不公平，刺激着相关群体更加浪费有限的医疗资源。

在这一时期，政府号召各类机构及人民群众在经济体制改革的过程中，要讲求国有企业的经营效益，强调建设自主经营、自负盈亏的经济主体，这从另一方面要求企业尽量减少原先背负的离退休人员的社会保险问题，特别是医疗保险问题。同时劳动力的自由流动逐渐放松，也使得原有的由企业、国家负责，在单位内封闭运行的劳保制度和医保制度难以适应经济发展的需要。在农村，由于家庭联产承包责任制的推行，农村集体经济迅速瓦解，农村合作医疗的主要资金来源被切断，合作社的取缔使合作医疗运行的组织基础丧失。基于城市与农村在医疗保障领域暴露出的问题，医疗保险制度的改革迫在眉睫。

3. 转型初期的医疗保险制度成为妨碍劳动力正常流动的绊脚石

改革开放初期，国有企业实行的还是固定用工制度，与之相适应和匹配的是企业职工劳动保障和公费医疗的福利保障制度。1984 年开始，国家经济体制改革逐渐提上日程，劳动力管理领域的制度改革随之跟进，1986 年实行劳动合同制度时，职工与企业签订劳动合同，意味着国有企业仅在有限契约范围内对职工承担保障责任，而这显然是与政府无限责任的公费、劳保制度与之相悖。于是从 1988 年开始，机关事业单位的公费医疗制度和国有企业的劳保医疗制度进行了初步改革。国有企业的裁员使得大量自由劳动力涌向市场，充分的劳动力供给成为劳动力市场活力的来源。而对于这一部分下岗的职工来说，由于失去了企业所提供的社会保障，未来的不确定性增加，规避风险的需求越发迫切。这就为医疗保险制度的改革和完善施加了更多的压力。

与此同时，企业在这一时期因为改革的原因，而出现了一定程度的活力释放，企业自身发展与严格的计划用工制度之间存在着矛盾，于是企业自发地从城市市民中招收了一部分个人，从农村招收了一些个人，即使企业想为这些人解决福利待遇问题，但却没有任何途径。看似不可思议的现象，起背后的原因是：所有的企业最终属于政府，包括人员工资的发放，都是在政府的统一计划框架之中，在政府未能解决系统性的就业矛盾问题之前，局部性的暂时缓解部分群体就业需求的措施不能成为固定的制度，否则极易引起大范围的新矛盾，所以，对于当时在国有企业内工作的计划外用工一律不能给予完整的福利待遇，包括医疗保险；反过来看，如果连医疗保险福利都不能享受的话，企业员工因为健康因素而被迫退出劳动力市场的情况就成为一种必然的现象了。政府选择这样做，即保证了国有企业眼前对劳动力的需求，又避免了给企业增加负担。虽然这样做的目的部分化解了眼前的矛盾，但是，对于劳动力的个人发展，对于劳动力市场的形成，都是极为不利的。

（二）1992—2002 年的劳动力市场及医疗保险制度改革

1. 劳动制度改革与劳动力市场的形成

1992 年开始的国有企业"减员增效"和"员工下岗"。这一阶段主要是随着社会主义市场经济体制在政治上的确立，中国也开始探索建立现代企业制度，建立现代劳动力市场制度成为当时中国劳动制度改革的急切目标，同时国有企业在"减员增效"改革措施的推动下，开始大规模的裁减员工，掀起了国有企业的下岗热潮。一方面，从原先国有企业中释放出来的劳动力为建成劳动力市场提供了充足的劳动力资源，另一方面，帮助各类企业克服各种经营中的困难，也是摆在政府眼前的难题。

20 世纪 90 年代后期开始的企业改制和员工置换身份。到 20 世纪 90 年代后期，国有企业实施改制，简单来说就是实现股份化和私有化的过程，伴随这一过程，企业员工身份也发生了转变，劳动者与公有制最后的联系被切断，真正成为市场经济条件下除了自身劳动力以外一无所有的劳动者，由此我国劳动力市场正式建成。

2. 社会化的医疗保险制度被提上议事日程并开始实施

1988 年中国开始对机关事业单位的公费医疗制度和国有企业的劳保医疗制度进行初步改革，劳保医疗和公费医疗改革的方向是实现医疗费用的社会统筹，引入社会保险机制，约束就医供需双方的行为。但是，在当时的体制下，这方面的改革进展缓慢，一直到 1993 年党的十四届三中全会通过《关于建立社会主义市场经济体制若干问题的决议》中明确指出"城镇职工养老和医疗保险由单位和个人共同负担，实行社会统筹和个人账户相结合"，这标志中国开始正式朝着社会基本医疗保险制度的方向迈进。1994 年江苏省镇江市和江西省九江市开始进行统账结合的医疗保险制度的改革试点，到 1998 年结合"两江"试点等改革的经验，国务院颁布《关于建立城镇职工基本医疗保险制度的决定》，确立了统账结合的医疗保险制度，要求 1999 年内全国基本建立职工基本医疗保险制度。

中国的医疗保险制度正式开始从福利性、政府无限责任的公费、劳保制度，逐步过渡到政府有限责任的服从于劳动力市场发展需要的社会医疗保险制度，而改革所面对的问题，是在一个具有城乡差距、区域差距的社会中，如何尽最大可能实现医疗资源的公平分配，以及在一个人口众多、经济尚不发达、老龄化速度快、疾病情况多元化和医疗费用高速增长的社会中，如何用廉价的成本提供高效优质的服务，总结来说就是如何实现公平和效率的问题。它既要在解决老百姓医疗问题方面发挥积极有效的作用，又要在对应的劳动力市场发育水平的框架中提供恰当的保障水平，每一年的医疗保险资金在运行中出现的任何保守节约政策和任何的冒进做法，都可能招致上级的批评，甚至等同于处罚的政治批评。

在这一时期，中国的社会医疗保险呈现出的五花八门的表现形式，除了最主要的城镇职工医疗保险外，失地农民医疗保险、灵活就业人员医疗保险、乡镇居民医疗保险、农民医疗保险等针对不同群体的探索形式层出不穷。

3. 服务于劳动力市场发展要求是同期社会医疗保险政策的基本原则

这一时期，中国医疗保险制度的基本思路是"低水平、广覆盖、双方负担、统账结合"。执行这一思路的根本原因，有的学者认为，这是中国的财政实力等一系列约束条件所致。这样的假设并不存在，在中国一些地区，一些基层官员为了职位晋升，刻意讨好当地居民的各种福利竞赛现象时常出现，特别是在临近换届时，一些福利锦标赛的竞争活动常常到了被上级政府发文遏止的地步。经过理性的思考，以及我们和基层政府官员的深入交流后，我们认为，中国政府清醒地意识到本国的医疗保障制度不完全是一种福利制度，更多的是一种配合了劳动力市场发展的社会政策，其发展水平，需要与地方经济政策、劳动力市场政策相配套。否则，两方面的政策都难以取得预期的效果。

（三）2002 年以后市场经济条件下的劳动力市场及医疗保险制度改革

1. 社会主义市场经济体制下的劳动力市场政策

中国确立社会主义市场经济体制以后，特别是中国正式加入 WTO 以后，各级各地政府均从制度上和实体上建立了新型的劳动力市场，企业用人体制机制得到了很大的解放，劳动者也有了更多的选择自主权。中国政府自己把这一时期的就业政策定义为"积极的就业政策"和"更加积极的就业政策"，这一政策主要是指在实施宏观经济政策扩大就业机会的同时采取扶持政策和有效措施，鼓励劳动者自主创业，促进企业吸纳就业，帮助困难群体再就业，缓解就业压力，促进社会和政治稳定。在过去的十多年时间里，"积极的就业政策"还可细分为4个版本，从1.0到4.0，每一个阶段都有不同的关注点，内涵也在不断地拓展提升。1.0版，关注的主要是下岗失业人员；2.0版，已涵盖了所有就业群体，期间颁布实施《就业促进法》，纳入法制轨道；3.0版的贡献在于围绕稳定就业提出一系列政策措施，体现了"更加积极"的特色；4.0版，则围绕着如何进一步促进就业，特别是着力促进创业出台了一整套政策。

其中，离我们最近的4.0版最大的亮点是突出了创业，把鼓励创业与促进就业更有效地结合在了一起。就业方针的调整完善是一致的。过去的就业方针是"劳动者自主就业、市场调节就业、政府促进就业"，中国共产党的十八大报告中将其增加5个字，将最后一句改为"政府促进就业和鼓励创业"。新一届政府进一步提出要打造"大众创业，万众创新"的新引擎。积极就业政策4.0特别强调"创业"，是对新时期就业方针的细化和具体化，也是对"双创"的具体化。

在这一时期，中国的劳动力市场在保证就业规模的同时，开始平衡灵活性与就业质量之间的关系。劳动力市场的灵活性主要指企业具有较高的用工自由度和自主权以及免受不当干预的权利，在中国，通俗地说，就是那些能够促进就业的各种有效手段；而就业质量，常常与劳动力市场的安全性联系在一起，也就是指劳动者依法享有平等就业机会、就业岗位、失业保障和免受不公平待遇的权利。当前，中国劳动力市场的灵活性与安全性又出现了"一刀切"的悖论，一方面体制内劳动力市场过于安全，人员流动困难，企业用工自主性较低，另一方面，体制外劳动力市场过于灵活，劳动者流动过快，使得劳动者权益仍然难以获得理想的保障。

2. 社会医疗保险制度促进了市场经济体制下的劳动力市场发展

这一时期，除了继续做实城镇职工医疗保险制度及相关的管理机制外，2002 年中共中央、国务院出台《关于进一步加强农村卫生工作决定》是完善中国医疗保险体系的主要标志性事件。这个《决定》明确指出"建立和完善农村合作医疗制度和医疗互助制度"，2003 年国务院转发卫生部等部门《关于建立新型农村合作医疗制度意见》，全国确定了包括云南在内的四个试点省份。通过给予农民设立社会性的普惠制的医疗保险制度，鼓励了广大农村剩余劳动力更加自由地进入劳动力市场，即使选择经济较为落后的城市地区打工，无法参加城镇地区的医疗保险，也可以在农村老家获得或多或少的医疗保障。

随着城镇劳动力市场的逐步完善和人口城市化的进程，中国政府在解决了城镇职工和农民的医疗保障问题后，开始关注城镇非就业居民的医疗保障问题。2007 年国务院《关于开展城镇居民基本医疗保险试点的指导意见》，为城镇居民提供医疗保障。自此覆盖城镇职工、居民、农村居民的"全民医保"体系框架初步形成。现行的医疗保险制度主要由城镇

职工基本医疗保险、城镇居民基本医疗保险和新型农村合作
医疗三大板块构成，三个板块的制度安排分别对城镇职工、
城镇居民以及农业人口提供了医疗保障。

　　随着各项鼓励性的参保措施的实施，以及各种医保制度
之间的竞争，中国社会医疗保险的体系不但内容逐渐完整，
被医疗保险覆盖的人群规模也逐渐扩大，从图 1 可以看到，
中国在扩大就业规模的同时，参加医疗保险的群体规模也在
迅速上升，其增长速度甚至超过了同期就业规模的增长速度。

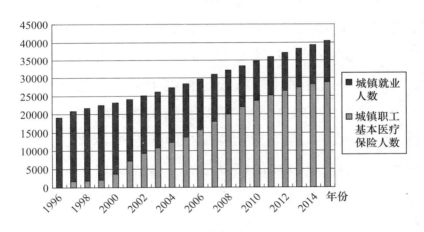

图 1　　1996—2016 年中国就业人数及参加城镇
职工基本医疗保险的人数（万人）

3. 这一时期医疗保险政策中的基本原则

　　中国的医疗保险制度中的一个基本原则是要坚持"统账
结合"。如两个账户分别核算，设置统筹资金的起付标准和最
高支付限额。但是，这种方案没有明示以何种方式决定这两
个账户的支付范围，中央政府把起付标准和划分标准的负担
比例问题交给统筹地区自己决定。两者之间应该如何合并、

如何管理此类问题以及如何运行，并没有给出任何约束性的
政策规定。在国际上，统账结合的主要模式，并不能被证明
是一种较为完善的运行手段，但是，中国政府从实际出发，
坚持把医疗保障作为一种从属于经济发展的社会政策工具，
围绕政策的服务目标，巧妙地避开了关于政策自身效率的
争论。

执行统账结合方式的医疗保险制度，能够较好地体现公
平性和互助性，增加国家和个人的责任分担的透明度，加强
政府对医疗费用的控制，能够让政府希望的适度性原则在实
践中得到落地。统账结合方式，主要在门诊费用上大做文章，
这个途径可宽可窄；门槛也可高可低；自己支付比例可多可
少，对不同的患者而言，从一定程度上来说，是公平的。当
然，与这种制度相配合的，需要有效的供方控制机制，也就
是说，需要以公立医院为主的医疗卫生服务体系。政府既是
运行复合式的付费制度的操盘手；又要能够成为对定点医院
进行有效监管的监督者。只有这样，双管齐下的运行模式才
能有效运行，才能在劳动力市场运行中发挥政策设计者的
目标。

4. 医疗保险制度设计中的"脱节"机制并非制度缺陷

这一时期，劳动力市场出现了前所未有的大规模流动，
也出现了前所未有的福利诱惑。作为中央政府，需要在国家
层面既维护劳动力的高流动性，也为了避免区域间竞争造成
的经济损失，各相关部门一直在小心谨慎地推进医疗保险领
域的相关改革。下面我们介绍两个看似不利于劳动者更好享
受医疗福利的机制。

（1）医疗保险的非携带性

所谓医疗保险的可携带性是指参保人工作单位、工作地点变动时，或者从一项医疗保险计划转到另一项医疗保险计划时，已经获得或正在获得的医疗保险权益可以被保留、维系或转移以避免福利受损的能力。参照上述标准不难发现，新农合具有突出的"非携带"特征。第一，"新农合"要求农村人口只能户籍地参保，而不能随着农民工务工地点变动随时参保。第二，与本地报销相比，异地报销的起付线更高，而报销比例却更低。第三，虽然从政策上看农民工进城务工以后，新农合是可以转为城镇医疗保险的，但由于不同社保制度之间筹资方式、筹资额度、保障程度等方面的规定差异很大，实际操作时还存在困难。

（2）麻烦的目录制管理

在城镇职工医疗保险的管理机制中，最突出的是实行目录制管理，即为确保医保资金的有效使用，减少不必要的医疗资源浪费和挥霍，通过制定药品目录、和医疗设施服务标准等来对医疗资源使用进行有效管理。2000年，中国出台第一版城镇职工基本医疗保险药品目录，并在2004年出台第二版城镇职工医疗保险药品目录并使用至今。通过制定目录对医疗资源进行有效管理确实在很大程度上实现了原先的设定目标，遏制了医疗费用过快增长的趋势，减少了不必要的医疗资源的浪费。在此基础上，基本药物制度作为国家医改方案的重要内容之一被列入2009年的医改工作内容之中，而基本药目录作为未来城镇居民基本医疗保险和新型农村合作医疗的主要目录，其将扮演一个比现有的医保目录更加基础的目录的角色。

目前，目录制管理仍存在着较多的问题，一是医生选择药品的权利被严重地限制，无法根据患者的情况灵活地选择药品；二是患者无法及时享受到最新的医疗技术和产品的服务，限制了患者充分享受治疗的权利；三是药品企业创新产品无法在短期内获得医疗保险的报销支持，产品销售始终面临瓶颈，限制了企业的创新意愿和能力。但是，所有这些限制性措施，都是为了确保医疗保险资金的安全运行，确保劳动力按照政府期望的调节方式在可控地流动。

（四）新经济形势下医改与劳动力市场

1. 劳动力市场的新特点

随着外部经济环境和经济形势的不断变化，当前中国劳动力市场呈现出了新的特点。其一，人口老龄化特征逐渐显现，改革开放以来实行了严格的计划生育政策，经过二十年左右的过渡期，补进劳动力市场的新锐劳动力数量开始下滑，而老龄人口的比重逐渐攀升，人口抚养比不断增大，社会负担沉重，由此引发的一系列社会问题逐渐显现。其二，人口红利的衰减使得经济转型升级的需求更加迫切。充足的劳动力所带来的人口红利兑现完成，劳动力工资水平不断上升，企业的用工成本增加，面对更加激烈的市场竞争，企业不得不加快结构调整和转型升级，追求资本对劳动的替代价值，于是开始削减雇员人数，劳动力市场出现劳动力溢出。其三，传统产业近饱和与新兴产业高门槛并存。一方面，随着社会主义市场经济的不断发展和日益成熟，很多传统产业领域呈现出接近饱和的状态，传统用工企业的盈利能力逐渐减弱，传统产业的利润空间越来越小；另一方面，新兴产业呈现高门槛的特征，表现为新兴产业发展所需要的高端人才紧缺，高额的用人成本和传统企业创业初期所面临的环境迥然不同。

从劳动者的角度来说，进入 21 世纪以来，人们的生活水平不断提高，健康意识逐渐觉醒，人们对自身健康水平的期待随之上升，对生活和工作环境提出了更高的标准和要求，特别是对工作环境中可能损害健康的因素尤为敏感，规避疾病所带来的健康风险和经济风险的需求增大。然而，随着集约化经济的发展，各产业更加地机械化、精细化、专业化，劳动力的劳动强度在不断增加，工作压力不断增大，对健康的负面影响不断积累，其外在表现为慢性疾病发病率的逐渐上升。因此，人们对健康水平的较高期待和高强度工作下日益显现的健康损耗之间产生矛盾，人们对医疗资源的需求快速上升，其上升幅度远远超过了经济增长水平。

2. 劳动力市场的灵活性与安全性的再平衡

新经济形势下，实现劳动力市场灵活性和安全性的基本平衡已经成为一项起码的社会共识。可是，经济结构的转型，一方面要加快劳动力流动，提高劳动力市场灵活性，以灵活性来应对经济发展新常态和经济结构转型升级所面临的就业压力；另一方面要加强对劳动者的就业保护和失业保障，传统的以农民工为主的弱势群体已经发生变化，一些大学生也成为了就业能力脆弱人群，但他们的心理预期和前一历史阶段的农民工完全不同，他们在安全性和就业质量方面的需求，如何得到满足，已成为增强广大人民群众的获得感的主要内容。

3. 城乡一体化的新型劳动力市场

随着城乡一体化的工作的迅速推进，城乡劳动力市场也迅速融合，过去按照学历划分的劳动力市场和人才的界限已经有利于模糊，有的地方已经完全合并。快速的城市化和大规模的劳动力流动，也使得三个基本保险系统覆盖的参保对象边界开始模糊，在基础数据资料不统一的情况下，出现了交叉覆盖、重复补贴现象，事实上，医疗保险制度按照人群分设的思路，不仅与城市化进程趋势不相适应，而且也容易造成医疗待遇的攀比和群体冲突，加大了管理难度，引发投机行为和道德风险。社会流动加速，医疗保险可携带性需求增大。城乡割裂的医疗保险制度越来越成为阻碍劳动力社会流动的壁垒，打破制度枷锁，实现全社会统一的医疗保险制度势在必行。因此，《中共中央国务院关于深化医药卫生体制改革的意见》明确指出，要"探索建立城乡一体化的基本医疗保障管理制度"。通过对现有三大基本医疗保险制度循序渐进的整合，降低劳动者在各个平台转化的成本，消除不同部门和职业在医疗保障上的歧视，促进劳动力市场的健康平稳运行。

4. 医疗保险制度对劳动力市场的影响

新农合明显减弱了农村劳动力外出务工的倾向。同时，对于已经在城镇工作的农民工群体，新型农村合作医疗制度则显著增强了其返乡的意愿。此外，城市不为农民工提供社会保障和社会福利，导致他们难以在城市定居而过早地退出城市劳动力市场。

5. 劳动力市场的新发展对医疗保险制度提出了新要求

从中国的发展经验来看，在中国正确地预防和解决这些劳动力市场问题的关键是建立和健全符合经济发展水平的社会保障制度，医疗保险制度的完善发展水平，也应该遵循这一基本准则。在中国共产党召开十九大的前夕，医疗保险领域，开始了以社会保险为主导，探索具有综合性和可携带性的医疗保障系统，在现有的以城职保、新农合、城居保等为主体的保障制度基础上，通过对各保障平台的整合，减少人们在各平台间参保与转换的限制，取消对不同部门和职业的歧视，使医疗保险真正服务于劳动者并促进劳动力市场健康运转的目的的政策已经启动。

四　进一步的讨论

通过对中国医疗保险制度如何促进本国劳动力市场发展，进而促进经济转型与发展的讨论，我们可以得到如下三条基本的经验：（1）中国实行的社会医疗保险制度始终把对应的历史阶段的社会主要矛盾放在制度设计的前提位置上；（2）不以完美的医疗保险制度为追求目标，适合的，才是最好的；（3）相比于复杂的制度设计，中国政府更偏向于执行易于落地的医疗保险制度。这些看起来通俗易懂的道理，在现实中真正做到，并不容易。为了帮助读者理解中国的"不得已而为之"的做法，笔者认为，我们需要在如下两个方面做到比较深入的理解，才能做到真正的思想解放。

（一）两个关系问题

1. 医疗保险制度与劳动力供给决策之间的关系

社会性的普惠制的医疗保险制度并不是一日建成的，即使从国际经验来看，任何发达国家的医疗保险制度的起源都是服务于劳动力市场、服务于经济发展需要的。中国医疗保险制度是根据户籍和职业特点而开始了政策逻辑的起点，劳动者通过参加工作，获得相应的医疗保险福利。我们要看到，如果只有一个完整的医疗保险制度，对于大多数劳动者而言，即使勤奋，或者增加劳动时间，也不能帮助他们在不同的医疗保险之间进行转移。对于一个转型社会中的人来说，会很容易失去进一步付出劳动的动力，而从眼前来看，利用制度的壁垒，却可以有效改变他们在劳动力市场中的表现情况。[1]

在面临负面健康冲击时，不同的劳动者的劳动力供给决策会有完全不同的表现。例如，享受城镇居民/新农合医疗保险的劳动者通常会选择大幅度降低劳动时间，导致这部分低收入人群的收入进一步降低。而中国现行的医疗保险体制存在结构性分割，享受不同医疗保险的劳动者面临着较大的医疗服务价差，这就导致分属于不同群体的劳动者，其收入差距进一步扩大。

2. 福利制度与道德风险关系

如果医疗保险能够有效降低个人在生病时的医疗费用的

---

① ［印度］阿马蒂亚·森：《以自由看待发展》，任赜、于真译，中国人民大学出版社 2002 年版。

支付水平，那么投保人所消费的医疗服务量就会必然需要比他们自付时消费的医疗服务量要多，否则，投保人没有足够的获得感。同时，医疗服务又是一个专业性很强的领域，相对于患者来说，医生具有更多的私人信息。在个人利益最大化的前提下，医生也倾向于诱导患者消费更多的医疗服务，或者向患者收取更多的医疗服务费。再次，由于双方均有利可图，为了各自共同的利益，医患双方极易结成同盟，共同欺诈医疗保险机构，以谋取保险费。如果过多地考虑福利享受者的便利性和福利水平，道德风险必然产生，无论是医保保险机构增加人力来减少风险，还是提高保费征收水平满足人民的需求，最后还是劳动力者群体蒙受更大的损失。

上述两个关系问题，我们必须要把这个问题放在福利制度的前端，否则，再好的政策，都会引来社会群体的负面情绪的效果。①

（二）中国实践的理论解释——"将健康融入所有政策"的成功范例

"将健康融入所有政策（Health in All Policies，HiAP）"是2013年6月世界卫生组织举办的第八届国际健康促进大会的主题。大会发表的《赫尔辛基宣言》将 HiAP 定义为一种以改善人群健康和健康公平为目标的公共政策制定方法，它系统地考虑这些公共政策可能带来的健康后果，寻求部门间

---

① ［美］罗伯特·诺奇克：《无政府、国家和乌托邦》，姚大志译，中国社会科学出版社 2008 年版；［美］迈克尔·J. 桑德尔：《自由主义与正义的局限》，万俊人等译，译林出版社 2012 年版。

协作，避免政策对健康造成不利影响。早在 1978 年，世界卫生组织的《阿拉木图宣言》中就提出了"将健康融入所有政策"的思想。但是，WHO 过多地强调健康目标的实现，不仅需要卫生部门的努力，也需要其他社会、经济部门参与，他们把工作的落脚点放在了健康目标上。特别是 1986 年，第一届全球健康促进大会上通过的《渥太华宪章》，提出建立健康的公共政策（healthy public policy），它要求把健康问题提到各个部门、各级领导的议事日程上，使他们了解决策对健康后果的影响并承担健康责任。2005 年、2013 年 WHO 都持类似的观点。但是，我们很少看到有哪个国家能够按照 WHO 推荐的政策取得什么成功的案例。即使 WHO 自己宣传的芬兰在慢性病防控领域实施 HiAP，南澳大利亚的"南澳战略计划"，不丹的"国民幸福指数"，印度的烟草控制，纳米比亚的多部门艾滋病防控，瑞典减少道路交通伤害的跨部门合作等经验，其实都是卫生部门自身的成绩，并没有触及其他社会经济部门。

中国政府的在医疗保险政策领域的思路，却反其道而行之，我们把政策的落脚点放在了促进劳动力市场、促进经济转型方面，在配合其他部门工作的同时，自身也取得了巨大的发展。

因此，中国政府逐渐把"将健康融入所有政策"的理论理解为一种社会政策工具，虽然是一种跨部门的治理，但更多的任务却放在了自身的任务框架之内，在促进其他部门的工作成绩之中，实现自身的发展目标。

（三）结论

劳动力市场的发展与医疗保险制度的变革有着密切的联系，两者共同服务于不同社会背景下经济形势的需要，但是，中国政府更善于把握劳动力市场的发展与医疗保险制度建立过程中的主要矛盾方面。自 20 世纪 80 年代以来的所有保障性制度的发展演绎过程中，以医疗保险制度为代表的社会福利政策紧紧地服务于劳动力市场的转型与发展，并在 21 世纪初形成的较为成熟的医疗保险制度体系后，又反作用于劳动力供给决策过程。在新时期新的社会经济形势下，面对劳动力市场呈现出新的特点，面对人们的健康意识逐渐觉醒的挑战，中国政府在医疗保险领域中的基本原则还将继续坚持和发展。

下　篇

President of Chinese Academy of Social Sciences, Wang Weiguang's Speech

Wang Weiguang *

Respected President Alizadeh,
Ambassador Wei Jinghua,
Ladies and Gentlemen,
Good Morning!

It is a great pleasure for me to be here in Kuba, the beautiful capital city of Azerbaijan, for the Symposium on China-Azerbaijan Economic Development and Cooperation! First, please allow me to offer my heartiest congratulations on the opening of the symposium! Also, I would like to extend a warm welcome to all scholars here today and express my heart-felt thanks to our hosts for their hard work!

Today is the 25th Anniversary of the establishment of China-Azerbaijan Diplomatic Relations, also the 26th Anniversary of Azerbaijan's Independence. Over the past 26 years, Azerbaijan and its people have achieved great success in social and economic development, for which I would like to express my congratulations.

Ever since China and Azerbaijan established diplomatic relations, the two countries have maintained stable bilateral ties. As strategic partners, the two countries have enhanced mutual understanding and cooperation regarding bilateral and international affairs. In recent years, there have been more frequent exchanges of high-level visits, which marked a further development of their bilateral relations.

China and Azerbaijan, despite the geographical distance, have a long history of friendship between their people. China's Belt and Road Initiative, which was proposed by President Xi Jinping in 2013, has won warm response and active participation from Azerbaijan. In December of

---

* Wang Weiguang, then President of Chinese Academy of Social Sciences.

2015, President Ilham Aliyev visited China and signed the Memorandum of Understanding on Construction of the Silk Road Economic Belt, which marked that China-Azerbaijan ties has entered a new phase.

Ladies and gentlemen, Belt and Road Initiative was proposed for international cooperation in the new era on infrastructure, industrial capacity, trade facilitation, finance and cultural exchange, with an aim for common prosperity and opportunity. Toward this end, the Silk Road Fund and Asian Infrastructure Investment Bank were established. More measures for Belt and Road construction were proposed at the Belt and Road Form for International Cooperation held in May 2017, including a major funding boost – an extra 100 billion yuan to the existing Silk Road Fund. What's more, financial institutions will be encouraged to conduct overseas fund business in RMB with the estimated amount of about 300 billion yuan. Furthermore, China Development Bank and the Export-Import Bank of China will also set up special lending schemes worth 250 billion yuan equivalent and 130 billion yuan equivalent respectively to support Belt and Road cooperation on infrastructure, industrial capacity and financing.

Situated between Europe and Asia, Azerbaijan has enjoyed geographical advantages as the "heartland" and "cross-road" of Eurasia. Therefore, an enhanced China-Azerbaijan cooperation is conducive to promoting Eurasia connectivity and the development of countries along the Belt and Road. Both China and Azerbaijan will see new opportunities during the implementation of the Belt and Road Initiative. Bilateral cooperation between the two countries, currently focusing on petroleum refining and petrochemical industry, is likely to be expanded to other areas such as information, agriculture, tourism and transportation.

As the premier academic organization and comprehensive research center of China in the fields of philosophy and social sciences, Chinese Academy of Social Sciences has aimed for more academic exchanges between China and the world. In recent years, both China and Azerbaijan have witnessed more frequent exchanges in the filed of philosophy and social sciences, with more events for academic exchanges being jointly held by CASS, Embassy of Azerbaijan in China and Azerbaijan National Academy of Sciences. These events are very important for enhancing the mutual understanding and trust between the two countries.

Now, speaking at this symposium, I am looking forward to your valuable opinions and discussions.

Finally, I wish the symposium a great success. Thank you!

President of Azerbaijan National Academy of Sciences, Academician Akif Alizadeh's Speech

Akif Alizadeh*

Dear participants of the event!

Distinguished guests!

Ladies and gentlemen!

Let me, first of all, warmly welcome all of you here in Baku, Azerbaijan. The walls of this Round Hall of the Azerbaijani Academy of Science have witnessed to the countless scientific events, and today's event stands in the row of most significant ones of them. The Conference that we've gathered for is dedicated to the comprehensive cooperation between Azerbaijan and China – in economic area at the first place.

The People's Republic of China, undoubtedly, is one of the most influential economic powers in the modern world. And I believe that for Azerbaijan the strengthening of the economic and cultural ties with China is also of political importance. At the same time, Azerbaijan occupies a certain place in the Chinese economic expansion prospects which, once the process will reach a certain level, will generate political consequences as well. This is why I interpret the Conference topic as a multilateral one. It inevitably will include also the political, social and cultural dimensions, not only economic. We should look for new cooperation opportunities in all of these spheres. And this is, in my view, the most important challenge of the Conference. To achieve this outstanding goal we must intensively develop collaboration between our researchers, think-tanks and major scientific institutions which is a separate aspect of our general cooperation. And the Conference, that we are about to start, surely can be considered an important step in this direction.

Dear audience, as most of you may well know, the friendly relations and cooperation between Azerbaijan and China have a deep historical roots. In the ancient times, the Great Silk Road played a decisive role in the expansion of trade

* Akif Alizadeh, President of Azerbaijan National Academy of Sciences, Academician.

and cultural relations between our two countries. Fortunately, these historical traditions are not lost, and our relations are at a quite high level nowadays. The bilateral cooperation has been started immediately after the collapse of the Soviet Union. Noteworthy, when Azerbaijan declared its independence in 1991, China was one of the first countries who recognized us as a sovereign nation. Currently, our Chinese partners display great interest in a number of global economic projects in the Caucasus and Central Asia, especially to those transportation roads that will enable closer economic, cultural and even political cooperation in this broad region.

During his visit to China in 1994 former President of Azerbaijan Heydar Aliyev, whom we consider our national leader, confirmed that Azerbaijan recognizes China as a great player in the international political and economic affairs, and Azerbaijan is willing to benefit from the Chinese experience. By the way, within that historical trip he has also visited the Chinese Academy of Social Sciences where he delivered a brilliant speech about the political and economic affairs in the contemporary world and the role that our nations could play at international arena.

President Ilham Aliyev, who successfully continues to implement the National Leader's strategy, contributes a lot to the development of Azerbaijani-Chinese interrelations in all spheres of social life. He accomplished a highly fruitful visit to China and had productive negotiations with Chinese President Xi Jinping on the recreation of the Great Silk Road which in our days has been transformed into the "Belt and Road" Initiative. Chinese leadership evaluated that visit as a milestone in the history of our relations. It was stated that the consistent strengthening of Azerbaijan's economic leadership in the South Caucasus is a positive change favorable for the Azerbaijani-Chinese relations in the future. President Aliyev stressed out his commitment to the more active involvement of the Chinese businesses in various sectors of the economy of the Caucasus as a whole and of Azerbaijan in particular, adding that his government will do its best to assist Chinese business community to invest in the region.

Azerbaijan is situated in the geographic middle of the Great Silk Road and due to that, it is one of the key participants of the international transport corridor which interconnects the East and the West. This particularity gives us some advantages and, at the same time, puts on us huge responsibilities. Azerbaijan actively supports the "Belt and Road" Initiative from the very first moment. Despite a drop in global economic growth, decrease in the world oil prices and some political complications, the volume of trade between China and Azerbaijan is steadily increasing. Currently, China is one of the Azerbaijan's major trade partners. Our countries successfully cooperate on transportation, communication, agriculture, medicine, engineering, light industry, etc. The mutual investments also grow. Just compare: in 1993 the trade turnover between the two countries amounted to 1.5 million U.S. dollars, and now it is more than 770 million dollars. It means five hundred times increase in 25 years!

Taking this opportunity, I would like to confirm once again in front of our Chinese counterparts that we are proud of economic model which we succeed to establish within the past two decades. It's based on the major economic freedom of competition, pricing and trading across border at the first place. And, of course, it's based on the protection of property rights. This economic model along with our natural resources allowed us to exhibit an impressive economic performance over the past years. Now we are working hard to reach a qualitatively new stage of economic and social development. Our future progress will heavily depend on human resource development, advancement of science and education. To be an advanced country, we must multiply our national intellectual potential and establish a system which will open a gate for efficient application of knowledge.

Dear colleagues, it is, certainly, not a discovery to say that there is quite a strong correlation between economic development and scientific progress in the modern world. Moreover, they mutually determine each other. A well-developed economy provides at least financial basis for the scientific research which, in many fields is impossible anymore without solid technical facilities. In its turn, science and research appear to become inevitable drivers for the economic success providing it with new ideas, products and technological innovations.

This was one of the main motivations why we decided to preserve and preserved our Academy while many post-soviet countries abolished or completely restructured their academies. Some of these experiments can be considered relatively successful, while some others not that much. We also implemented a series of reforms in our Academy, and this transformation process continuously goes on. Our main goal is the development and implementation of a result-based system of the research work, which demands, besides everything else, a new approach to the financing of scientific research.

The first outcomes from our efforts have already been received. The most important matter, in my opinion, is that science and economy are getting closer to each other. Currently, Azerbaijan National Academy of Sciences (ANAS) institutes are tightly involved in development and implementation, or in some cases, in examination of the state programs for various sectors of the economy. These programs are to be approved by the President and they represent the main instrument in the planning of country's development. Specifically for fulfilling our responsibilities in this sphere we have established in our Academy the Council for Examination and Coordination of Innovative Projects.

We actively cooperate with the European scientific centers. Our institutes are heavily involved in the EU's research programs of different nature. When it comes to the development and introduction of innovations, we are committed to learn and benefit from every country's valuable experience.

ANAS plays a significant role in expansion of the innovation activities in the country. The large infrastructure has been created for this purpose within the Academy. It includes several technological centers and business incubators, but I have to mention our High Technologies Park at first place. It was established by the special decree of the President and all the resident companies operating under the Park's umbrella are exempt from taxes. This is a kind of testing ground for new ideas offered by our researchers.

Dear friends, I would like to underline with great satisfaction that in the recent years quite an efficient scientific relation has been established between Azerbaijani and Chinese academic institutions. And we are determined to expand these relations.

Two years ago, ANAS delegation led by Vice-president Habibbeyli visited Chinese Academy of Social Sciences. Significant agreements were signed. Then the working group on Azerbaijani-Chinese scientific relations was established under the Presidium of our Academy. Chinese Center at our Institute of Literature, which offers Chinese language courses both for our Academy's employees and for outsiders, is a good example of mutual interest. Some other ANAS institutes also work in cooperation with their counterparts in China carrying out joint research projects, conferences, symposiums and working discussions.

I am pleased to emphasize the cooperation between our economists. Professor Samedzade who is a prominent economist in Azerbaijan and one of the key-speakers at this Conference, published a massive book about China's economy some years ago. Cooperation between Azerbaijani and Chinese economists was firmly intensified after Professor Muzaffarli's visit to China, during which he delivered a lecture at the Insititute of Economics, CASS. I realized from his opening speech, that Chinese experts exhibit a certain interest in the methodology developed by our researchers to measure the level of an economy's liberalism. I am confident that this methodology can constitute a solid ground for joint research – especially since liberalization of the economy has brought very positive results both in Azerbaijan and in China.

I hope that the cooperation between our countries' national academies will further strengthen in the nearest future. Today's Conference is of great importance from this point. I believe that the presentations and discussions will be interesting and fruitful, and I wish every success to all of you!

Chinese Ambassador to the Republic of Azerbaijan, Wei Jinghua's Speech

Wei Jinghua *

Respected President Alizadeh,
President Wang Weiguang,
Distinguished Scholars,
Ladies and Gentlemen:

It is a great pleasure for me to be here, for the Symposium on China-Azerbaijan Economic Development and Cooperation jointly held by Azerbaijan National Academy of Sciences (ANAS) and Chinese Academy of Social Sciences (CASS). On behalf of Chinese Embassy in Azerbaijan, I would like to express my congratulations on the event.

Chinese Academy of Social Sciences is the most authoritative think-tank for Chinese government and Azerbaijan National Academy of Sciences, along with its eminent scholars, has been playing an irreplaceable role in Azerbaijan's economic and social development. The symposium, jointly held by the two influential academic institutions, will certainly give new impetus to China-Azerbaijan cooperation.

Sino-Azerbaijani friendship has a long history. Over 2000 years ago, the peoples of both countries were connected by the ancient Silk Road. In December of 2015, President Ilham Aliyev visited China and signed the Memorandum of Understanding on Construction of the Silk Road Economic Belt, which opened promising prospects for bilateral relations.

The Belt and Road Initiative proposed by China aimed for common development and prosperity in the new era. It will align China's development with that of the countries along the routes, and combine the Chinese Dream and the dream of their peoples. Toward this end, we should carry forward the open and inclusive spirit of the Silk Road for peace, mutual learning and win-win cooperation.

---

* Wei Jinghua, Chinese Ambassador to the Republic of Azerbaijan.

Azerbaijan, situated between Europe and Asia, has been one of the most important countries along the Belt and Road, a founding member of Asian Infrastructure Investment Bank, and a SCO dialogue partner. In May 2017, the delegation headed by Shahin Mustafayeve, Minister of Economic Development, participated in the Belt and Road Form for International Cooperation. China will work with Azerbaijan to boost mutual political trust, enhance mutually beneficial cooperation and promote people-to-people bond. I believe that through our joint efforts the Sino-Azerbaijani friendship, enhanced by bilateral cooperation on the Belt and Road, will become even stronger.

Hopefully, the joint efforts of ANAS and CASS will better facilitate the Belt and Road construction and China-Azerbaijan bilateral relation. Finally, I wish this symposium a great success. Wishing President Alizadeh, President Wang Weiguang and all guests health and success.

Thank you!

The Factor of Science in the Light of the Strategy of "One Iron Silk Road" and the "Belt and Road" Initiative

Isa Habibbeyli*

As it is known, for its level of development the People's Republic of China is one of the leading states in the world. This country's development can be compared with that of the USA and the most developed European countries. In this sense, it is not logical to compare the level of development of the Republic of Azerbaijan, one of the young states, which has recently gained its independence, with the People's Republic of China, one of the giant states of the world. Nevertheless, one can draw comparisons and parallels between the two countries from the points of view of their places in the region, position they have obtained, history and contemporaneity. For instance, China is one of the cradles of the ancient civilization in the world. In this regard, China can be compared with the civilization of Egypt. Azerbaijan is also one of the centres of the most ancient civilization in the Caucasus. It was in the Azykh cave in Azerbaijan that the lower jaw bone of the primitive man settled in this region 350-400 thousand years ago was discovered. *Azykhantrop* is an ancient historical mark of Azerbaijan. The drawings on the rocks of Gamigaya and Gobustan reflect the lifestyle of the ancient human societies in our country. In this sense, the Azerbaijani civilization is a great bridge between the civilizations of Egypt and China. The Eastern civilization has developed passing through this bridge. And for centuries Azerbaijan has made its great contributions to the world civilization.

Caravan routes developed in Azerbaijan back in the periods before our era. These routes made their contributions to the development of culture and science, along with trade. Also, the caravan routes resulted in the

---

* Isa Habibbeyli, Vice-President of the ANAS, Academician.

construction of numerous infrastructures along the route: caravanserais were established, fire-worshipping places and temples were built. This development is a historical process. The transfer of the caravan routes into the Silk Road resulted in the expansion of Azerbaijan's geography of caravan routes. Azerbaijan held the central position and one of the key places on the caravan routes, on the Silk Road stretching from Europe to China. Not only economy, trade, but also culture and science moved from East to West and from West to East through Azerbaijan. This facilitated the integration of Azerbaijani culture and science into the world as well as the inflow of the world cultures, scientific ideas into the country through the Silk Road. Due to that, in the 11-13th centuries Azerbaijan was one of the main centres of the Eastern Renaissance. While one of the greatest principles of this process was the revival of antique Greek and Roman culture and science through Arabic in the Caucasus, Azerbaijan, in the caravan world, the second principle was associated with the fact that the Silk Road stretching from China to the West passed through Azerbaijan.

The Silk Road gave birth to the phenomenon of the Eastern Renaissance in Azerbaijan in the 11-12th centuries. This was also the Azerbaijani Renaissance characterized by its own peculiarities, though it constituted the organic part of the Islamic Renaissance as a whole. Especially, focusing attention to the national features in the development of trades which are considered the most important features of the Renaissance culture such as pottery, goldsmithing, coppersmithing, weaving, etc. and an extensive use of the regional ornaments in architecture... also defined the individual characteristics of the Azerbaijani Renaissance. This phenomenon of Renaissance has great works in Azerbaijan. The outstanding poets, scholars, architects such as Nizami Ganjavi, Gatran Tabrizi, Afzalladin Khagani, Mahsati Ganjavi, Ajami Nakhchivani, Nasiraddin Tusi are mighty creators of the Azerbaijani Renaissance literature, science and culture. The prominent personalities matured in the light of the great ideas generated as a result of the processes taking place on the Great Silk Road stretching from China to the West developed as the creators of great culture. In the same period the merger of Eastern and Western civilizations owing to the Great Silk Road raised the socio-cultural scene to the level of Renaissance.

China has been one of the powerful centers and locomotives of both the Eastern and Western Renaissance. The ancient Silk Road played a great part in that country. The integration processes shaped by the Silk Road indicate that the cultural dialogue has occurred in Azerbaijan since the very ancient times. Beginning from the years of independence this policy has been pursued at the state level in our country. The International Scientific Conference "The Great Silk Road" held at the initiative of the national leader of the Azerbaijani people Heydar Aliyev became the manifestation of the present-day strategy of the independent state. Today in the People's Republic of China the "Belt and Road" Initiative is recognized as the priority of the country. While, the independent Azerbaijani state has built the first Iron Silk Road of the 21th century. Baku-Tbilisi-Kars Railroad, which was put into service in October 2017, is the Iron Silk Road of the 21th century. Baku-Tbilisi-Kars Iron Silk Road will cover a vast territory from Europe to China via Azerbaijan. The ancient Silk Road is the great civilizational movement of mankind that started in the 3 to 2th centuries B.C. and continued up to the 13-14th centuries A.D. And through Baku-Tbilisi-Kars Iron Silk Road new economic-cultural bridges will appear between Europe and Asia, and give an impetus to the great development. This is an important international project which will uphold the world countries united in the light of the idea of the project of the People's Republic of China "Belt and Road" Initiative, and on the basis of Baku-Tbilisi-Kars Iron Silk Road, whose author is Azerbaijan. Besides, China is recognized as a peaceful country not intervening in military and political conflicts in the world and region. Despite being artificially drawn into the war and conflict, the Republic of Azerbaijan is carrying out in the Caucasus the function similar to that of the People's Republic of China as one of the countries trying to solve the military-political conflicts through dialogue and in the framework of international legal norms. Today Azerbaijan enjoys normal relations based on the mutual cooperation with the world countries, especially the states of the region.

In the People's Republic of China the economic reforms constitute the guideline in the general development of the country. At the same time, the fields of entrepreneurship are developing fast in China. Entrepreneurship, economic development and access to the world are among the priorities in Azerbaijan too. Given all this, we consider that the Chinese-Azerbaijani cooperation is of great historical importance and has a significant perspective. The multi-aspect relations between the countries have offered wide opportunities for the mutual cooperation in the 21th century. The Chinese capital is active in Azerbaijan's oil industry, information technology and other fields.

As it is stated in the speech of the President of the Chinese Academy of Social Sciences, science is already holding a special place in the integration process. The opportunities provided in the agreements signed in 2015 between the National Academy of Sciences of Azerbaijan and the Chinese Academy of Social Sciences substantiate a wider development of the scientific relations in our countries. I find it necessary to point out that in the period of independence the foundations for the Azerbaijani-Chinese scientific relations were laid by the national leader of the Azerbaijani people Heydar Aliyev. The national leader Heydar Aliyev's trip to the Chinese Academy of Social Sciences during his visit to the People's Republic of China in 1994 and the ideas expressed in his speech with deep insight, the suggested obligations have turned into firm foundations for the scientific relations between our countries. Also, the interstate relations founded by the outstanding state figure Heydar Aliyev and now successfully continued by the President of our country Ilham Aliyev stimulate and precondition the integration as well as development with the People's Republic of China in all the spheres including science in Azerbaijan. A new wave has already appeared in the Azerbaijani-Chinese scientific relations. A profound monographic work on the Chinese economy has been published by Academician Ziyad Samadzadeh. The staff member of the Centre for Strategic Studies under the President of the Republic of Azerbaijan has developed and published a major Azerbaijani-Chinese dictionary. The staff members of the ANAS Institute of Literature after Nizami Ganjavi took twice the Chinese language examinations in 2017 and obtained high scores. Also, Confucius Centre has been opened in ANAS. Fruitful relations of cooperation have been established between ANAS Institute of Economics and the appropriate scientific institutions of the Chinese Academy of Social Sciences. The trip of the big delegation headed by the President of the Chinese Academy of Social Sciences to Azerbaijan will further deepen the integration in the Azerbaijani-Chinese scientific relations hitherto developed in literature and economics. I think that the "Belt and Road" Initiative of the People's Republic of China and Baku-Tbilisi-Kars Iron Silk Road of the Republic of Azerbaijan will make its great contribution to further extension of the scientific relations of the countries situated on the Silk Road including Azerbaijan. Azerbaijan and China will re-build and further develop their mutual scientific activities in the frames of the joint projects in art, architecture, economics, and social-cultural development. This will increase manifolds the role and significance of the factor of science in the development of both the countries: the Republic of Azerbaijan as well as the People's Republic of China.

Azerbaijani and Chinese Economies in the Mirror of the Research on the Liberalism-Dirigisme of the Economy

Nazim Muzaffarli *

Distinguished President of the Azerbaijan National Academy of Sciences, Academician Akif Alizadeh,

Distinguished President of the Chinese Academy of Social Sciences, Academician Wang Weiguang,

H.E. Ambassador of the People's Republic of China to the Republic of Azerbaijan, Mr. Wei Jinghua,

Distinguished representatives of the Government and the Parliament,

Dear colleagues and media representatives!

I'm deeply pleased to welcome all of you on behalf of the ANAS Institute of Economics at the Conference dedicated to the Azerbaijani- Chinese Economic Cooperation.

This is the first conference of such a format and has a remarkable background. In accordance with the understanding reached during the Azerbaijan National Academy of Sciences (ANAS) leadership visit to China, last year I had the honor to deliver a lecture at the Institute of Economics of the Chinese Academy of Social Sciences. My main purpose was to inform our Chinese colleagues about our research on the measurement of the government interference in the economy and defining the area of optimality in the interrelation between its liberalism and dirigisme. The lecture was accepted with a certain interest, and in June of this year the high-level delegation from the Institute of Economics, CASS led by Professor Pei visited our Institute to get acquainted more closely with that particular research. Our staff has developed and delivered a number of presentations. The idea of the Conference on Azerbaijani-Chinese economic cooperation was born in those detailed and productive discussions.

It is, of course, a source of pride for Azerbaijani economists that theoretical and applied research conducted at the ANAS Institute of Economics causes a certain, albeit not very high, international interest. Our main research topic,

---

* Nazim Muzaffarli, Prof., Director ANAS Institute of Economics.

as many of you know, is related to the social and economic problems of the post-oil economy establishment in Azerbaijan. Improvement of the government regulation of economy, investigation of the balance intervals between the rightness (liberalism) and leftness (dirigisme) of the economy are the constituent parts of that general research.

I believe the modern history of economic theory may well be interpreted also as a confrontation between liberalism and dirigisme. In contemporary world, political competition within countries (and sometimes even between countries) is built on the contradiction between these two philosophies (ideologies) which appears to be one of the main driving forces of political-economic progress in modern world.

The main singularity of our Institute's research in this sphere is that we are now able to measure (quantitatively assess) the level of the liberalism-dirigisme of the economy. For that we have developed a methodology and produced a tool, which is a composite index that we call *Index of Leftness (Rightness) of Economy — IL(R)E*. This is an indicator annually being published by the Institute of Economics since 2014. The latest research covers 95 countries with different level of economic development and representing various regions of the world.[①]

The methodological groundwork of the research is that we differentiate the forms of government intervention in the economy and allocated its "model-shaping" forms in a separate group. Economic models established in different countries are distinguished, first of all, by the level of these forms of government intervention, i.e. any economy can be considered more liberal or more dirigist compared to other economy only based on the evaluation of the level of this type of interventions. The peculiarity of the model-shaping government interventions in the economy is that they are bipolar: in normal, their reduction is aimed on the improvement of the business environment, and their increase is aimed on the strengthening of the people's social protection. For example, both objectives pursued by the regulation of foreign trade that, in fact, mutually exclude one another — the freedom of imports and domestic market protection — have a right to exist. They are like two values with the constant sum, i.e. an increase of one implies a decrease of another. It is fundamentally impossible to increase

---

① *IL(R)E – 2016: The Level of Liberalism-Dirigisme of the Economy;* available at: economics.com.az.

freedom of imports and reinforce market protection for the same goods and services (or for the country as a whole) simultaneously.

The complication derives from the fact that there are not purely liberal (i.e. based only on market self-regulation mechanisms) or totally dirigist (i.e. regulated solely by the government) economies. The economy of this kind is impossible even theoretically. All the economies are located at intermediate points of the conventional scale, the left pole of which is extreme dirigisme of the economy and the right pole — its extreme liberalism. In any particular country and at any given time, the economy acquires certain degree of leftness (rightness) depending on the extent of model-shaping forms of the government intervention in economy. The higher the level of these forms of government intervention, the lefter the economy, and vice versa, relative rightness of the economy indicates lower intervention.

The *Index of Leftness (Rightness) of Economy* is based on these methodological provisions, and is a weighted average of six sub-indices: Public Finance, Price Regulation, Foreign Trade, Licensing, Employment Regulation and Minimum Wage. Data for calculation of sub-indices, in turn, are retrieved from the relevant international statistical sources.

There is not any overall (universal for all economies) optimal value of *IL(R)E*. As it can be easily detected in the Diagram below, relation between *IL(R)E* and economic growth is weak both in countries with GDP per capita above 35 thousand International dollars (intermittent logarithmic curve), and, especially, in all others (solid logarithmic curve).

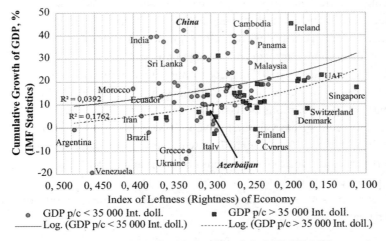

Fig. 1 *IL (R) E vs Real GDP Cumulative Growth in 2012-2016 (95 countries, 2011=100%)*

Countries with a liberal or dirigist economy can be equally successful — both in the economic development and in rising of public welfare. Some countries achieve the greater social and economic success due to the rightness of their economy, while the others — to its leftness. In addition, the optimality limits of Index for a single country also are subject to change over time — due to a variety of economic and non-economic factors.

Nevertheless, the cumulative economic growth for several years in any particular country provides a certain ground to define how close the IL(R)E of that country is to its optimal level — the methodology called indicative. It can also be useful in evaluation of government regulation changes in separate sectors of the economy. If government introduces more liberal (or dirigist) regulation in any sector of the economy, and as a result, the development pace of that sector becomes higher than that of other sectors (or higher than overall economic growth rate), then policies are chosen properly and reforms of same nature should be continued.

The working on *IL(R)E — 2016* was coincided in time with the Azerbaijani economy's adaptation to the post-oil stage. By that time the implementation of a set of new economic reform programs — the *"Strategic Roadmaps for the National Economy and Its Main Sectors"*— has already started. Practically, all the "model-shaping reforms" envisaged by the "Strategic Roadmaps" are of right-liberal character. Our latest Report confirms that reforms of this nature should continue, because at present the model-shaping government intervention in the economy has deviated from the "optimal ratio field" of liberalism and dirigisme towards the second. The potential for liberalization of the economy is high. In the current situation, liberal reforms are a necessary, although not sufficient, condition for accelerating economic growth and raising public welfare.

All these issues — with respect to both the Azerbaijani and Chinese economies — will be discussed in detail at our Conference. I hope that the "paired" presentations will also be of interest to the participants of the Conference. For each problem, we will hear two reports — one from Azerbaijan, the other from China. This will allow us to assess the proximity and differences between the approaches of Azerbaijani and Chinese experts to the issues under discussion.

A wish of success to the speakers and all the participants of the Conference!

Liberalism Potencial of Economic Models: Comparative Analysis of China and Azerbaijan

Mayis Gulaliyev*

1. Introduction

Rapid expansion of all aspects of international economic relations realizes through the expansion of liberalization in the national economy through the influence of globalization. The liberalization of the national economy serves as a countrywide projection of the globalization process. The World Trade Organization, Transnational Companies, International Financial Institutions and many other international organizations require the liberalization of national economies, as the major instruments of globalization. Therefore, in the modern era, each country faces the choice of two opposite directions: to ensure liberalization in the country's economy by joining globalization challenges, or to strengthen government intervention in the economy to protect the internal market.

There is not a single country in the world that does not have a foreign economic activity, going with an absolutely autarky path. There is not a country that is completely transparent to finance and migrants for all kinds of goods and services by joining globalization calls either. The necessity of foreign economic activity for any country is doubtless. But every country seeks to make the best use of the opportunities created by globalization and to maintain the domestic market. The contradiction between the globalization process and the autarky shows itself as a contradiction between liberalization and dirigisme in the national economy. Each country seeks to ensure that the economy's liberality is at the same level as the development of business environment and protection of the domestic market.

The ratio between economy liberalism and dirigisme changes from country to country. This ratio may depend on the level of economic development of countries, regional features, historical development level of the society, national identity and other determinants. For example, level of liberalism in the economy of Japan is not equal to level of liberalism in the German or Swedish economy. Likewise, level of

* Mayis Gulaliyev, PhD, Institute of Economics, Azerbaijan National Academy of Sciences.

liberalization of Georgian and Iranian economies located in the same region differ significantly.

Globalization is a legal and political environment outside of national countries, but in constant contact with national countries. This environment is dynamic and always evolving. In this process, economic relations are formed between the two types of elements, which are qualitatively different from each other. First, it is the link between economic system of any country and institutions that play a key role in the formation and development of the globalization process. The second one is related to economic relations among the countries that enter the world economy in one way or another. This environment also encourages national countries to improve continually their legislation and foreign economic activity. This improvement is carried out only in two ways — increase of the state's intervention in the economy (dirigisme) or decrease of the state's intervention in the economy (liberalization). The constant change of economic policy in the direction of dirigisme or liberalism is the event that belongs to history of economic development of each country. By expanding globalization, no country can do absolutely liberal or definite dirigisme politics. However, each country determines the direction of development by choosing "more dirigisme" or "more liberal" economic model than the other. Such economic models influence on the effectiveness of all economic activities of the country, including foreign economic activity.

2. Review of Literature

Research devoted to macroeconomic impacts of the model-shaping forms of state intervention (in particular, ration of the state ownership in the economy, price regulation, balancing of foreign trade, regulation of licensed economic activity fields, minimum wage, employment) in economics are frequently shown in the economic literature.

Economic literature has different approaches to the economic effects of nationalization and privatization and the relation between these two contradictory processes. For example, B.Holmstrom and P. Milgrom (1991) and A.Shleifer (1998) claim that though privatization ensures an increase in revenues, this is due to the reduction of other social costs. Guriev and Rachinsky believe that privatization creates strong interest groups and these groups have a significant impact on the country's economic policies (Guriev, Sergei, and Andrei Rachinsky (2005)). In particular, if political, legal and economic institutions are weak in the country, interest groups created as a result of privatization can become private monopolists. In this case, it is impossible to form a competitive environment for the development of the market economy (Mara Faccio, 2006). However, in the economic conditions where private entrepreneurship is poor and state-ownership is dominant, even democratic governance remains unable to resolve the issue of efficiency and social well-being.

Investigators can be divided into two groups in the approach to the privatization policy. The first group thinks that privatization is important for economic development and poverty alleviation. Based on the theoretical arguments made by C.Shapiro and R.Willing (1990), and also by J. Laffont and J.Tirole (1991), unlike state ownership, conflict of interest in privately owned companies is less found. In the public sector, the state acts as a proprietor, a governor, and a regulator. On the other hand, state creates favorable conditions for the state-owned companies, which prevents competition.

Study by A.Boardman, C.Lauren and A.Vining (2002) on the evaluation of the effectiveness of privatization confirms that after privatization, business profitability and labor productivity are rising. Summarizing the results of more than 150 researches on the effectiveness of public and private enterprises and results of privatization in various countries, B.Villalonga notes that at least three-fourth of these studies are aimed at justifying the effectiveness of private companies.

On the other hand, in countries where privatization has positive economic and socio-economic effects, such impacts may not be sustainable. In this case, nationalization-privatization processes play a role as an instrument of state regulation of the economy by substituting one another at a certain level (Chua, Amy L.,1995). S. Kobrin (1984), analyzing the nationalization process in 79 countries in the 1960s and 1979s, concluded that the process began in 1960 and reached its peak level in the early 1970s. In the following years, the process weakens. This study was expanded slightly by M. Minor (1994) and covered the period by 1993 over 95 countries. According to M. Minor's research, the process was reversed in the late 1980s, replacing the nationalization process with privatization process. Research made by O. Manzano and F. Monaldi (2008) prove that there is a tendency for the privatization process to be replaced by nationalization after the 2008 financial crisis.

Supporters of privatization believe that profits in private enterprises increase the effectiveness of entrepreneurs and managers (Radu Vranceanu, 2013) as a major motive. Some researchers argue that while the enterprise is owned by the state, workers are more inclined to increase labor productivity and stimulate to actively operate (UNDP, 2015).

There are different approaches to the impact of fiscal policy on GDP. Ramey and Shapiro (1998) approached the fiscal policy in a "narrow sense" and concluded that changes in public expenses make serious changes in the demand. They analyzed the impact of public expenses on the sectors and offered the same model of the two sectors. Two-sector model provides more information about possible changes in quantities compared to a single-sector model.

Other researchers, such as U. Edelberg, M. Eichenbaum, J. Fisher (1999), who continue to deal with such an approach, analyzed the effects of public procurement on the economy in the U.S. economy and achieved results consistent with the results of Ramey and Shapiro. Based on the data of 1997, they come to the conclusion that public procurement creates positive changes in the economy. According to the results of this study, real income, domestic investment, consumption volume decrease, as public procurement, product release, employment, foreign investment volumes increase. Reduction of real income is useful for alternative business cycle models. Fatás and Mihov (2001) identify fiscal shocks and consider increasing government expenses as interference in the economy. They conclude that increase in the amount of private investment during the intervention of the state in the economy is more than the amount that compensates for the reduction in private consumption. One of the major results that their fiscal policy has been compared to the dynamic effects of macroeconomic variables is that increase in government spending leads to increasing of consumption and employment. Empirical analysis of the macroeconomic impacts of fiscal policy suggests that increase in government spending influence on increasing of private consumption, but not the growth of investments.

We also see the same outcome in the results of a study conducted by Blanchard and Perotti (2002). Thus, fiscal shocks have a positive impact on product release and private consumption volume, negative impact on the volume of private. Studies conducted by Mountford and Uhlig (2005) reveal that fiscal shocks have a negative impact on domestic and foreign investment. Similar studies in other countries, such as Canada, Germany, Australia, and the UK, also show the same result, the fiscal policy has a positive impact on private consumption, negative on private investment, and in some cases there is no effect (Perotti, R., 2004). The fact that such studies do not cover other countries and, in particular, with the U.S. economy, does not allow for determining empirical patterns of fiscal policy influencing on macroeconomic indicators, in particular, on production release, investment and consumption volume. The main difficulty in conducting such research is that it is difficult to obtain accurate information on public finances in most countries.

R. Perotti (2004) explores the effects of fiscal policy on the volume of GDP, inflation, and income norm in 5 OECD member countries through the method of vector autoregression: (1) the fiscal policy has little impact on GDP. Only in the United States in the 80s of the last century, these effects were higher; 2) there is no reliable evidence that economic effects of tax reduction are higher than the economic impact of tax increases; 3) impact of increasing government spending shocks and taxes on GDP and its components is gradually weakening. After 1980, these impacts, particularly on private investment, were mostly negative; 4) after 1980, impact of government spending on interest rates was positive; 5) impact of government spending on inflation has also been weak (Perotti, R., 2004).

The calculations made by De Castro and Hernández de Cos (2006) show that there is a positive correlation between government spending and the total production volume in the short term, and that the government spending in the medium and long term causes high inflation and less total productivity. Interesting results were obtained in studies conducted in Germany and Italy. Thus, Heppke-Falk and others (2006) study the impact of positive shocks of government spending on total productions and consumption of private sector in Germany, and conclude that a positive shock in government spending increases the total productivity and consumption of the private sector. But it should be taken into account that such increases are not so great. The study conducted by Giordano and others (2007) on Italy also gives the same result. Research by Biau and Girard also shows that cumulative multiplication of public spending is more than one. The empirical calculations for France show that government spending on private consumption and private investment is positive.

Studies conducted by D. Barlow (2006), A.Panagaria (2004), M.Chui and others (2002) related to the effects of trade liberalization on economic growth also indicate that nature of the relationship between these indicators is not universal, and it varies from the country to the country for short-term and long-term periods.

Studies show that nature of the relationship between the foreign trade sub-index and FDI-to-GDP ratio is also dependent on the level of liberalism-dirigisme of foreign trade and is sensitive to the change of this level. In countries where the relation of FDI on GDP is greater than 20%, foreign trade regime is relatively liberal and the foreign trade sub-index is less than 0.2. Research on the impact of trade openness on the FDI volume also proves that there is no universal relationship between these indicators. According to the result of research dedicated to study of relation between trade openness and FDI for 25 Sub-Saharan African countries between 1977-2009, there is a cause-and-effect relation between these two indicators for selected countries.

Research dedicated to the impact of level of trade transparency on foreign economic activity, in particular growth rate of volume of exports and imports show that the liberalization of trade in some countries has a positive impact on the growth rate of volume of exports and imports (Chaudhary M. Aslam and Amin Baber, 2012). The impact of the trade openness on the total export is noticeably felt and expected. Each country is interested in expanding exports. Being of positive of these impacts for total import, as well as the dependence of the change in the import and export volumes on trade openness is universal law.

In most countries, minimum wage is determined based on living standards and is defined by legislation. In economic literature, there are various methods for calculating the living standard as a human right. Plato and Aristotle in ancient Greece, T. Aquinas in the Middle Ages, and A.Smith in the 18th century, emphasized the necessity of determining minimum limit for living (Stabile, D.R., 2008).

Most researchers think that high levels of minimum wage have a negative impact on the employment of young people and low-skilled workers. On the other hand, many studies have shown that rise in the level of minimum wage does not have a significant impact on the household income of the poor population, as well as the low-skilled workforce. Changes in level of minimum wage influence on the involvement of young people in secondary and higher education institutions and their graduation from university education (Neumar D.,1995). On the other hand, increase in minimum wages adversely affects the income distribution among households by impacting on the consumption of poor households. (Marc T. Law, 2016).

The impact of "minimum wage" on economic growth, socio-economic development, foreign economic activity and other areas in economic literature is of special interest. Most countries are trying to reduce poverty by interfering with the minimum wage. It is assumed that income of households living below the poverty line increases according to the increase in the level of minimum wage. However, studies indicate that the use of level of minimum wage in poverty reduction is not a very successful path (Card D. and Krueger A.B., 1995). Increase in minimum wage also affects the level of unemployment. By increasing the minimum wage, resignation of less-skilled staff may result in their replacement with high-skill or middle-skill employees (Neumark D., 2014). Studies conducted by Lustig and McLeod (1996) as well as Clemens and Uither (2014) have also led to similar results. Dube (2013) claims in its research that its minimum and maximum margins are to minimize the negative impact of minimum wages on employment. On the other hand, the dependence of such relationships on time should be taken into account. Dube argues that the relationship between minimum wage and employment is not a cause-and-effect relationship.

The likelihood of a direct or indirect relationship between the level of minimum wage and employment and living standards also contributes to its economic growth. On the other hand, minimum wage may also have a positive or negative impact on economic growth through collecting or investing. The impacts of the minimum wage on the economic growth may also be related to the impact of the change in minimum wage levels on labor productivity (Samuel Kwabena Obeng, 2015).

In another study, as a result of increase in labor cost as a mechanism for the impact of the minimum wage on the economic growth, the increase in product prices and the decline in profits can have a negative impact on the real GDP. On the other hand, if the minimum wage increases, the income of low-skilled employees, who continue to work increase in relation with those who have lost their jobs and company owners and volume of GDP increases as the marginal tendency of such workers to consumption increases (Sabia, J. J., 2015).

The impact of the minimum wage level on international trade may be linked to the impact of the first on the labor market. Slaughter (1999) emphasized the impact of more international trade on the minimum wage in its research. In his view, international trade changes the demand in the labor market and wage structure. Freeman (1995) explained increase in pressure on low-skilled labor markets through import activity from low-wage countries. Thus, the increase in imports from these countries reduces the demand for low-skilled labor in the country. If the level of minimum wage (W_e) in the exporting country is lower than $(W_e < W_i)$ the importing country (W_i), then the trade of goods created by low-skilled labor becomes possible. If $W_e/W_i \sim 1$, the trade of such goods goes down in these countries.

In his research, Chihiro Inaba (2014) tried to explain the impact of the minimum wage level on international trade through the impact of the minimum wage level on the production of high and low-tech goods. It assumes that developed countries (North) produce two types of goods (high and low-tech goods), but developing countries (South) — one type (only low-tech goods). In this case, the difference in minimum wage between these countries will affect the trade of low-tech goods. The rise in the level of minimum wage in developing countries contributes to the declining of low-tech goods in developed countries. Such decline in these countries increases the demand for labor in low-technology products.

In the mid-and second half of the last century, these problems have attracted the attention of researchers. George J. Stigler (1946), Richard A. Lester (1960), Lawrence F. Katz and Krueger (1992), David Card (1992) studied the impact of the minimum wage on employment. According to George J. Stigler's research, identification of the minimum wage does not stimulate the increase in public employment, but rather stimulates the increase in unemployment. However, research by Lawrence F. Katz and Krueger (1992) has led to the fact that the state's intervention in the economy has not increased unemployment. Recent studies by David Card and Alan Krueger (1993) on the impact of minimum wage on employment in the Fast Food industry have also proven that there is no serious contradiction between these two indicators. Further studies have not shown that minimum wage has a negative impact on employment.

However, all investigations have shown that the state's intervention into the economy does not constitute a bi-polarity, a contradiction between the business environment and social protection of workers. Just such interventions of the state tend to push the country's economy to the "right" (further liberalization) or to the "left" (dirigisme). In this sense, the model-shaping forms of state intervention can be measured in the same size and quantified by composite index. This method of evaluation was proposed by N.

Muzaffarli (2014), later developed by the Economic Research Group of the Institute of Economics of ANAS.

According to research conducted by N. Muzaffarli and others (2017), the economic model of each country is directly related to the state's interference in the economy. When the interference of the state in the economy effects (a) property relations, (b) social protection measures, and (c) economic freedom of action, the content of this economic system varies considerably. The essence of the economic model is determined by the proportion of liberalism with administrative. The same thing differentiates the economic system of any country from others.

It should be noted that not all forms of state intervention in the economy have three types of influence. For example, most of the government's interventions to reduce corruption in the economy do not relate to the model-shaping forms of state intervention.

As the economic model of each country is determined by the model-shaping forms of state intervention in the economy, these interventions always give rise to discussions among public-political groups that are committed to forming an economic policy. Interestingly, regardless of the classification of economic models, only model-shaping forms of state intervention in the economy reflect itself as the discussion subject of political parties.

The state's "vectors" of intervention in the economy can be as numerous as endless. On the other hand, the fact that the state interferes with any particular economic field may have only two opposite directions: "right" and "left", or "down" and "upward". That is why the final vector of characterization of state intervention in different economic activities will have two directions. The absolute value and direction of the final vector determine the static position of the "mixed" economic system at any time and characterize the trend of development dynamics.

Among the "vectors" characterizing state intervention in the mixed economic system, it is possible to distinguish between their "presence" or "absence" as the state's responsibility for the social protection of the population and the improvement of the business environment. The state and its institutions should take appropriate steps to ensure the social protection of the population and, if necessary, to intervene in the economy. Such interventions in the economy can slow economic growth by limiting the business environment. Thus, some vectors characterizing the state intervention focus on the social protection side of the mixed economic system "to the left", and the direction of the business environment to the "right".

State intervention in the economy can be measured. In the one-dimensional coordinate system with the left and right axis, the degree of state intervention and its dynamics can be analyzed by the location of the economic system. Quantitative measurement of state interference in the economy has great methodological significance. The increase in this intervention, tendency to the "left" of economy (or vice versa, the decline in state intervention, tendency to the right) results in serious macroeconomic and social consequences.

Thus, model-shaping forms of state intervention in the economy are: 1) development of entrepreneurship through the social protection of the population; 2) state property with private property; 3) dichotomy between individualism and collectivism. Therefore, political parties try to use this dichotomy for their political interests. Political parties transform model-shaping forms of state intervention in the economy not only into the subject of discussion, but even form the new economic model of the country by increasing or decreasing such state intervention of government. The newly formed economic model is long lasting, if it ensures the optimal development of the country's economy or otherwise, it changes quickly.

3. The Relevance of the Research

Two countries, China and Azerbaijan, have been selected for the research. These countries, which differ greatly from the size of their population and territory, have a different economic development history. The economic development models of these countries are essentially different. Quantitative assessment of the economic development model of both countries based on the development dynamics of the state's economy and macroeconomic impacts of these models can enable the idea of how close the selected model to "optimism" is.

4. Contribution of the Research to World Science

By setting the economic development model of each country on the basis of model-shaping forms of intervention, it is possible to define the "optimal" degree of state intervention in the economy by identifying the peculiarity and dynamics of development. A comparative study of such models between the two countries — China and Azerbaijan, which are significantly different from each other, provides a methodology that enables comparative analysis of other countries. On the basis of such analyzes, it is possible to measure the extent to which the state interferes with the economy and the effectiveness of such interventions in the economic development model of each country.

5. Purpose of the Study

The aim of the research is to determine the effectiveness of macroeconomic impacts of state interference in the economy by comparing the level of liberalism or dirigisme of the economic model of the Chinese economy with the results on the economy of Azerbaijan. The article reviews economic characteristics of the Chinese and Azerbaijani economies, some elements of economic relations between China and Azerbaijan, comparison of the various components of the model-shaping forms of intervention in the economy of both countries and dynamics of components, econometric analysis of the macroeconomic effects of the components of the economic development model of the two countries are studied.

6. Methods

In the study, the methodology of the *Index of Leftness (Rightness) of Economy – IL(R)E* of the Institute of Economics of ANAS was used. Seven forms of intervention, model-shaping forms of intervention in the economy of state, are taken as the basis: 1) share of state-ownership in the economy; 2) volume of public finance; 3) price regulation; 4) regulation of foreign trade; 5) application of licensing; 6) employment regulation and 7) application of minimum wage.

A different methodology has been applied to determine the level of each intervention form. The share of the public sector in the economy is: 1) the share of the public sector in the total number of employed population in the country; 2) the share of the public sector in the total amount of main funds of the country; 3) the share of the public sector in the volume of GDP in the country; 4) the share of the public sector in the number of enterprises in the country; 5) composite index, such as the "size of the public sector", calculating as the numerical average of the share of investment in the main funds of public sector in total investment in the country.

7. The Main Results

The growth rates of Chinese and Azerbaijani economies are sharply different from average indicator over the world. In the decline period of the Azerbaijani economy (1991-1993), the economic growth rate in China was around 14%. Economic reforms in Azerbaijan began to show positive effects in 1995. In 1998-2004, the economic growth rate in both countries was approximately identical. However, as a result of the large-scale implementation of oil contracts in 2005-2007, the rate of economic growth in Azerbaijan was higher than the average global indicator and China's economic growth rate. In recent years, as a result of the decline in oil prices in the world market and the decline in oil production, the rate of economic growth in Azerbaijan has dropped dramatically. The devaluation of Manat in 2015 and 2016 accelerated the decline of economic growth rate (Fig. 1).

In China and Azerbaijan, GDP per capita with current U.S. dollar does not differ sharply until 2005. In the period from 2005 to 2014, GDP per capita in Azerbaijan was ahead of China's indicators. But after 2014, Azerbaijan is far behind in comparison to China. Unfortunately, this indicator has declined in the last 3 years. It should be noted that GDP per capita in both countries is considerably lower than the world average (Fig. 2).

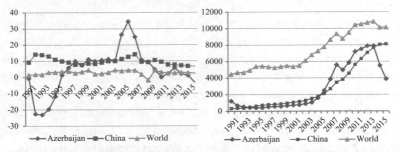

Fig. 1 GDP growth (China, Azerbaijan and world)

Fig. 2 GDP per capita (China, Azerbaijan & World)

However, according to the calculations on purchasing power parity, GDP per capita in both countries has a steady growing dynamics, and Azerbaijan is ahead of China and worldwide in this indicator (Fig. 3).

After gaining independence, Azerbaijan has significantly expanded its foreign economic relations. Azerbaijan is one of the world's leading countries in terms of share of exports in GDP. In some years the volume of exports exceeded 50% of GDP. It increased by 86% in 1992, and 68% in 2007. In 1998, the figure was less than 20% in exports, with the lowest share of GDP. According to this indicator, Azerbaijan has always been above world average over the past 25 years. In China, the share of exports in GDP is around 20% to 30%. Only in 2005 to 2008, this figure was between 30% to 40% (Fig. 4). Except for these years, China's share of exports in GDP is less than the average worldwide. It is not correct to associate serious differences between China and Azerbaijan with differences in levels of globalization or liberalization. Thus, oil and gas have a major role in the export of Azerbaijan. If such calculation is carried out on non-oil products, then it will be known that this volume is very small for Azerbaijan.

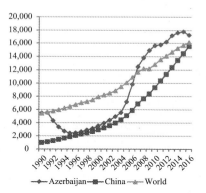

Fig. 3 GDP per capita (PPP) (China, Azerbaijan & World)

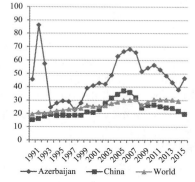

Fig. 4 Export share in GDP (%)

The volume of imports in Azerbaijan's foreign trade is also high. The share of imports in GDP in Azerbaijan is more than 40% since 2000. This is much higher than the world average. For China, this figure is around 20% excluding the period between 2003 and 2009, and is slightly lower than the world average (Fig. 5).

High dependence of the Azerbaijani economy on foreign trade activity is reflected in the share of trade balance in GDP. After gaining independence, share in GDP of negative balance of Azerbaijan's trade rose to 30% in some years (for example, in 1998). After 2005, foreign trade balance was mostly positive. This figure dropped to 3% after the devaluation of Manat, though this figure exceeds 40% in some years. The share of China's foreign trade balance in the GDP has always been positive in the last 25 years from 0-10%. Comparison of these indicators also suggests that the dependence of the Chinese economy on the foreign trade activity is little in addition; it possesses positive stable balance of foreign trade. It is largely dependent on the scale of the country's economy. Smaller economies are heavily dependent on foreign trade balance (Fig. 6).

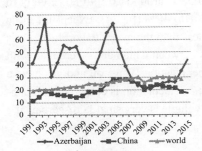

Fig. 5 Import share of GDP (%)   **Fig. 6 Trade balance share in GDP (%)**

China has an important position among foreign trade partners of Azerbaijan. However, imports are substantially higher than exports in this regard. Only in 2008 the volume of imports and exports was approximately equal. The volume of imports from China is constantly increasing. Export volumes are fewer than imports, but are not sustainable and vary from year to year (Fig. 7).

Azerbaijan's economic relation with China is much weaker than relations with CIS countries, especially with Russia. China's share in Azerbaijan's export activity was even around 1% in some years (Fig. 8). However, imports from China are continuously increasing. Though the volume of imports from the CIS countries are more than China, it has a growing dynamic (Fig. 9).

Although the economies of China and Azerbaijan differ dramatically from one another by scale, GDP per capita and human development levels in each of these countries provide a comparative analysis of both economic models (Fig.10). The main point of interest is that (1) the closeness of the economic outcomes of these countries depends on the extent to which they apply the economic models; (2) the economic models in which these countries apply, may change the economic outcome; (3) the type of potential for the development of existing economic models in each country to further improve economic outcomes.

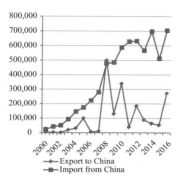

Fig. 7 Trade turnover between China and Azerbaijan (thousand US dollars)

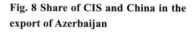

Fig. 8 Share of CIS and China in the export of Azerbaijan

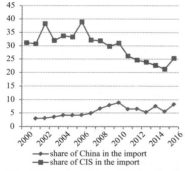

Fig. 9 Share of CIS and China in the import of Azerbaijan

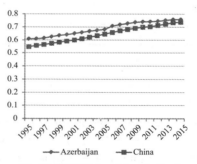

Fig. 10 HDI (China &Azerbaijan)

Let's first compare the main contours of Chinese and Azerbaijani economic models based on the above methodology. As we have mentioned, when we say an economic model, we mean the static system of model-shaping forms of intervention in the economy, and this model describes at what level the state intervenes in the economy. The *Index of Leftness (Rightness) of Economy – IL(R)E*, calculated for both countries based on six sub-indexes, allows to characterize the level of intervention of the state in the economy in certain approximation.These sub-indexes include: 1) public finance sub-index; 2) price regulation sub-index; 3) foreign trade sub-index; 4) licensing sub-index; 5) minimum wage sub-index and

6) employment regulation sub-index. For China, the estimated prices for these sub-indexes for 2007-2016 are given in Table 1.

Table 1 *IL(R)E* **on China and dynamics of sub-indexes**

	Public finance	Regulation of prices	Foreign trade	Licensing	Regulation of employment	Minimum wage	IL(R)E
	SF_t	P_t	FT_t	L_t	E_t	MW_t	$IS(S)I_t$
2007	0.476	0.245	0.347	0.588	0.4075	0.439	0.4265
2008	0.482	0.211	0.347	0.517	0.4075	0.418	0.4106
2009	0.527	0.208	0.378	0.458	0.43	0.439	0.4260
2010	0.444	0.196	0.375	0.430	0.46	0.435	0.3987
2011	0.453	0.176	0.380	0.378	0.46	0.422	0.3902
2012	0.458	0.169	0.394	0.323	0.46	0.435	0.3868
2013	0.461	0.165	0.392	0.307	0.46	0.443	0.3857
2014	0.464	0.165	0.360	0.126	0.46	0.463	0.3595
2015	0.479	0.167	0.360	0.126	0.46	0.482	0.3670
2016	0.499	0.182	0.347	0.126	0.46	0.487	0.3739

Note: Calculated by the author.

In the Chinese economic model formed on these sub-indexes, level of intervention in the economy on public finance increased slightly in 2007-2009, but dropped sharply in 2010 and continued to grow in subsequent years. However, in this area in 2016, interference is somewhat higher than in 2007. The interference of the state in pricing policy has been steadily decreasing for the last 10 years. However, in 2015 and 2016 the level of intervention has increased slightly compared to 2014 (Fig. 11).

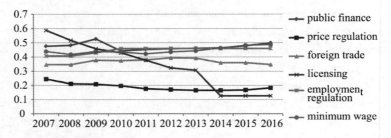

Fig. 11 Dynamics of sub-indexes on China

The state intervention in the foreign trade regime in China during the period between 2007 and 2012 increase, but it shows a decline in approximately the same rate in subsequent years. Thus, the level of intervention in 2016 was up to the level of 2008. The state intervention in the licensing system has dropped continuously between 2007 and 2014. In following years it remains stable. The slight increase in employment and minimum wage sub-indexes between 2007 and 2016 indicates an increase in government intervention in this area.

The composite index calculated based on these sub-indexes in China — *Index of Leftness (Rightness) of Economy* generally indicates that China's economy has been liberalized in the last decade. While the level of intervention in the economy of index in 2009, 2015 and 2016 have slightly increased, compared to 2007, however, the Chinese economy can be considered quite liberal in 2016.

Table 2 *IL(R)E* on Azerbaijan and dynamics of sub-indexes

	Public finance	*Regulation of prices*	*Foreign trade*	*Licensing*	*Regulation of employment*	*Minimum wage*	*IL(R)E*
	SF_t	P_t	FT_t	L_t	E_t	MW_t	$IS(S)I_t$
2007	0.341	0.317	0.361	0.204	0.272	0.195	0.291
2008	0.360	0.240	0.358	0.178	0.270	0.161	0.277
2009	0.373	0.294	0.358	0.152	0.284	0.227	0.296
2010	0.363	0.260	0.344	0.140	0.230	0.218	0.276
2011	0.374	0.211	0.342	0.143	0.230	0.177	0.267
2012	0.383	0.208	0.333	0.139	0.306	0.190	0.280
2013	0.390	0.210	0.333	0.136	0.360	0.202	0.291
2014	0.381	0.215	0.333	0.139	0.251	0.200	0.274
2015	0.392	0.316	0.337	0.097	0.316	0.218	0.297
2016	0.401	0.439	0.338	0.122	0.378	0.200	0.327

Note: Calculated by the author.

Studies conducted across 95 countries, including China and Azerbaijan, show that decrease in government intervention in foreign trade is necessary for economic development, but not enough. In other words, the less interference by the state in foreign trade activities is not accompanied by the economic development. In developed countries, the state interferes with foreign trade, but this interference does not exceed a certain limit. For emerging economies, freedom of foreign trade is not always accompanied by economic development. The foreign trade sub-index of Azerbaijan has been steadily declining in the last 15 years. Some protectionist steps have been taken after the devaluation of national currency in Azerbaijan. However, the positive link between freedom of foreign trade and economic growth for Azerbaijan gives grounds to say that protectionist actions can have a negative effect (Gulaliyev and others., 2017).

In the last 10 years, the state-funded sub-index has been increasing trend in Azerbaijan. However, studies show that there is no universal link between the public finance sub-index and volume of GDP, and the nature of the relationship between these two indicators is related to the economic characteristics of each country. There is a positive correlation between the public finances sub-index and the GDP volume for Azerbaijan (Gulaliyev M., 2017).

Research shows that over the last 10 years, Azerbaijan has faced a higher level of regulation of public finances, employment and prices, and further liberalization of licensing, foreign trade and the minimum wage. Due to a higher level of price regulation, the *Index of Leftness (Rightness) of Economy* has increased slightly over the last two years (Fig. 12).

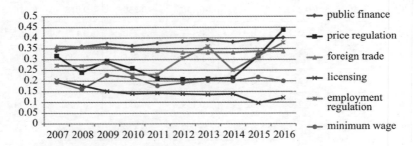

Fig. 12 Dynamics of sub-indexes on Azerbaijan

The mutual comparison of *IL(R)E* in China and Azerbaijan suggests that state intervention in the Chinese economy is relatively high compared to Azerbaijan. Nevertheless, in the past 10 years, the level of intervention in China is generally decreasing. In Azerbaijan, periodic increase-decrease is observed. Another point of interest is the gradual closing of the level of liberalism in the Chinese and Azerbaijani economies, which are significantly different in scale. The continuous liberalization of the Chinese economy has slowed down not only in the past two years, but even "leftness" is observed. Protectionist reforms in Azerbaijan significantly increased state intervention in the country's economy.

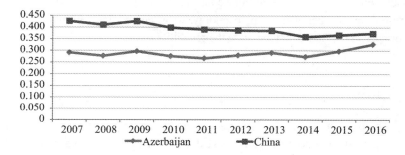

Fig. 13 Dynamics of *IL(R)E* on Azerbaijan and China

Research shows that reforms in the liberalization of Chinese economy have a negative impact on GDP growth. In Azerbaijan, the relationship between the level of economic liberalization and economic growth in the non-oil sector is positive.

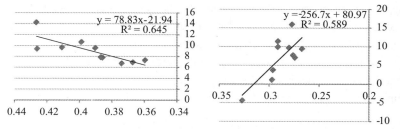

Fig.14 Correlation between GDP growth (Y-axis) and IL(R)E (X-axis) in China

Fig. 15 Correlation between GDP growth (Y-axis) and IL(R)E (X-axis) in Azerbaijan

8. Analysis of Received Results

China and Azerbaijan cannot be regarded as a prerequisite for evaluating the degree of intervention of the state with the above-mentioned methodology. The essence of model-shaping forms of intervention in the economy are related to the weight of state-owned enterprises in the economy. The methodology mentioned does not take into account the level of state ownership. Because that it was not possible for the two countries to obtain the necessary indicators to identify the weight of state ownership in the economy. As a methodology, the other deficiency is that the model-shaping forms are defined for the last 10 years. The lack of observations reduces the reliability of economic growth or other macroeconomic indicators in both countries in determining their dependence on the level of liberalism in the economy. As a methodology, eliminating both shortages in the future may increase the reliability of the results.

9. Conclusions

Thus, by analyzing the dynamics of model-shaping forms of intervention of state in the economy over the last decade, one can conclude that: 1) the liberalization of Chinese economy in modern conditions does not have a positive impact on economic development; 2) In China, there is a need to strengthen some model-shaping forms of intervention. There is a need for additional research on each of them to identify such model-shaping intervention forms; 3) As a result of the protectionist measures implemented in Azerbaijan in recent years, tendency to the "left" of economy has a negative impact on economic growth; 4) The current state of the Azerbaijani economy is far below the level of "optimal" liberalization it can possess. Therefore, the economy of the country needs to be further liberalized; 5) Investigations on macro-level and sectoral levels should continue in Azerbaijan's economy to identify the need for more liberalization of "which" forms, as well as "how much" liberalization of model-shaping forms.

On the Sustainable and Qualitative Development of Chinese Economy, Creation of a Modernized Economic System

Ziyad Samadzada*

The global processes that take place in the world exceed the state limits, information technologies, computer technology combine states and regions far beyond one another.

An interesting aspect in the People's Republic of China is that these processes are evolving over the evolutionary stage rather than the fantastic speed specific to some countries. For example, some countries have been able to enter the world economy through the liberalization of the economy hastily. But a huge country like China enters the world economy by strengthening its national economy and ensuring the economic security. In 1978 that is before beginning the reforms China's GDP per capita was 9 times lower than the corresponding figure for Russia.

Incompatibilities in the structure of the economy, poverty of the majority of the population, high level of unemployment, and the low level of other key figures led this huge country to an abyss which of the result was severe, dangerous for the world.

All these raised the tension in Chinese society. The Communist Party quickly lost its reputation. In such a situation, Deng Xiaoping has announced a strategy for the country to escape the disintegration. This strategy primarily meant radical changes in economic policy. Evaluated as a rare event in the 20th century, this strategy covered various spheres of economic life.

One of the principal aspects was that increasing the role of the Communist Party which is considered as a ruling party in the reform process was regarded as an important factor of China's more rapid progress, and it was important to give special consideration to the ideological support of reforms. In other words, it was decided

* Ziyad Samadzada, Academic, Chairman of the Committee for Economic Policy, Industry, Entrepreneurship of the National Assembly of the Republic of Azerbaijan.Scientific director of the Public Union "One Path, One Way Economic Analysis and Collaboration".

to make innovations in the economy without changing the country's political system.

The Chinese people didn't strike a moral blow to the elderly and skillfully used ideological forms and methods that emerged from realism and allowed applying benefits of socialist economy and the market economy but not magnificent slogans in the country in the reform process. The country should be saved. There was no other way out. China has found an effective way of making reforms without "shock therapy".

The revival plan was a challenge to spirit of national patriotism of successors of the country's rich culture which is an ancient center of human civilization, historically powerful state, and which has not seen any country as an opponent for many years and then has been a semi-colonial country. This plan met main purposes of the Chinese people, and therefore encouraged the mobilization of its building activity. The revival plan has formed the main line of the government's practical activities with the ruling party in essence and the elimination of the country's economic recession has become a major duty of all foreign and domestic policy. The long-term nature of the program has given historic optimism to Chinese society.

In a word, in contrast to the other socialist countries, the Communist Party of China was not only the initiator of reforms but also a guarantor and organizer of their implementation.

In the course of reforms, Deng Xiaoping also commented on one issue: "The planned economy is not yet socialism. There is also planning in a full privatization, and the market economy is not capitalism".

Such a position has diminished the desires of those who were in favor of the planned economy against the market economy.

In December 1978, after the long debates in the Third Plenum of the 11th Central Committee of the Communist Party of China, the "open door" principle for the outside world was adopted. The stage-by-stage implementation of reforms has been identified.

In China, the reforms first began in the village. This decision which was contrary to the West's recommendations, that is to start the reforms from the agrarian sector first of all was a great risk, but at the same time it was a very correct step. After all, the situation in the Chinese village was even worse. At the beginning of 1980s, poverty rate in the Chinese village was very high. Food products were provided with coupon in the city. And in the villages, the income of 250 million people was lower than the official poverty rate.

Therefore, the Communist Party of China decided to apply market relations firstly in the agrarian sector, which gave its positive results.

China prepared to enter the World Trade Organization very seriously. Therefore, it thoroughly analyzed rules of entering the world market, and made every effort to produce more competitive products not losing in the free market trade and achieved remarkable results. China's export capabilities are now very high. The figures characterizing export and import clearly prove this. China's exchange reserves, including gold, exceeded $3 trillion, which is 3.6 times more than in 2005. Artificial reduction in money circulation in the country is not allowed, domestic demand is stimulated, and changing the consumer price index are systematically analyzed and controlled.

One of the most important issues is that radicalism in economic reforms was not allowed, property forms were not confronted. The government preferred to take precautionary measures in order to increase the effectiveness of the use of public property, as well as to create conditions for the development of property forms on the basis of competition principles and made relevant amendments to the laws in order to prevent them from being confronted.

Our research shows that China's "economic miracle" which is impressive all over the world for its development speed, scale and outcomes, is largely related to the creative approach to property relations today.

The Chinese believe that pushing failures, socio-economic pains that manifest themselves in some cases off on socialism is defamation of the history, falsification of historical facts, disrespect and treachery of the holy spirit and works, sufferings of our great forefathers, but nothing else.

One of the aspects taking attention in the conversations and disputes we had in China with scientists and specialists was that they didn't claim that Chinese economic model was a single development model. They are in favor of using the world experience, regardless of the country in which it is achieved, if this is good.

World experience shows that many undeveloped countries have not been able to ensure a high rate of development despite financial assistance. In other words, none of the undeveloped for a long time, but currently developing countries has achieved a progress like China in a short period of time.

China pursues the liberalization of economy consistently, patiently which doesn't belong to any state and put forward the protection of the national state interests and the minimization of social losses. On the one hand, the government abandons the economy by refusing administrative-domination methods and on the other hand, it is getting closer to it with the need for the regulation of the economy.

And the China's experience proves once again that thinking of "market solves everything" in the country being in a transitional period, having a very complex situation is a very wrong idea and those who live with this idea are probably unaware of the world experience or there is no problem of the national economy's revival for them.

It was especially highlighted in the congress of Chinese communists held in 2017 that the country's economic policy and the latest challenges will be continued taking into account changes in the world and national interests.

The government considers the refusal of the ideas of socialism in the management of economy as an unforgivable mistake.

In 2017, GDP per capita for purchasing parity in China was $16,600, which is 2.8 times more than in 2005. The GDP growth rate in the country has been much higher than the world average for 40 years.

There are many concepts about "open economy" in the scientific economic literature. The Chinese government's economic policy and its successes once again prove that the open economy should have certain limits. Free economic development, without any regulation, can damage national interests, national security and state independence.

Most of the developing countries have been suffering from the implementation of radical concept of the open economy and application of bad competition methods up to now. However, when the concept of open economy is implemented deliberately, any country can achieve great success in entering the world economy.

Today, in China, a multidisciplinary and harmonious functional structure ensuring the Chinese economy's openness for the outside world has been created in the coastal zone, bordering regions and internal continental regions base which have no analogues in the world for scale. Each of these regions plays a role of a "window" and mediator in the development of economy directed to the foreign market, increasing the currency revenues and importing advanced techniques and technologies from abroad.

As a result of successful "open door" policy, China has risen to the second place in the world in terms of foreign capital involvement.

All regulatory documents defining the mechanism for the import and export management, realization of import and export goods, the rules for the fight against dumping and dotations have been adopted in the country. These legal acts helped to improve the foreign trade management mechanism, as well as created a rule in the foreign economic relations and thereby increased the international reputation of the country.

Thanks to the "open door" policy and rapid development of economic cooperation with foreign countries, the structure of the Chinese economy has improved significantly; the country's exchange reserves have increased several times, which has become an important factor ensuring the country's economic security.

Today, China is a country that has a serious impact on the global economy.

Investments of foreign companies in the Chinese economy continue to grow rapidly even now. Foreign investors explain their great interests in the Chinese market with the huge potential of this market, its great scale. Moreover, the high interest in the Chinese market is related to this country's proximity to rapidly developing markets in Asia, low transaction costs and direct support of export by the government.

In general, today China is known as a country with attractive investment climate, a very flexible market and a relatively expensive workforce, and all these favorable factors don't remain outside the attention of foreign investors. Foreign investors ever pay attention to the fact that China has an ancient culture and rich history, the Chinese always remember their investors, adherence to traditions, and commitment to the homeland.

The Chinese government simplifies the rules of involving investment in the country year by year. A great importance is given to the activities of mixed enterprises with the involvement of various organizational structures, including foreign capital. Such enterprises are established with the Chinese company, enterprise or economic organization by foreign legal or physical entity in the country.

China has created trade and economic relations with more than 220 countries and regions of the world now. The experience of the past 40 years shows that thanks to the implementation of "open door" policy for the outside world and active foreign trade, it is possible to use the opportunities of either domestic market or the international markets more fully, and favorable conditions are created for maneuvering with material resources.

The average annual GDP growth rate in the People's Republic of China has been 2-3 times higher than the global average over the past 15 years. It is enough to show that over the last 5 years, the increase in the gross domestic product was between 7% to 8% with comparable prices. And this is a very high indicator of development in the conditions of increased risks in the global economy. And its absolute amount was $13 trillion and $20 trillion due to the purchasing parity in 2017. This is the second highest indicator among the world countries. Undoubtedly, such economic development is directly related to the fact that the country has a strong investment flow and that the production-based investments are increasing rapidly. We have already mentioned above that Chinese government strengthens the financial basis of the country's economic development year by year. Thus, gross weight in GDP is 2 times higher than the world average. The average annual growth rate of total investments in the country's economy is 2 times higher than growth rate of gross domestic product. Interestingly, the role of the budget in investment funds allocated to the economy of country tends to increase. This tendency has intensified after the crisis in the world financial market. It is known that budget expenditure are acting as one of the most important mechanisms of the government's regulation policy in the economic development process, the presence of the budget in the identification and implementation of economic development directions reflects the interests of the government, and increases the aggregate demand. As a result, the money supply in circulation increases, investment activity and development opportunities of production infrastructure are expanding.

The rapid and dynamic development of the Chinese economy undoubtedly requires an objective assessment of the role of the state in the economy. In short, we would like to express some of our thoughts by referring to the experience of China and other states.

In general, how much should the optimal level of government intervention in the economy be? What should be the ratio between the public sector and the private sector? How should this ratio be changed? Can all economy be concentrated in the private sector? There is, was and of course will be hot disputes, investigations around these questions.

Starting from the second half of the twentieth century, the issue of the state's role in the economy is in the focus of the most influential organizations in the world, heads of state, economists and politicians. From the development history of the twentieth century, it is known that the role of the state in the economy in a number of Western countries, including the USA has been different at every stage of development. The concepts that defend increasing the impact of the state on the economy in some periods and management of economy mainly based on the market relations in some periods have been proposed. Today, radical registrants should be reminded that U.S. presidents Roosevelt and Johnson's ideas about forming a big community in the U.S. were realized because that they were able to create a powerful impact mechanism for the state's economy, and the country was pulled out of the crisis by the state.

Problems such as control of inflation, increasing employment, economic activity, creating social protection system were directly solved by the government's involvement and leadership.

It should be noted that in the world economic literature, there are various views on the role of the state in the development of economy and the society in general. Of course it is not possible to investigate them in details. However, it should be accepted that the issue of the interference of the state to the economy depends on the specific conditions of each country, its historical development, level of socioeconomic development, and the domestic political situation. It is an incorrect idea to prepare the same scenario in this issue for all countries.

Chinese experts say that since there is no ideological content, the market is neutral, universal, secular and it does not mean that the transition to the PRC does not mean the choice of a new social development path, nor the use of any foreign model. If the Chinese government takes something from any country and applies it, it does not mean that the country is more civilized, more democratic, but means that China's imports from that country are more in line with China's national interests.

In general, the problem of the state's interference in the economy, both in the developed and developing countries, including China, will remain relevant both in the near and far in the future. We must continually follow these processes, analyze them, and use them in terms of the the national state interests.

The government of China concentrated on monetary policy to remove the country from the crisis, currency regulation, strengthening the legal framework for reforms, creating conditions for the protection of other forms of ownership along with state property, gradual formation of healthy competition environment, domestic market protection, preparation of programs to help increase employment and control over them and all these gave positive results.

The government considers definition of effective ration between consumption and harvesting, regulation of industry and agricultural products exchange, increasing control over the use of financial funds, increasing cash flows to the treasury as important prerequisites of economic development.

One of the important problems of people throughout history has been the issue on the provision of food to the people.

In the reform process, the government of China led its people to the right direction, right policy to use all the means to ensure abundance of food and to solve this serious problem.

An interesting tendency in the production and international trade of world's agricultural products is also evident. This is the fact that, despite the increase in the production of the world's agricultural products, its role in the world trade decreases. Over the past 40 years, the share of food and agricultural products declined more than 2 times, which is one of the main reasons of why this is the solution of the food problem in China with a population of more than 1.3 billion, taking measures to eliminate hunger.

Here, proven methods and management techniques in the world experience in agrarian process are applied; their application opportunities in local conditions are investigated and successfully used in positive results. We want to mention once again that food supply of the country with a population of more than 1.3 billion people is of really a global significance of human achievement.

One of the key points attracting attention is that here a villager is more interested in productivity, but not in the expansion of planting areas.

The government of China pays special attention to mitigate the differences between the levels of the income of the people in the regions, cities and villages. Of course, it is very difficult to fully adjust it. However, it is interesting that important works are done to reduce the differences between the per capita incomes of the urban population and the corresponding indicator in rural areas in the period covered by about 40 years.

Measures are taken to increase economic activity in small towns and settlements, which also allow them to effectively use workforce and to eliminate discrepancies in the development of a number of regions, villages, to create regional markets, and to optimize area and territorial structure of national economy in total.

One of the important directions of development strategy of agrarian sector that is the main factors of its implementation is the technical progress, raising the cultural level of village population, training the personnel who were master of modern technologies. Measures serving the agrarian sector development show once again that implementation of economic reforms in systematic and logical sequence by the head of the state come from the main line of the economic policy. And the main line is that increasing the modeling level of agrarian sector in total, development of economy dynamically and qualitatively should effectively eliminate the discrepancies in its field-territorial structure.

The most amazing miracle is that in a world where food security faces serious challenges, this huge country has successfully solved these problems.

The long-term research carried out by the author suggests that China today demonstrates such a high level of development of global tensions, which is a logical consequence of the state policy that meets the national interests in the country.[1]

I would also say that the launch of Europe-Caucasus-Asia transport corridor was in the spotlight long ago. But the objective conditions for its implementation were limited. It was impossible to realize this idea during USSR period, because there was a single transport system in the country. The cargo was sending from Europe to China and neighboring countries transiting through Russia and Kazakhstan and this was considered as an important, strategically important road. In such a situation, USSR government couldn't have agreed with the opening of a new transport corridor and its transit through Transcaucasia, Central Asian Republics due to its nature. The USSR collapsed and new independent states emerged in its territory and this created objective conditions for the realization of this transport corridor. The European Union raised a development of such a program, the importance of launch of Europe-Caucasus-Asia corridor as a global issue for its great inters and strengthening the independence of new independent states. In the twentieth century's decade, the Chinese government made a big-

---

[1] Chairperson of the Parliamentary Committee on Economic Policy, Industry and Entrepreneurship, Academician Ziyad Samadzade published two books – *The Economic Miracle of China*, *China in the Global World Economy* in Russian and Azerbaijani languages, more than a dozen of books on China's economy, a special number of the "Economics" newspaper dedicated to the 55th anniversary of the People's Republic of China. In April 2001, the International Scientific-Theoretical Conference titled "Transition from planned economy to market economy and economic development model" was held in Baku with great success. The Union of Economists of Azerbaijan, the Embassy of the People's Republic of China and the Institute of People's Diplomacy were the organizers of that conference. The mentioned conference was widely covered by the mass media and caught great interest of the experts.

scale initiative.

In the history of every nation, there are such events whose correct assessment and solution become a strong factor of everlasting development. The realization of "One pipeline one road" project of the Europe-Caucasus-Asia transport corridor is one of these events. Because Azerbaijan is in the center of this transport corridor; is a point which connects two continents. The economic-political potential, capacity of this transport corridor is a so extensive which this is a constant capital, constant political position, constant stable development, permanent active participation in international economic relations for our republic.

Therefore, I consider the Baku Summit as one of the most important achievements of Azerbaijani diplomacy and Azerbaijan's foreign policy and I consider this summit to be the most important than the international assemblies held in recent years.

The leadership of the People's Republic of China state that it was emphasized that the "Belt and Road" Initiative is not only important for China but also for the world. I would like to say with pleasure that at the meeting of the chairman of the People's Republic of China with Ilham Aliyev, the President of the Republic of Azerbaijan, it was promoted highlighted that the realization of the "Belt and Road" Initiative has been expanded beneficial cooperation opportunities between the two countries.

At the 19th congress of the Chinese Communist Party, fundamental tasks were put forward in relation with the further development of the country, which I consider to mention some of them. These tasks include first of all achieving to ensure the greatest victory of socialism, which is distinguished by Chinese specification at the new stage, implementing a new concept of development, building a modernized economic system, deepening structural reforms for faster and more qualitative development of the real sector, accelerating the creation of innovation-type state, implementing growth strategy, balanced and coordinated strategy of the regions, rapidly improving the socialist market economic system, ensuring better and high-quality living of Chinese people by effectively utilizing all opportunities for a systematic and consistent implementation of the "Belt and Road" Initiative is Initiative. I am pleased to state that China-Azerbaijan relations are developing in all areas with confidence. The friendly relations between the two countries are aimed at the restoration of the ancient silk road of Azerbaijan, the development of cooperation with the "Belt and Road" Initiative, including the opening of the

Baku Sea Port, Baku-Tbilisi-Kars Railway in Azerbaijan, located between Asia Europe Establishment of the Alat Economic Zone on the Baku coast of the Caspian Sea will further develop Azerbaijan's economic relations, which will contribute to the economic and social progress of our countries.

Government Regulation of the Pension System: Cross-country Comparative Analysis

Rasmiya Abdullayeva*

1. Hypothesis

How does the liberalization have an influence on the pension system and is it possible to measure the level of the government regualtion of the pension system? Research of Institute of Economics proves that in most cases liberalism gives a positive effect on the social-economic development. However, constructive potential of economic liberalism is not everlasting, it means, first of all, at some stages there is certain end for liberalization of the economy. Secondly, after certain level (before the last level) liberalism may bring out immanent shortage (the market sinister) in free market in a destructive way.

That is why one of the main (and very difficult) duties of economic science is to define effective ranges of liberalism (accordingly, state regulation) for each certain country during specific time frame. This duty is urgent for Azerbaijan as well. Azerbaijan National Academy of Sciences (ANAS) Institute of Economics' recent research proves that liberalism of Azerbaijani economy has not reached its last effective level and in the nearest future it will be a necessary condition for acceleration of country's economic development and reinforcement of the social protection of population, although not a satisfactory condition (Muzaffarli, 2016). Therefore, by liberalizing pension system and creating non-state pension provision, one of the main demand of the period is to ease the social burden of the government and to increase the reinforcement of social protection.

One of the difference of pension funds from different social protected chain is that this system is able to liberalize. In this case the political economic ideology of government, performing leftness and rightness economical politic which affect to the structure of pension system and the proportion of state and non-state pension funds. Referring to the political and economic ideology, first of all, it intends relation of

---

* PhD, Associate Professor, Institute of Economics, Azerbaijan National Academy of Sciences.
  Email: resmiyyesabir@gmail.com

government to economic liberalism and dirigisme. First ideology is about how to reduce government's model intervention to economy, the second one is by contrast, which means to increase. Leftness established on the basis of dirigisme and rightness based of liberalism announce its recent improvement of public welfare purposes. According to leftness political and economic ideology, the "shortest" and possible way to reach this goal is to carry out regulatory measures by government, while based on rightness ideology, the solution is to "release" economy from the pass. The competition between these two philosophies (leftness and rightness) is the main driving forces of political and economic development in the modern world (Muzaffarli 2014).

Generally, pension system is formed under the influence of a number of political, economic, demographic and social factors. Regardless of the political and economic ideology, while implementation pension reforms each government has obligated to take into account the current development level of the economy, the demographic situation, the mentality of the population (the nature of the economic psychology) and its capacity to strength social protection, also, it needs to forecast the near future for each aspects. Therefore, the ideology of liberalism or dirigisme which government follows is less important for the establishment of the pension system than comparing to other sectors of economy.

2. Methodology

Based on the study of various classifications, quantitative evaluation of the pension system is compulsory condition for the optimization of pension provision. From this point of view, the level of liberalization of the pension system, i.e., governmental intervention measurement, is very important in this system.

Based on some authors, lack of pension costs is more specific for poor countries and more costs are specific for rich countries (Pallares-Miralles, Romero and Whitehouse, 2012). In fact, this idea is wrong. Because, though a number of economically highly developed countries' public pension costs are less, overall, pensions, replacement rate, pension income are high enough. The reason for this is the strong development in the private pension system. The country's pension costs depend on the level of government interference in the country's pension system rather the fact of how poor or rich the country is. Experience shows that intervention of the government to pension system is not directly but indirectly (by stimulating the establishment and development of the private pension system) can enhance social protection of pensioners. This is a universal pattern and can be attributed to all components of social welfare. N. Muzaffarli proved that, formally "not" "socially oriented", by meaning not presented as rightness economics, formally could be called more social oriented rather than so-called "social oriented" economy and in most cases it is. (Muzaffarli, 2014).

Our research proved, that there is no index measuring government's intervention to pension system's performance in the world. For the first time, by the Institute of Economics of Azerbaijan National Academy of Sciencesthe index measuring government's intervention to pension system's performance (Pension System Liberalization Index, PSLI) has been calculated. Primarily, not having the necessary statistic information dates the Index has been calculated on the base of one- ratio of investments in private pension funds valued in various financial instruments to GDP.

But the following indicators will be taken into notice in the future calculations:

-the ratio of the private and public sector in the pension system;

-the ratio of the private pension assets (%, GDP);

-the restrictions of the management of the of the private and public pension assets;

-socialinsurance taxes, etc.

PSLI is calculated in accordance of the Institute of Economics of Azerbaijan National Academy of Sciences annually published Leftness Economy (Rightness) Index methodology (IL(R)E, 2015), and it is being calculated based on the ratio of investments in private pension funds valued in various financial instruments to GDP. The goal is to measure government's intervention to pension system's performance. PSLI changes between 0-1: "0" shows pension system's "absolute rightness" (the government does not interfere to pension system at all), "1" shows "absolute leftness" (pension system regulated by the government).

The ratio of private pension funds investment to GDP indexed by the formula *(Vi - Vmin) / (Vmax - Vmin)*.

Among the countries included in the ranking with the ratio of investment in private pension funds to GDP, Denmark is the country with the largest number (205.9%), but the least number is in Azerbaijan (0). That is why Vmax and Vmin were replaced accordingly with 250 and 0. Statistical source is database of the Organization for Economic Cooperation and Development for 2015. (OECD, 2016).

In the initial stage PSLI was calculated for 54 countries.

3. The Results and Their Interpretation

Below is the table where is shown the ratio of private pension investment held by various financial vehicles to GDP and based on this PSLI calculation is presented in comparison with economy leftness (rightness) (Fig.1-Fig.2). Countries are listed based on ratio of pension funds to GDP from maximum to minimum.

According to PSLI the most rightness country is Denmark (0.176) and the Netherland (0.286). As per IL(R)E, both countries, either Denmark (0.190) or the Netherlands (0.317) are the rightness countries. Based of IL(R)E, the most leftness county is France (0.416), PSLI also considers it leftness (0.965)

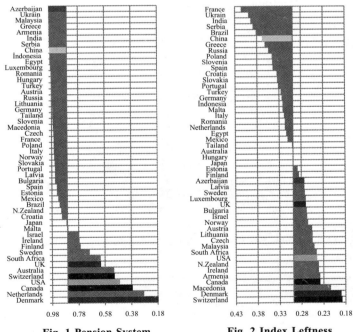

Fig. 1 Pension System Liberalization Index

Fig. 2 Index Leftness (Rightness) Economy

Source: Calculations were done based on OECD, 2016 and IL(R)E, 2015.

Some countries (Germany, France, Turkey, etc.) are in the leftness for both IL(R)E and PSLI.

PSLI results are shown in visual form in Fig. 3. The relative central indicator of the scale (0.850) is higher than the geometric centre of the scale (0.500). It means that pension system is inclined more to the left rather to the right in researched countries. Azerbaijan takes place at the extremely left point (Fig. 3).

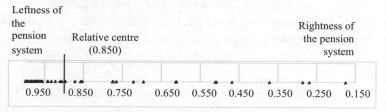

Fig. 3 The Pension System Liberal Index *(54 countries, 2015)*

The maintained results are similar with the indexes of some internatioanal organisations (Fig. 4).

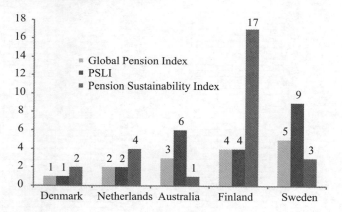

Fig. 4 Ranking of Global Pension Index, PSLI, Pension Sustainability Index (5 countries, 2015)

Source: Melbourne Mercer Global Pension Index (2016), Pension Sustainnability Index (2016).

According to the above-mentioned Global Pension Index (GPI), in 2015 Denmark (81.7) and the Netherlands (80.5) are in the 1st and 2nd places among 25 countries. GPI is calculated based on three sub-indices – Adequacy (40%), sustainability (35%) and integration (25%). Countries are divided into 6 categories (A – the highest, E – the lowest category) As per the report for the year 2015, categorization was done as follows – Denmark and the Netherlands – "A", Australia – "B +", Chile, Great Britain, Canada, Finland, Switzerland, Sweden – "B". The highest level of public sector in pensions is in France (57.4) – "C", Japan (44.1) and China (48.0), and they have been included in the category – "D". (Melbourne Mercer Global Pension Index, 2016). According to PSLI and GPI reports, Denmark's pension system is the most liberal (rightness) system in the world (in both cases - among the investigated countries). In the scale of IL(R)E Denmark is close to the right pole. The Netherlands, Canada, USA, Australia have liberal pension system, and they are located in the right pole in PSLI scale. We may come to the conclusion that as a rule those countries which has less governmental model intervention in the economy are more liberal.

Since 2011, UN publishes *Pension Sustainability Index* (PSI) which assess the long-term financial sustainability of pension systems and on this basis, the need for extent level of pension reforms in individual countries. PSI is calculated as per decimal scale for 54 countries. 10 points shows the least need for reform in the country, 1 point shows the government's high need for it. Top 5 in PSI's 2016 ranking are Australia (8.08), Denmark (7.93), Sweden (7.81), the Netherlands (7.75) and Norway (7.59). USA (7.23) is in 10th place, Chile (7.23) is in 11th, the UK is in 12th (7.20). *(Pension Sustainability Index, 2016)*. Apparently, the countries which highly ranked in PSLI, have a better position on the PSI.

Global Age Watch Index (GAWI) which evaluates the financial situation of pensioners and the health status is being calculated based on 4 indicators (financial situation, health level, personal potential and a favorable condition). As per GAWI's report the top ten countries are Switzerland, Norway, Sweden, Germany, Canada, the Netherlands, Iceland, Japan, the United States and the United Kingdom.*(Global Age Watch Index, 2015)*. In GAWI report either in top 5 or in top 10, there are "leftness" and "rightness" economic countries. In Switzerland which is in first place, the share of the private sector pension system is 71%.

PSLI pension system differs a lot from other calculated indexes. GPI evaluates adequate retirement income, the sustainability of the pension system and the private sector role in formation of the pension revenues, PSI shows financial sustainability of pension systems, GAWI estimates the financial situation of pensioners, however, PSLI calculates the level of liberalization in pension system and assess the role of socio-economic development of individual countries.

4. Determinants of Liberalization

But of course, the formation and development of pension systems are not only defined by the degree of their liberal-dirigist but also affected by a number of other determinants, including demographic, economic and social factors (Fig. 5).

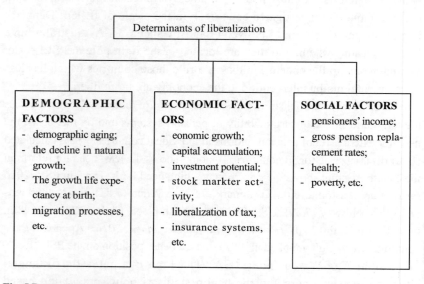

Fig. 5 Determinants of Liberalization

5. Demographic Factors

In this study, demographic factors are the process of aging of the population, the decline in natural growth, life expectancy at birth and migration processes. According to the classification of UN experts, if the population aged 65 and over are 4% or less – it is considered young people, between 4%-7%-on the eve of aging, 7% and above is considered aged population. *(Muradov, 2003)*. In the 21th century, significant changes will occur in the age structure of the population in most countries of the world. According to UN statistics, in 2015, 12.2% of the world's population was older people (65 and older). According to forecasts, in

2050 this figures will be 16.0% and in 2100 it will increase up to 22.7%. In 2015, the highest share of the composition of the population and the working-age population were Moldova (74.3%) and China (73.2%). In 2100, the corresponding figures will decrease, such as, it will be 57.9% in Moldova and 52.8% in China. The lowest indicator (49.0%) of the composition of the working population will be in Singapore in 2100. *(UN World Population Prospects, 2015).*

Demographic changes will manifest itself in the rate of the retirement age of the population as to working-age population. Figure 6 shows the ratio forecast of pension age population as to the proportion of the working-age population till 2100. The predictions help us to understand that some serious problems in pension provision will occur in the future. As shown in the diagram, by 2100 in most countries of the world, the ratio of the pension age population as to the working-age population will increase. The highest results will be in Singapore (82.3%), Albania (72.6%) and Korea (71.5%).

According to estimates of *Global Aging Watch Index*, the share of the population over the age of 60 will be 16.5% in 2030, but in 2050 it will be 21.5%. *(Global AgeWatch Index, 2015).* In 2015 this figures were 12.3%. In world's developed countries compared to 2015, in 2050 the ratio of the population aged over 65 as to the able-bodied population will increase from 32.2% to 58.5% in Germany, from 43.4% to 70% in Japan, from 21.4% to 36.5% in the U.S.. However, this trend is not just for developed countries, as noted earlier, it will be typical for most governments. For example, in Georgia in the respective period of time, the same figure will increase from 20.4% to 42.8% and in Azerbaijan figures will change from 7.8% to 26.3%.

Based on United Nations classification, Azerbaijan is on the eve of the aging population: In 2015, the share of aged 65 and over was 5.6%. However, in the near future, Azerbaijan is expected to be in the list of countries with aging populations. It is forecasted that in 2020 corresponding figures will increase to 7.35%, in 2050 it will be 16.95% and in 2100 figures will increase till 23.9. In addition to it, the share of the able-bodied population will decrease, the figure 72.5% which was in 2015 will decrease to 60% in 2100. All these show that the government will have aggravation of the social burden *(UN World Population Prospects, 2015).*

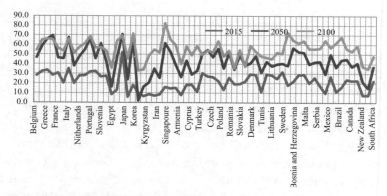

Fig. 6 Ratio of the population 65 + to the able-bodied population (15-64)
(62 coutries, 2015,%)

Source: UN World Population Prospects, 2015.

Of course, this is a serious change and a reduction in the number of workers per pensioner in future means aggravation of the social burden. In order to comply with this, governments will have to deduct the pension costs (Bonoli, 2000), or will be forced to increase the retirement age. Thus, developed and developing countries pay special attention to the factors listed in pension policy development. Thus, developed and developing countries pay special attention to the listed factors while forming pension policy. A similar trend was observed in Azerbaijan, it is necessary to make the liberal reforms in the pension system.

6. Economic Factors

In the scientific literature economic the factors affecting the pension system are as follows: the level of economic development of the country, capital accumulation, investment potential, stock market activity, liberalization of tax and insurance systems.

In case that other conditions (eg retirement age) remain unchanged, in order to meet total pension payments, the government either should increase compulsory social insurance allocations or must reduce the benefits of pension. Both steps, particularly the reduction of pensions is politically very unpopular and all governments are trying to avoid it. Sometimes the "social tax", so-called compulsory social insurance increase fees in terms of business development are not effective and economic growth may weaken because of it.

In this case, the solution can be acceptable by all social groups could be the creation of non-government pension system. In addition, employers and employees by investing voluntarily their funds to private pension funds may expand investment opportunities for pension funds and indirectly, entrepreneurs. The experience of developed countries shows that, the formation of non-government pension system (creating private pension funds) plays an important role in the revival of investment climate and in general in economic development. In fact, in some countries, assets of private pension funds exceeds GDP. Non-government pension provision is an important tool to help a positive impact on the economic development of the country, mitigating the social burden of the government, the possibility of further expanding their insured workers, and prevent the outflow of highly skilled workers from large enterprises.

Though, the first non-government pension plan was created in 1875 in the U.S., development of such funds began in Western European countries after World War II. Currently, based on capacity of the world's pension funds (governmental and private), 13 countries (Australia, Brazil, Canada, France, Germany, Hong Kong, Ireland, Japan, Netherlands, South Africa, Switzerland, UK, USA) have significant role. Sometimes, these countries are being called as "P13". In some reports, among those countries, 7 countries (Australia, Canada, Japan, the Netherlands, Switzerland, UK, U.S.) are being distinguished as "P7".

In world financial markets pension funds (especially, private pension funds) have a special role. In 2015, the total amount of investments in private pension funds in P7 countries was over than 31.32 trillion USD. The highest private pension funds investments is the United States (23.85 trillion USD). The creation of an enabling environment for private pension funds take rapid action for their assets. In 2005-2015, private pension funds investments were increased by 1.6 time in the U.S., 1.8 times in the Netherlands, and 1.6 times in the UK.

As mentioned, capacity of investments in the non-governmental pension funds is quite high in countries with liberal pension systems, in some countries (USA, Australia, the Netherlands, Canada and Switzerland) it even exceeds GDP. Figure 7-Figure 9 reflect the change of PSLI in 2005,

2010 and 2015 for P7 countries. Due to the lack of statistical information on investment in private pension funds, Japan was not included in the calculation and was not conducted in scales for the respective period.

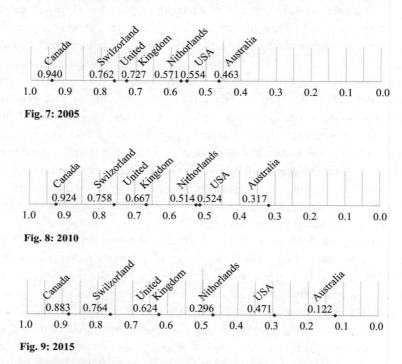

Fig. 7: 2005

Fig. 8: 2010

Fig. 9: 2015

Fig.7-Fig.9 Pension System Liberal Index (P7 countries, 2005, 2010, 2015)

Source: Calculations were done based on OECD, 2016.

As seen, in 2005-2015, liberalization of the pension systems continued in P7 countries. In 2005 PSLI in Australia was 0.463 and in 2015 it dropped to 0.122. During the same period of time, PSLI decreased in the U.S. from 0.554 to 0.471; in the UK from 0.727 to 0.624; and in Canada from 0.940 to 0.883, only in Switzerland it has increased from 0.762 to 0.764. But leftness inclination was not sustainable in Switzerland, rightness started to be observed in 2011-2012.

As mentioned, investments in private pension funds play an important role in the economic development of countries. The following figure shows dependence of investments in private pension funds and GDP in the U.S.

(Fig.10).

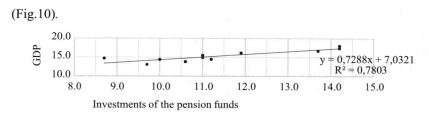

Fig.10 Correlasion the investment of the private pension funds with GDP in USA (billion, US dollars, 2005-2015)

Source : Calculations were done based on OECD, 2016.

We may see from the Figure that, the correlation between investments in private pension funds and GDP is high in the U.S. (r = 0.8833).

Interestingly, countries with pension funds' assets are those countries that made rightness (liberal) reforms. This fact can be interpreted so that, depending how less the government intrusive to pension system, pension organizations will be developing so much. Countries with the biggest pension funds have more private foundations. For example, in 2011 the share of private sector was 89% in the UK, 86% in Australia, 72% in the U.S., 71% in Switzerland and 70% in the Netherlands.

In the U.S. and the UK the ratio of the non-governmental pension funds investment to GDP was respectively 79.4% and 97.4% in 2015. In countries such as Germany (6.6%), France (0.6%) where governmental pension funds are dominating, the ratio of pension assets to GDP is less than 10% (Fig.11).

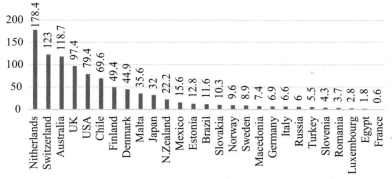

Fig.11 The ratio of the investment of the private pension funds to GDP (27 countries, 2015, %)

Source: Calculations were done based on OECD, 2016.

As mentioned, apart from the funds of private pension funds, there are the pension funds that are also available in a variety of financial instruments. Along with private pension funds there have more capacity. Such as, the ratio of private pension investments in various financial instruments to GDP is 205.9% in Denmark, 178.4% in the Netherlands, 157.2% in Iceland,156.9% in Canada, and in the U.S. 132.9%.

7. Social Factors

Liberalization of the pension systems and social determinants include pensioners' income, health, poverty and this kind of other factors.

To characterize the social status of pensioners, a number of indicators are being used. Usually, those indicators are average pension wealth accumulated during the period of employment of pensioners and the level of pensions (including its relative performance), which is related to the level of poverty among pensioners. The table below reflects the data of the average pension wealth accumulated during the period of employment (Table 1).

Table 1 Gross pension wealth (25 countries, thousand US dollars, 2015)

Countries	Men	Women
Australia	802	856
Austria	539	598
Belgium	401	462
Canada	357	400
Chili	100	101
Czech Republic	128	148
Denmark	943	1,054
Estonia	120	152
Finland	520	618
France	435	522
Germany	467	544
Greece	249	281
Hungary	131	154
Iceland	601	668
Irland	336	379

(Contd.)

Countries	Men	Women
Israel	398	427
Italy	454	518
Japan	371	426
Korea	253	296
Luxembourg	1, 015	1,170
Mexico	42	44
The Netherlands	1, 083	1,248
New Zealand	428	483
Norway	863	1, 000
Poland	88	104

Source: OECD – Pensions at Glance (2015).

In countries where the figure is high (the Netherlands, Luxembourg and Denmark) pension system is more liberal. Countries with the high average of pension wealth have very low social insurance rates for employees or employers. The figures are as follow, in Denmark employees 2.7% and 0 for employers, in Luxembourg both employers and employees 11.0% and in the Netherlands employees 13.9%, and 9.7% for employers. In several countries with liberalized pension system, social insurance rates for employees and employers are respectively as follows, in the United States 5.1% and 8.9%, in Australia 0 and 5.6%, in Ireland 0.4% and 7.2%, in Chile 7.0% and 0, in Switzerland for both employees and employers are 5.9% and 0 in New Zealand. In contrast, the countries with the highest share of public pension provision have figures as follows in France 9.5% and 30.6%, in Germany 17.3% and 16.4%, and in Italy 7.2% and 24.3% (OECD, 2013).

One of the key indicators that characterize the social status of pensioners is gross pension replacement rates (for example, the ratio of pension to the average monthly wage).

In 2014, the gross pension replacement rates was as follows for Netherlands 90.5%, Denmark 67.5%, Canada 36.7%, U.S. 35.2%, Japan 35.1%, respectively, the highest score was noticed in India (96.5%).

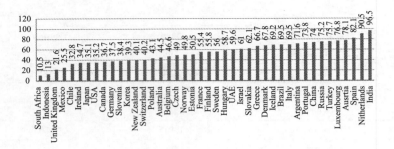

Fig.12 Gross pension replacement rates (ration to the pre-retirement earnings)
(42 countries, men, 2014, %)

Source: OECD, 2014.

Apparently, there isn't a strong dependency between the relative level of pensions (in any case, the relative level of this indicator) and liberal level of pension system, by this meaning, the relative level of pensions can be up or down in countries with liberalized pension system or in countries where public pensions provision are high.

Another indicator of the social status of among pensioners is the level of poverty. The figure below shows the poverty level of pensioners for some countries (Fig. 13).

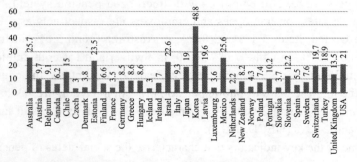

Fig.13 Poverty levbel of 65+ (retirement age) (35 countries, 2014,%)

Source: OECD Income Distribution Database.

Among comparable countries, in 2014 the highest poverty level of pensioners was in South Korea (48,8%). This indicator in Israel was 22.6%, in Australia 25.7%, in U.S. 21.0%, in Japan 19.0%, in Chile 15.0%, in the UK 13.5%, in Germany 8.5%, in Canada 6.2%, in Norway 4.3%, in France

3.5%, and in Netherlands 2.2%. As mentioned in the previous case, poverty among pensioners does not depend on the level of pension system liberalism: in countries with leftness or rightness pension system the poverty level among pensioners may differ. However, the lowest poverty level among pensioners was in the Netherlands where the pension system was more liberalized.

We may say the same idea about the share of pension income in the total amount of the revenue. Such as, in the structure of income among 65+ aged people, the share of income may be high or low in countries with governmental or private pension system (by meaning, rightness or leftness pension system). For example, in 2015, these figures were in France 100.0%, in the U.S. 92.1%, in Canada 91.6%, in the Netherlands 87.3%, and in Germany 86.9% *(OECD Income Distribution Database, 2015)*.

There are several factors that need to liberalize the pension system in Azerbaijan. Among them, demographic aging process, progressive deterioration of social burden on the state and the low standard of living of pensioners are important ones. An interesting aspect is that neighbor countries (Kyrgyzstan, Georgia, Armenia) with weaker economy than Azerbaijan have the non-state pension system.

Thus, administrate reforms, (raising the retirement age, "Accumulation" – the adding elements), meet expectation neither of the government nor the people (especially pensioners). In Azerbaijan, pension provision is under governmental monopoly (extreme leftness system) and it needs to be partially liberalized (rightness system).

8. Conclusions

• There is a worldwide demographic aging process going on, the number of pension for aged people increases, the number of employees for each pensioners decreases and there is the heavy social burden for countries. Because of all these reasons, it is necessary to make liberal reforms in the pension system. Demographic aging is also happening in Azerbaijan and in near future it will gradually accelerate.
• The government can intervene directly or non-directly (for example, by stimulating the formation of the private pension system) to pension

provision and can strengthen social protection of pensioners this way.

• There are several factors that need to liberalize the pension system in Azerbaijan. Among them demographic aging process, progressive deterioration of social burden on the state and the low standard of living of pensioners are important ones.

• Thus, administrate reforms (raising the retirement age, "Accumulation"– the adding elements), meet expectation neither of the government nor the people (especially pensioners). In Azerbaijan, pension provision is under governmental monopoly (extreme leftness system) and it needs to be partially liberalized (rightness system). The preliminary PSLI results also support this theory.

The "Belt and Road" Initiative and Sino-Azerbaijani Economic Cooperation

Pei Changhong*

Ever since China and Azerbaijan established diplomatic relations, the two countries have maintained stable bilateral ties, with more frequent exchange of high-level visits, political trust being enhanced and economic cooperation being advanced steadily. So far, China has become the fifth largest trading partner and the third largest source of imports of Azerbaijan. Areas of bilateral cooperation, originally focused on imports and exports, have been expanded to include hydrocarbon exploration, building materials production, information and communication and agriculture. It is widely believed that China's "Belt and Road" Initiative, which has won warm response and active participation from Azerbaijan, offers an unprecedented opportunity for the economic transition of countries dependent on traditional energy, particularly for countries along the land and maritime Silk Roads. Therefore, a closer look at the Sino-Azerbaijani economic cooperation within the "Belt and Road" framework is conducive to expanding mutually-beneficial cooperation and promoting the common development between the two countries.

1. Global FDI Fluctuation and China's Growing ODI

Global FDI inflows, having reached a peak of $1.97 trillion in 2007, began to decline after the global financial crisis, and went down again after a slight increase in 2011. In 2015, it went upward to around $1.8 trillion and is expected to go further upward in 2017 after the slight decrease in 2016.

According to the *World Investment Report 2017* issued by the United Nations Conference on Trade and Development (hereinafter referred to as UNCTAD) on 15th June 2017, global flows of foreign direct investment in 2016 fell by about 2

---

* Pei Changhong, Researcher, Institute of Economics, Chinese Academy of Social Sciences.

per cent, to $1.75 trillion and was expected to rise by 5% in 2017, to $1.8 trillion before going up to $1.85 trillion in 2018.

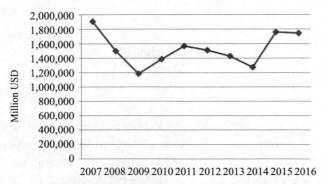

Fig.1 Global FDI after the Financial Crisis (*Inflow, Million USD)*

In 2000, Chinese government initiated the "going global" strategy to encourage outward foreign investment, which rose rapidly during the period of the "12th Five-year Plan". Chinese outward FDI reached $68.81 billion in 2010, before it jumped to $107.84 billion in 2013 (covering all sectors). According to the *World Investment Report 2017: Investment and the Digital Economy,* issued by UNCTAD, while the FDI of developing countries in Asia dropped by 15%, China made itself the world's second largest investor in 2016, with an outward flow of $183 billion.

According to the statistics issued by China's Ministry of Commerce and the State Administration of Foreign Exchange, Chinese enterprises ranked the second among global investors for the second time, with their ODI outflow amounting to $183.2 billion in 2016, which included a $170.1 billion non-financial outbound direct investment.The rapid increase in China's ODI contributed substantially to its economic transition by allowing Chinese products, equipment, technology and services to "go global". In the meantime, it brought much benefit to the world economy by promoting growth in the host countries. Statistical evidence shows that with the sales volume amounting to $1.5 trillion in 2016, Chinese enterprises overseas contributed $40 billion worth of taxation as well as 1.5 million jobs to the host countries. Thanks to Chinese government's efforts to raise investor's risk awareness and its thorough review of outward investment projects, irrational investment overseas was effectively curbed during the first half of 2017.

China's ODI during the period tended to be more rational and fell by 42.9% to ¥331.1 billion ($50.9 billion). However, Chinese ODI in countries along the land and maritime Silk Roads dropped by just 3.6%, much lower than the overall 42.9%. Since more emphasis was placed on physical investment, Chinese ODI in manufacturing did not fall as much as in real estate, culture, sports and entertainment. Several large merger and acquisition projects went smoothly. Additionally, the turnover generated by China's foreign contracted projects rose by 7.2%, to ¥462.2 billion.

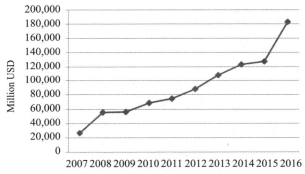

Fig. 2 China's ODI *(Outflow, Million USD)*

2. China's "Belt and Road" Investment

State-owned enterprises and Central government-led enterprises are the pioneers and main force of China's ODI in countries along the land and maritime Silk Roads. Such enterprises are motivated primarily by the desire to expand international product and service markets, capture local markets, increase global market share and improve profitability, and secondarily by government policies. With the "Belt and Road" Initiative being implemented, an increasing number of Chinese enterprises, most of which are state-owned in first-tier cities, started to invest in countries along the land and maritime Silk Roads.[①]

The location choices of China's ODI are subject to cultural differences, levels of economic development, geographic locations as well as international relations. According to the statistics issued by China's Ministry of Commerce,

---

① Top ten largest Investors in China are Guangdong, Shanghai, Shandong, Jiangsu, Zhejiang, Liaoning, Tianjin, Hunan, Yunnan.

Chinese enterprises' non-financial ODI in the 53 countries along the land and maritime Silk Roads reached $14.53 billion, 2% down from the year earlier; the 8,158 contracts entered into with 61 countries along the Silk Roads were worth $126.03 billion, 36% up from the year earlier; the $75.97 billion worth of turnover was 9.7% up from the year earlier.

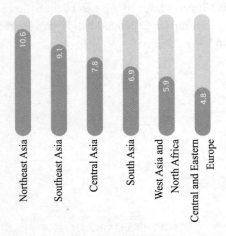

Fig. 3 Performance of Chinese Enterprises' Investment in the "Belt and Road" Regions (Scale 0~12)
Source: Public Record.

The areas and sectors toward which Chinese investments were directed, were different from country to country, due to the different conditions of each country and the complementarity of its economy to that of China's. Energy has been the primary and the most important area for Chinese investment, transportation comes second, and telecommunication technologies, which was considered part of information infrastructure, comes third.

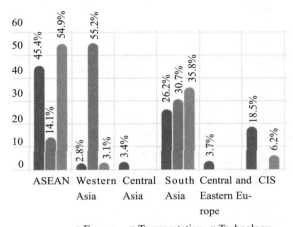

Fig.4 Destinations of China's "Belt and Road" ODI

Source: Public Record.

Although much has been accomplished as Chinese enterprises went out, potential risks should not be overlooked. During the period from January 2016 to March 2017, 215 cases of trade remedy investigations have been filed against Chinese enterprises, including anti-dumping, countervailing, anti-circumvention and safeguard investigations. The dispute resolutions show that 31% of the interviewed enterprises encountered civil suits or arbitration. The disputes mainly concerned purchase and sales contracts (worth less than 5 million or more than 100 million yuan). Such cases were mostly solved through reconciliation and mediation (with legal fees ranging from 100,000 to 500,000 yuan). What's worth mentioning here, is that the huge difference in the level of economic development among the "Belt and Road" countries, offered great opportunities for Chinese investors, but also induced potential risks for their "overseas investments". Research shows that 40% of the interviewed enterprises believe the major barriers to their investments are political instability, acts of terrorism, war, riot and military conflicts.

With the "Belt and Road" Initiative being implemented, Chinese enterprises will, to a larger extent, play by the international rules. Therefore, the key tasks for the Chinese government are to establish the mechanism, principle and procedures for solving disputes in investments while further completing the terms and conditions of bilateral investment protection agreement.

Central Asia
Possible political instability caused by power shifts
Energy nationalism
Terrorism
More fierce conflicts between the great powers

Middle East
Political instability
Rising pressure on Macro-economy
Terrorism
Risks induced by Exchange restrictions

Southeast Asia
Insufficient knowledge of the government and social conditions
Poor infrastructure
Terrorism and Separatism
More fierce conflicts between the great powers

Fig. 5 Risks to be Avoided in Regions Along the "Belt and Road"

Source: Public Record.

3. An Overview of China-Azerbaijani Economic Relations

Trade volume between China and Azerbaijan hit $100 million in 2000 before reaching $200 million in 2003. According to statistics issued by UNCTAD in 2010, the trade volume between the two amounted to $830 million, before it reached its peak, $900 million in 2014. However, as was shown by Chinese statistics, bilateral trade volume between the two countries reached $940 million in 2014, 16% down from the year earlier, with $640 million worth of exports and $300 million worth of imports on China's part, 25.8% down and 3.9% up respectively from the year earlier. In 2015, China-Azerbaijan trade volume reached $666 million, 29.3% down from the year earlier, with $440 million worth of exports and $226 million worth of imports on China's part, 31.7% and 24.2% down from the year earlier. According to Azerbaijani statistics, bilateral trade volume between the two countries reached $760 million, 14.3% down from the year earlier, which means China has become Azerbaijan's 13th largest trade partner and the fifth largest source of imports.

Table 1 Total Volume of Azerbaijani Export and Import to/from China and the World

(In Thousands of USD)

Year	Azerbaijan export to China	Azerbaijan export to World	Azerbaijan import from China	Azerbaijan import from World
2010	252,314.3	26,476,026	587,618.7	6,596,797
2011	135,397.4	34,494,900	628,250.2	9,732,869
2012	243,954.8	32,634,038	631,856.1	9,641,724
2013	188,286	31,702,945	568,160.1	10,763,392
2014	206,322.3	28,259,629	697,079.6	9,178,588
2015	148,678.8	15,586,052	512,505.3	9,211,126
2016	519,95.14	10,900,000	468,875.5	8,670,511

Source: *UNCTAD Database.*

The statistics issued by Azerbaijani Customs show that commodities exported to China were mainly fossil fuels, plastic, chemical and copper products, as well as leather, and mineral sands. Commodities imported from China were mainly mechanical appliances and parts, clothing and accessories, electrical appliances, audio-visual equipment, furniture, lamp and lantern, vehicle and auto parts. The UNCTAD report outlined the structure of trade between Azerbaijan and China as follows:

Table 2 Structure of Azerbaijani Exports to China

(In Thousands of USD)

Product	Primary commodities (SITC 0-4+68)	Chemical products (SITC 5)	Machinery and transport equipment (SITC 7)	Other manufactured goods (SITC 6 +8-667-68)
2010	240,175	11,836	162	141
2011	100,416	34,162	573	246
2012	219,355	23,886	599	115
2013	142,677	43,730	1,100	780
2014	133,719	67,034	59	5,511
2015	112,356	34,764	70	1,489
2016	32,596	18,192	182	1,024

Source: *UNCTAD Database.*

Table 3 Structure of Chinese Exports to Azerbaijan

(In Thousands of USD)

Product	Primary commodities (SITC 0-4+68)	Chemical products (SITC 5)	Machinery and transport equipment (SITC 7)	Other manufactured goods (SITC 6+8 -667-68)
2010	10,379	5,995	228,490	601,291
2011	11,874	7,059	298,463	575,155
2012	13,405	17,695	514,185	524,543
2013	18,186	21,832	353,505	475,046
2014	17,755	16,774	297,180	312,216
2015	10,728	13,441	165,607	250,095
2016	8,001	7,969	149,518	185,898

Source: *UNCTAD Database.*

The bilateral trade between China and Azerbaijan in 2016, according to the Azerbaijani Ministry of Commerce, rose by 73%, a substantial growth to $970 million, with $739 million worth of imports from China, which rose by 38%. In the same year, Azerbaijan has quadrupled its exports to China, mainly oil and gas, to $270 million. In the first half of 2017, the total value of Azerbaijani trade with China reached $670 million, with $335 million worth of imports from, and $340 million worth of exports to China. Its trade deficit has substantially narrowed with China. Commodities exported to China include fossil fuels, plastic and chemical products, as well as leather, beverages and liquor. Commodities imported from China are mechanical appliances and components, clothing and accessories, electrical appliances, audio-visual equipment, vehicle and auto parts, furniture, lanterns and lamps.

China, having worked with Azerbaijan on energy exploitation since 2001, had directly invested $712 million in its non-financial sectors by the end of 2016, with $615 million in areas like oil/gas exploitation and construction projects such as K&K oil field exploitation, the construction of cement plant, aluminum smelter and the curtain wall for the New Moon Palace in Baku. The main contractors are CNPC, China National Building Material Group, Sichuan Machinery and Shenyang Yuanda Enterprise Group.

Table 4 China's Outward FDI Flows in the World and Azerbaijan, 2007-2015

(In Millions of USD)

Country/ Region	2007	2008	2009	2010	2011	2012	2013	2014	2015
Total	26,506	55,907	56,529	68,811	74,654	87,804	107,844	123,120	145,667
Azerbaijan	-1.15	-0.66	1.73	0.37	17.68	0.34	-4.43	16.83	1.36

Source: Statistical Bulletin of China's Outward Foreign Direct Investment 2015.

Table 5 Azerbaijan's Outward and Inward FDI Flows, 2011-2016

(In Millions of USD)

Region/ economy	FDI inflow						FDI outflow					
	2011	2012	2013	2014	2015	2016	2011	2012	2013	2014	2015	2016
Azerbaijan	1465	2005	2632	4430	4048	4500	533	1192	1490	3230	3260	2574

Source: World Investment Report 2017.

UNCTAD statistics show that during the period from January to June 2011, Azerbaijan's inward FDI were $1,465 million, $2,005 million, $2,632 million, $4,430 million, $4,048 million and $4,500 million, most of which focused in the areas of oil and gas exploitation. Chinese enterprises have accomplished much in non-oil/gas areas. For instance, HUAWEI, a leading Chinese provider of information and communication solutions, has occupied after years of efforts, a substantial share of the Azerbaijani telecommunications market.

After the global financial crisis, the decline in world demand for oil and gas led to the sharp decrease in Azerbaijan's exports. The living conditions in the country have barely improved with its economic decline, trade deficit and currency devaluation. In 2013, Azerbaijan's new president, in an effort to transform its economic structure, proposed a new plan for non-oil industry, but the plan didn't yield good results. Foreign investment didn't help either. Against this backdrop, it is believed that the "Belt and Road" Initiative could help it achieve its goal of economic transformation.

In April of 2015, Azerbaijan became the founding member of the Asian Infrastructure Investment Bank, and then the SCO dialogue partner in July of the same year. In December of 2015, President Ilham

Aliyev visited China and signed the Memorandum of Understanding on Construction of the Silk Road Economic Belt, which meant that China-Azerbaijan ties entered a new phase. It is expected that the two countries will further deepen their cooperation on infrastructure and connectivity, so as to form synergy between Azerbaijan's 2020 plan and China's "Belt and Road" Initiative. The main efforts include: (a) To enhance the information connectivity between the two countries. Azerbaijan proposed in 2012 to build an information highway throughout Eurasia. The EU and UN have both attached great importance to the proposal. (b) To enhance the transportation connectivity. As the bridge between Europe and Asia, Azerbaijan is expected to bring the two continents together with the BTK rail line. On 3rd August 2015, the first test container train through the route China–Aktau–Alat arrived at Baku International Sea Trade Port, which means that Baku, after improving its capacity and efficiency, will become an important link between Asia and Europe. China will help Azerbaijan to modernize Baku port and invest in port infrastructure and the rail line connecting Europe and Asia. (c) To strengthen bilateral cooperation on agriculture and tourism. The world famous Caucasus Mountains in Azerbaijan, which encompass a variety of climate zones, have a rich abundance of agricultural and tourism resources. China's agricultural products, machinery, and technology are expected to be exported to Azerbaijan. The tourism resources in Caucasus and Caspian regions could be further developed by joint efforts. The development of both agriculture and tourism will increase the share of non-oil industry in the national economy. (d) To give full play to Baku's geopolitical and geographic advantages, shaping it into a five-star international transportation hub. The new Port of Baku at Alat is a transportation hub with a cargo-handling capacity of 27,000 containers, or 6 million tons (TEU), which will reach 25 million tons in 2020, when the construction of the new port is finished. China is expected to help Azerbaijan build at Baku, a free trade zone linking peripheral countries, an industrial zone and export processing zone like Shenzhen where products could be re-processed and added with additional value. (e) To advance cooperation between the industrial zones of the two countries. Qaradag, one of the 12 districts of Baku, and accounting for 51.3% of the total area of the Azerbaijani capital, covers an area of 1080 square kilometers, with a coastline around the Caspian sea of 106 kilometers. One of the key industrial zones in Azerbaijan, home to over 90 industrial enterprises, 22 of which are large ones, is known for production of oil, gas and construction materials. On 17th March 2016, the president of Azerbaijan signed an executive order, declaring the establishment of a free trade zone and special economic zone, both of which were directly under the control of Qaradag. The free trade zone under construction covers an area of 4,000 hectares, including part of the aforesaid Baku International Sea Trade Port. The priority for the industrial zone is to attract investment and build itself into an industrial park like the China-Belarus Industrial Park.

4. The Strategic Importance and Possibilities of Azerbaijan in the "Belt and Road" Initiative

The strategic importance is as follows:

First, Azerbaijan is situated in the center of the south route linking Asia and Europe (the north route refers to the central European rail line going through Kazakhstan, Russia and Europe), a potential base for China's manufactured goods to march into International markets. With Russia in the north, Georgia in the west, Iran, Turkey and Middle East countries in the south, and Kazakhstan and Turkmenistan linked through ports around the Caspian Sea, the country is an important transportation hub along the Eurasia south route. On 3rd August 2015, the first test container train through the route from China arrived at Baku International Sea Trade Port, after which, Azerbaijan, Kazakhstan, Georgia and Ukraine signed a protocol on the establishment of competitive preferential tariffs for cargo transportation. Since 1st June 2016, the Trans-Caspian International Transport Route officials have decided to apply the competitive tariffs for cargo transportation.

Second, with a rich abundance of hydrocarbon resources, Azerbaijan could become China's source of oil and gas imports. The volume of proved petroleum reserves is estimated to be 2 billion tons with geological reserves of about 4 billion tons. Shallowly buried and without many impurities, the petroleum reserve is easy to exploit. Ranking first among the three Caucasian countries in terms of hydrocarbon resources, Azerbaijan has proven gas reserves of 2.55 trillion cubic meters, and prospective reserves of about 6 trillion cubic meters. Apart from oil and gas, the country has abundant agricultural and fishing resources.

Furthermore, Azerbaijan's participation in the "Belt and Road" Initiative will maximize the bilateral interests, which bring benefits to China's engagement in world diplomacy and economic affairs. Because of its rich natural resources, Azerbaijan has long been regarded as Europe's solution to Russian energy control. For this reason, there has been fierce competition for Azerbaijani resource between America and Russia.

Behind the pending issue of Nagorno-Karabakh, is the competition between America and Russia. Despite the setbacks and painful memories in the area, Azerbaijan sticks to the principle of balanced diplomacy as well as economic and political independence. In order to avoid Russian control over its petroleum resources, Azerbaijan collaborated with Turkey, Georgia and Kazakhstan on the construction of the BTC Pipeline, which in a sense, broke the Russian monopoly of oil resources in Central Asia. The economic benefit yielded during the construction of the Silk Road Economic Belt will help maintain the stability of the area by enabling Azerbaijan to minimize its dependence on the West and alleviate Russia's discontentment over its tightening relation with the West. Also, it will help China increase its influence in the region.

Last but not least, a closer tie between China and Azerbaijan is conducive to building an international front against terrorism. In East Turkistan, the separatist force in China could hide itself and build up its power in Islamic countries. By further advancing bilateral economic cooperation, China and Azerbaijan may join forces to cut off East Turkistan's connection to international terrorist forces.

The basic strategic concepts are:

First, to shape China into Azerbaijan's important export market for oil and gas, diversifying its exports basket so as to reduce Russian and European competition for its petroleum resources.

Since the opening of the BTC Pipeline in 2006, Azerbaijan has exported over 50 million tons of oil to Europe through the pipeline, which practically makes the Baku – Novorossiysk Pipeline (with a terminal in Russia) barely useful. In order to counter Russian control of gas, the EU further advanced its cooperation with Azerbaijan in 2011 by proposing the Southern Gas Corridor project, which consists of the Nabucco Gas Pipeline from Turkey to Austria, the Trans Adriatic Pipeline from Greece to Italy, the White Stream Pipeline from Georgia to Ukraine and the ITGI from Turkey to Italy. The project, once completed, will be a devastating blow to Russia's energy hegemony. In response, Russia spent huge amount of money on the South Stream plan but given the fact that the groundwork for the Southern Gas Corridor project has been completed, Russia will be gradually eliminated from the competition for energy in Transcaucasia. Therefore, how the Russian punishment will be imposed on Azerbaijan becomes a big concern. Despite Azerbaijan's friendly gestures, like participating in a Moscow Parade, it is inevitable that the country (Azerbaijan) will further advance its cooperation with the West on oil, gas and electricity. Some even believe that Azerbaijan will sooner or later, seek military protection from the West and become a member of NATO. In general, Azerbaijan's politics are largely dependent on its export of oil and gas.

China has a huge potential market for Azerbaijan's oil and gas exports, which are expected to account for 10% of the total volume of Azerbaijan's total volume of export trade.

Second, to encourage Chinese enterprises to invest in the non-oil and gas industries, so as to increase the international market share for Chinese products, and help with Azerbaijan's economic transformation.

One of the aims of the China-Belarus Industrial Park is to open up the Eurasia market for Chinese products. Azerbaijan, lying along the southern Silk Road, and with a 1000 kilometers market linking Eastern Europe, Middle East and the Commonwealth of Independent States, is a potential base for the processing and reprocessing of Chinese products. Therefore, Chinese enterprises should be encouraged to invest in Azerbaijan, particularly in building an export processing zone and a free trade zone. Chinese outward investment, together with the geological advantages of Azerbaijan, will help the country to develop its non-oil industry and transform its economy.

5. Strategic Measures for China-Azerbaijan Economic Cooperation

First and foremost, efforts should be made to improve the infrastructure. Both Kazakhstan and Turkmenistan, facing Azerbaijan across the Caspian Sea, have built oil pipelines to China. Chinese enterprises can be encouraged to participate in building the new Baku port so as to increase its storage of oil and gas while improving the efficiency of shipping companies. By linking the new port to the railway and pipelines in Kazakhstan and Turkmenistan, Azerbaijan will diversify the market for its energy. In this sense, the construction of new Baku port will be given priority in the "Belt and Road" Cooperation between China and Azerbaijan. Meanwhile, Baku could be shaped into one of the major stops on the China-Europe Railway Line. The successful operation of the Yiwu-Xinjiang-Europe and the Zhengzhou-Europe railway lines proved that it is feasible to extend the lines to Baku, which will create favorable conditions for logistics and expanding trade and production.

Second, joint efforts should be made to build free trade zones (export processing zones under Customs Supervision). Right now, under the leadership of the vice premier, Azerbaijan has established a special agent for the construction of a free trade zone. According to the plan, a new port and a free trade zone will be established 70 kilometers south of Baku. Chinese enterprises are expected to participate in the construction as the primary developers and investors. China should respond and participate after a careful study of the feasibility. Large enterprises could be encouraged to develop the primary projects of the park, while favorable terms could be offered to attract investment.

Given the fact that Azerbaijan's annual import of commodities, including mechanical and electrical equipment, vehicle and auto parts, black metal and food, building materials and ceramic products, has reached $10 billion, Import Substitution Industrialization should be adopted to develop its non-oil industries before expanding its exports. As for China, efforts should be made to encourage its export enterprises to establish production and assembly lines in Azerbaijan so as to increase its exports to peripheral markets.

Third, introduce solar energy technology and investment from China. Azerbaijan's wealth conditions are suitable for generating solar energy. The equipment, technology and investment from China could help with developing clean diversified energies.

Fourth, introduce Chinese agricultural technology to develop water-saving agriculture. Located in a Temperate Climate Zone and with a relatively small population, Azerbaijan has a large amount of arable land and rich experience in farming. Both the cost and risk for investing in agriculture and livestock farming are lower. China and Azerbaijan should advance their cooperation on agriculture and the exchange of agricultural technologies. Apart from inviting agricultural officers and experts from Azerbaijan for communication, China could also encourage agricultural enterprises to invest in Azerbaijan.

Fifth, develop the service trade and infrastructure for tourism. With its unique folk culture and tourism resources, Azerbaijan has huge potential for tourism and the health industry. Chinese enterprises should be encouraged to invest in hospitality, transportation and infrastructure of the health industry.

Sixth, weave an aerial silk road. Facilities connectivity is a major part of the "Belt and Road" Initiative. To bring China and Azerbaijan closer, more air routes should be opened. Right now, there are only two direct air routes between China and Azerbaijan. There should be at least three more. Chinese airlines could be encouraged to open new routes to Kuba.

Seventh, promote cultural exchange. Bilateral cooperation on natural sciences, social sciences and education should be encouraged. Apart from establishing a Confucius Institute in Azerbaijan, a China-Azerbaijan Institution could be established in Chinese universities, with an aim to cultivate talents for trade between the two countries. What's more, exchange of students and scholars should be included in government agenda.

Eighth, joint efforts should be made to establish "Belt and Road" Study Centers. To seek cooperation and development within the "Belt and Road" framework has become the common interest of both countries. How to achieve shared growth through discussion and collaboration is the common subject for scholars both in China and Azerbaijan. Therefore, it is necessary to establish study centers for China-Azerbaijan Economic Cooperation within the "Belt and Road" framework.

Economic Outlook for China's
13th Five-year Plan

Chang Xin*

Two major trends will shape China's economy during the period of the 13th Five-year Plan: first, a shift from high-speed growth to a medium-to-high level. Annual growth rate in the period dropped to around 6.5%, as a result of declining supply-side growth caused by the change in total factor productivity and the limitation imposed by the supply of labor, capital and resource. Other reasons for the fall of growth are negative output gaps caused by the deficiency of effective demands, as well as the change in real estate markets caused by demographic shifts and the reallocation of residents assets.

Second, changes in the economic structure. Once troubled by the imbalance between domestic and external demands, as well as consumption and investment, China's economic growth, previously dependent on investment and exports, will be further promoted by consumption, investment and exports; the industrial structure, which was characterized by the disproportion between the primary, secondary and tertiary industries, will be optimized to facilitate economic growth; technological innovation will replace factory input as the main engine of growth since all factory productivity contributed very little to economic growth.

1. The Main Trend: from High-speed to Medium-high Growth

Generally, China's growth has slowed down ever since the global financial crisis. Its GDP growth rate fell sharply from 14.2% in the second quarter of 2007 to 6.7% in the third quarter of 2016 (remaining steady after the fourth quarter of 2016); annual growth rate has seen an obvious slowdown, from 14.2% in 2007 to 6.7% in 2016 (fig.1). The change in

---

* Chang Xin, Researcher, Institute of Economics, Chinese Academy of Social Sciences.

China's growth, from a double-digit high-speed to medium-high speed of 7-8%, was caused by the joint forces of the long-term growing-tendency and short-term cyclical fluctuation. The trend is expected to continue throughout the period of the 13th Five-year Plan.

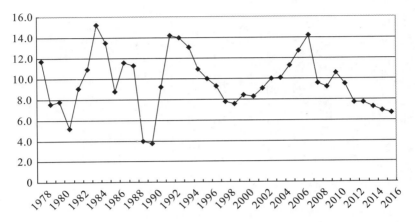

Fig. 1 China's Annual GDP Growth Rate (%)

Source: National Bureau of Statistics of China.

1.1 The Long-term Growing Trend

The declining supply-side growth is closely related to the periodical changes in the pattern of factor supply. The changes are as follows.

1.1.1 The Change in Labor Supply

There has been a change in the fast-growing trend of labor supply over the past few years due to the rapid demographic change. First, the working-age population fell sharply from 14.91 million in 2006 to 8.94 million in 2007 and continued falling. Since the middle of the 12th Five-year Plan period, there has been another change. The working-age population (age 15-59) in 2012, accounting for 69.2% of the total population, dropped 3.45 million, a 0.6% fall from late 2011. This was the first absolute decline over a long period of time. In 2013, the working-age population (16-59)[1] saw a 2.44

---

[1] In *Statistical Communique of The People's Republic of China on the 2013 National Economic and Social Development*, the standard for age group division was adjusted from age 15-59 to 16-59, so as to ensure the compliance with China's Labor Law.

million decline from last year, accounting for 67.6% of the total population. In the following years, the declining tendency continued (Fig. 2).

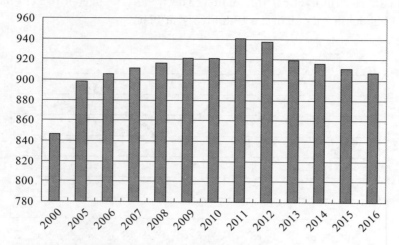

Fig. 2 Change in China's Working-age Population (million)

Source: National Bureau of Statistics of China.

Demographic changes in China have led to the change in dependency ratio. Beginning in 2012, both children and old-age dependency started to rise (Fig. 3). During the period of the 13th Five-year Plan, the demographic dividend and the positive effective of labor supply on economy may continue to decline.

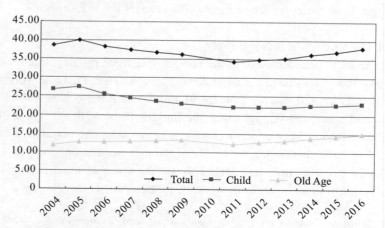

Fig. 3 Changes in China's Dependency Ratio (%)

Source: National Bureau of Statistics of China.

1.1.2 Changes in Capital Supply

China has been a high-saving country as suggested by Table 1, where the national saving rate and the savings rate for residential sector, enterprises sector and government sector[1] from 1992 to 2015 are listed. The table shows that from 2007 to 2011, the national savings rate had been above 50%, total savings rates generally around 47% to 49.5% (5% for government, 20% for enterprises and 25% for households), well above countries with 20% of national savings rate (Fig. 4). For this reason, China has ranked among the top-savings countries such as Japan and South Korea.

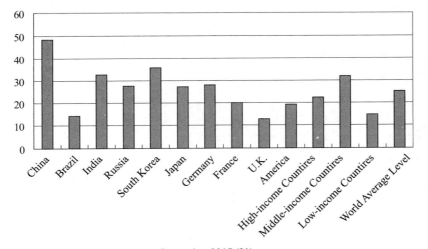

Fig. 4 National Savings across Countries, 2015 (%)

Notes: Statistics for low-income countries is from 2014.
Source: World Bank WDI Database.

---

① China started to compile cash flow statement in 1992 and have produced all together 21 of the statements during the period from 1992-2015. In this paper, cash flow statement (Commodity Trading) is used to calculate the national saving rate and sector saving rate. In cash flow statement, China's economy is divided into five sectors: non-financial sector, financial sector, government sector, residential sector, and foreign sector. Both financial and non-financial sectors can be placed under enterprise sector whereas the residential sector, enterprises sector and government sector under the category of national sector. The total savings of the three is known as national savings. National saving rate refers to the ratio of national savings to the disposable income of all national sectors. The saving rate for each sector refers to the ratio of savings of each sector to the national disposable income. The sum of saving rate of the three sectors equals national saving rate, namely National Saving Rate = Residential Saving Rate+ Enterprise Saving Rate + Government Saving Rate.

Table 1 China's National and Sector Savings, 1992-2012 (%)

	National	Residential	Enterprise	Government
1992	40.29	21.08	13.33	5.89
1993	41.72	19.32	16.15	6.24
1994	42.73	21.49	16.02	5.22
1995	41.62	20.04	16.7	4.88
1996	40.32	21.32	13.57	5.43
1997	40.76	20.75	14.73	5.65
1998	39.98	20.39	14.33	5.27
1999	38.61	18.55	14.31	5.75
2000	37.6	21	17.9	-1.4
2001	38.5	20.6	18.9	-1.1
2002	40.2	20.3	19.3	0.6
2003	43.1	21.7	19.9	1.4
2004	45.7	20.6	22.5	2.6
2005	46.5	21.5	21.6	3.3
2006	48.2	22.4	21.5	4.2
2007	50.9	23.1	22.1	5.7
2008	51.9	23.3	22.7	5.9
2009	50.6	24.4	21.2	4.9
2010	51.8	25.4	21.2	5.2
2011	50.6	24.8	20	5.8
2012	49.5	25.2	18.5	5.8
2013	48.3	23.6	19.8	5
2014	49.1	23	20.5	5.6
2015	47.2	22.8	19.8	4.5

Source: China Statistical Yearbook.

　　Although the high-savings trend is unlikely to change in the short-term, China's aging population started to pose problems. The old-age population (age 65 and above) has kept rising since the foundation of People's Republic of China, particularly in recent years (Fig. 5). The change has resulted in a decline in the high-savings rate, which is expected to continue during the period of the 13th Five-year Plan. The declining savings rate will lead to a falling rate of capital formation, which means the positive influence of capital accumulation on economic growth will decrease.

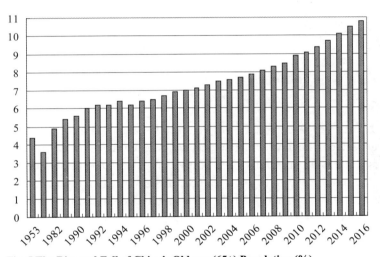

Fig. 5 The Rise and Fall of China's Old-age (65+) Population (%)

Source: National Bureau of Statistic of China.

1.1.3 More Limitations Imposed by Resource and Environment

　　In recent years, both the speed and intensity of China's energy consumption have kept increasing. Here is a comparative perspective on the total energy consumption per unit of GDP across countries. In 2014, China's energy use (kg per $ 1,000 of GDP) was 175.3, 113.1 for high-income countries, 138 for middle-income countries and 126.7 as the world's average use. China's energy consumption per unit of GDP was 1.5 times as much as that of the high-income countries, 1.3 times as much as middle-income counties and 1.4 times as much as the world's average level. As shown below, energy consumption in 2014 was 134.2 for America, 87 for Germany, 93 for Japan, 96.6 for Brazil, 118.3 for India and 195.6 for Russia. China's level of energy consumption is well above developed countries and emerging economies (Russia excluded) (Fig. 6).

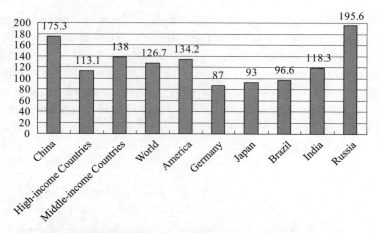

Fig. 6 Energy Consumption Per Unit of GDP Across the World, 2014 (kg)

Source: World Bank WDI Database.

Apart from resources, the environment has imposed more limitations on the growth of China, where pollutants emission has been on the rise in recent years. Here is a comparative perspective on pollutants emission per unit of GDP across the world. In 2014, carbon dioxide emission (kg per $ of GDP) of China was 0.59, and 0.26 for high-income countries, 0.39 for middle-income countries, 0.34 for the world's average level. China's carbon dioxide emission per unit of GDP was 2.3 times as much as high-income countries, 1.5 times as much as middle-income countries and 1.7 times as much as the world's average level. The total emission was 0.32 for America, 0.2 for Germany, 0.26 for Japan, 0.17 for Brazil, 0.32 for India and 0.47 for Russia. As shown in Figure 7, China's carbon dioxide emission per unit of GDP was well above that of the developed countries and emerging economies. The limitations imposed by resources and the environment are expected to continue during the period of the 13th Five-year Plan, which means the growth overly dependent on factor input will slow down.

With the positive effect of the aforementioned factors being weakened, total factor productivity didn't function properly to boost economic growth. Because the marginal output of the capital from the service sector has been lower than the manufacturing sector, a transition from manufacturing to service sectors will increase the production rate. What's more, as China's technology catches up with developed countries, the spillover effect of technology imports has been weakened, which is a major cause for the reduction of the potential growth rate.

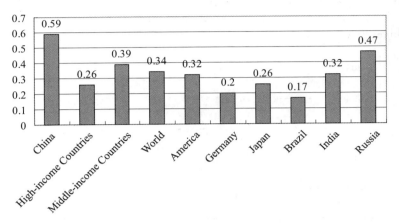

Fig. 7 Carbon Dioxide Emission Per Unit of GDP Across the World, 2014 (kg)

Source: World Bank WDI Database.

1.2 The Short-term Cyclical Fluctuation

The negative output gap of the demand-side was mainly caused by insufficient effective demands. Upward movements in the 21st Century have been driven mainly but investment and exports which kept being weakened since the global financial crisis.

1.2.1 Sustained Weak Demands for Exports

Since 2008, the current account surplus as a percentage of GDP has dropped sharply from the peak of 10% in 2007 to around 2% in recent years (1.7% in 2016), remaining within a reasonable range[①]. Trade surplus in

---

[①] In the past, there was no consensus within the academia regarding the proper amount of surplus. Since the beginning of the 21st Century, international community, with growing concerns over the global imbalances, started to take current account surplus seriously. In 2007, IFM adopted the Decision on Bilateral Surveillance over Members' Policies, calling for its members to deal the external instability, including large current account surplus. Although a cap of 4 per cent on large current account surpluses and deficits was proposed at the G20 Summit in Seoul, an agreement was not reached on an universal measure. In December 2011, European Union enters into force with a new set of rules for economic and fiscal surveillance known as the "Six-Pack", with one of the alert indicators being "backward moving average current account balance as a percent of GDP, with the a threshold of +6% of GDP and –4% of GDP". (see *China's Balance of Payments Report 2011*)

goods and services (% of GDP) fell from the peak of 8.7% to 2.5% in recent years (2.2% in 2016) (Fig. 8). This is an evidence of the external imbalance being corrected as well as the effect of changes on both international and domestic economies.

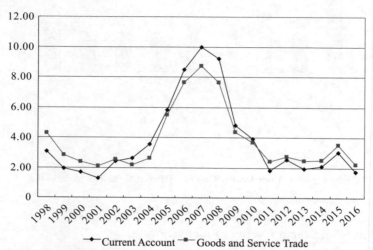

→ Current Account　→ Goods and Service Trade

Fig. 8 The Balance of Current Account, Goods and Service (% of GDP)

Source: National Bureau of Statistic, State Administration of Foreign Exchange.

The global economic situation contributed to China's sustained weak demand for exports. After the global financial crisis, the world economy ended its long period of stable growth and entered a period of "new normal" characterized by sustained low growth. The potential growth rate (or growing tendency) of both developed and developing economies has dropped. Growth rate of the former dropped by 0.5% to 1%, while the latter by 1.5% to 2%. Christine Lagarde, IMF Managing Director, repeatedly mentioned that the world economy was threatened by a mediocre era of low growth for a long time. Judging from the current situation, developed economies are being haunted by a "productivity crisis", seeing a decline both in the growth rate of labor productivity and total factor productivity after the global financial crisis. Former U.S. Treasury Secretary Lawrence Summers even issued a warning against "secular stagnation". Under such circumstances, the world economy will not be able to offer strong external demands.

China's weak export demands were also subject to domestic influence. For instance, rising labor costs, caused by a labor shortage. The cost of

China's labor supply has kept rising after the global financial crisis. As shown in Fig. 9, the growth rate of migrant workers' monthly wages rose to 19.3% and 21.2% in 2010 and 2011, even after China's GDP growth rate fell to under 8% in 2012. Undoubtedly, in this situation, China had lost its labor cost advantage in the fierce competition for exports.

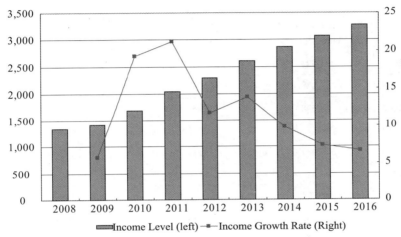

Fig. 9 Migrant Workers' Average Monthly Wages and Growth Rate (¥, %)

Source: Investigation Reports on Rural Migrant Workers in China and the author's calculation.

1.2.2 Sustainability of Investment Demands Being Challenged

With its investment being increased, China's economy has overly depended on investment over the past few years, resulting in a deterioration of its investment efficiency. Capital-output ratio has been rising since the mid-1990s, from below 3 to above 3. This means that there has been an increase in capital stock required for output per unit and a decline in the capital output; what's more, Incremental Capital-Output Ratio (ICOR: the ratio of investment to growth which is equal to the reciprocal of the marginal product of capital) has also been rising since mid-1990s, from 3 to around 5 (the world's average level being 2). This means a deterioration of marginal productivity of capital. Normally, an ICOR of 3 represents a high level of production efficiency, which proved that the fast growth of investment will not be sustained. For a better look at investment efficiency, we might as well scrutinize the amount of fixed asset investment necessary for generating next unit of GDP. As shown in Table 2, since the global financial crisis, there has been an obvious increase in ICOR, which rose sharply from 2.77 in 2007 to 12.47 in 2015. This proves that whether or not the high growth of investment is sustainable remained an issue.

Table 2 Changes in China's Investment Efficiency

	Total Investment in Fixed Assets of the Year (¥100 Million)	GDP Growth of the Year (¥100 Million)	Fixed Asset Investment/ GDP Growth
2007	137,323.9	49,495.9	2.77
2008	172,828.4	48,235.1	3.58
2009	224,598.8	26,857.4	8.36
2010	251,683.8	60,610	4.15
2011	311,485.1	71,591.2	4.35
2012	374,694.7	45,838.1	8.17
2013	446,294.1	49,375.1	9.04
2014	512,760.7	48,119.9	10.66
2015	561,999.8	45,078.1	12.47
2016	606,465.7	55,075.1	11.01

Notes: Index for the fixed asset investment was adjusted from RMB 0.5 million to RMB 5 million (real estate investment and rural household investment excluded).

Source: National Bureau of Statistics, calculated by the author.

Another factor affecting investment demands is the change in the demands for real estate investment. Judging from the long-term trends of real estate markets, two types of changes are worthy of our attention.

First, changes in population age structure. The cycle of real estate investment is closely related to population structure. A major change in China's population age structure is that population with demands for housing will begin to fall after reaching a peak. People approaching the marriageable age, namely those who are in need of a new house, will reach a peak. This is caused by the constant decline in birth rate and natural population growth rate after the baby boom in 1980s (Fig. 10). These changes may weaken the demands in real estate markets as well as the major support of house price.

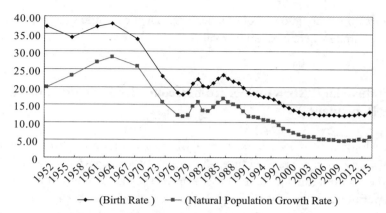

— (Birth Rate)   —■— (Natural Population Growth Rate)

Fig. 10 China's Birth Rate and Natural Population Growth Rate (‰)

Source: National Bureau of Statistics of China.

Second, the re-distribution of resident assets. As one of residents' most important assets, real estate has accounted for 60% of total assets and 90% of non-financial assets. In contrast, financial assets such as banking products, stocks, funds, trusts and insurances, accounted for a relatively smaller share, about 1/3 of total assets. With the house price being expected to fall, real estate as investment lost its attraction. As the rate of return on financial assets starts to rise, residents' wealth is being directed from real estate to financial assets. Within a country's financial structure, the ratio of financial assets to physical assets often tends to rise before it becomes stable. The effect of wealth re-distribution is an important factor affecting the mid or long-term trend of real estate markets.

Therefore, real estate markets have been transformed, from a period of shortage to a period of property surplus. The problem of supply-exceeds-demand is more pressing in 3rd or 4th tier cities, where demands are weakened due to the high level of inventory and the lack of inward movement of population.

Therefore, during the period of China's 13th Five-year Plan or in a longer period, to sustain China's economic growth, efforts should be made to reshape its economic structure and growth engine. In order to increase demand, the problem of imbalance between investment and consumption should be solved. Meanwhile, domestic demand should be expanded to ensure a stable and sustained growth; to boost demand on the total-factor-productivity-side, issues of technology innovation and low contribution of TFP (total factor productivity) to economic growth must be coped with. This requires the renovation of old modes of production while introducing new modes through technological innovation.

2. Industrial Restructuring: from Second-tier Dependent to Third-tier Dependent

Along with the acceleration of China's industrialization since the beginning of the 21st Century, the intensity and capital to labor ratio in the manufacturing sector has been on the rise. Since 2008, capital deepening has caused the replacement of labor with capital. While employment in the manufacturing sector began to fall, employment in the service sector did not rise either. The contribution of the service sector to employment is still relatively low although it overtook the primary and secondary industries in 1994 and 2011 as the major attraction of the labor force (Fig. 11). As shown in Table 3 for high-income countries, the share of employment in service sectors in total employment reached 74%, middle-income countries being 50%, the world's average level 47.5% and China being 42.4% in 2016. How to increase the flexibility of employment in the service sector is one of the main tasks for industrial restructuring during the period of the 13th Five-year Plan.

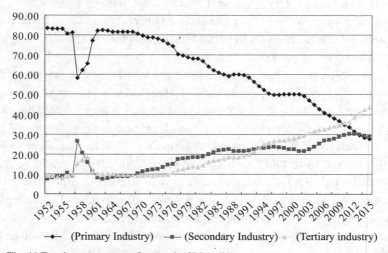

Fig. 11 Employment across Sectors in China (%)

Source: National Bureau of Statistics.

Table 3 Service Sector's Contribution to GDP and Total Employment (%)

	Share of GDP	**Share of Total Employment**
China	51.6	42.4
Brazil	73.3	77.3
Germany	68.9	70.9
India	53.8	26.6
Japan	70	69.3
Russia	62.8	66.1
America	78.9	79.9
High-income Countries	74.2	74
Middle-income Countries	59.2	50
World's Average Level	69	47.5

Notes: The item Share of GDP, data of Japan, America, High-income Countries and the World's Average Level were from statistics in 2015, the rest from 2016. The item Share of Total Employment, data of India and the World's Average Level were from statistics in 2010, the rest from 2015.
Source: World Ban WDI Database.

As shown above, China's service sector has been promoted in recent years. In 2013, the service sector exceeded the industrial sector in terms of its share of GDP (Fig. 12), but compared with other economies, either developed or developing, China's service sector still has a relatively smaller share, 22.6% lower than high-income economies, 7.6% lower than middle-income economies and 17.4% lower than the World's average level (Table 3). The wide gap between China's service sector and that of other countries, imposes limitations on its ability to create employment. It is estimated that the service sector's share of total employment has been around 50%, and its share of GDP is around 25%. For developed countries, the service sector's share of total employment has been above 50%, some even reaching 60%-70% while their share of GDP is around 30% to 40% or higher. This means that China's service sector is somewhat lagging behind.

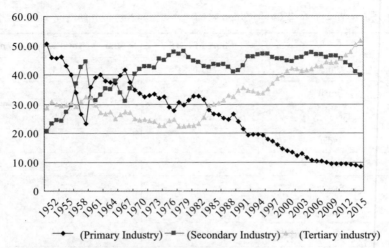

Fig. 12 Sector-wise Contribution of GDP in China (%)

Source: National Bureau of Statistic of China.

There are many factors affecting the development of China's service sector, particularly the sector of productive services. The most prominent one is the limitation imposed by China's economic system and monopoly. Compared with traditional sectors such as wholesaling, retailing, food service, transportation and social services, service sectors in China are less marketable, with prices being regulated by government, market access to be eased and barriers to entry to be eliminated. Established enterprises and new enterprises are competing under unequal conditions. The marketplace has been monopolized by state-owned business since private capital finds it extremely difficult to enter. Take the total investment in service sector (rural household excluded) in 2016 for example: investments made by state-owned enterprises account for 49.4% of the total. Such investment, which accounts for 11.2 % in wholesaling and retailing, 14.3% in accommodating and food service, 28.8% in real estate, 31.3% in science and technology, 35.2% in residence service and maintenance, 37% in rental and business service, 42% in financial sector, 44.8% in information, software and info-technology, 47.8% in culture, sports and entertainment. In the other five sectors, investment made by state-owned enterprises accounted for over 50% of the total: 81.2% in public administration, social security and social organization, 78.1% in water project, environment, public facilities administration, 76.7% in transportation, warehouse, postal service, 74.4% in education, 61.2% in health-care and social works. The predominant role of state-owned investment affected the efficiency and the overall development of the service sector. In other words, the lack of competition has become the major barrier to the service industry. Therefore, efforts should be made to change the situation, so as to unleash the full potential of employment. During the period of the 13th Five-year Plan, a deeper reform should be initiated on the service industry: sector monopoly should be eliminated, market access should be eased, and private capital should be encouraged to participate in the competition.

3. Demands Adjustment: from Investment Demands to Consumer Demands

Although China's consumer demand has witnessed a steady rise since the beginning of the 21st Century, the imbalance between consumption growth and investment expansion led to a yearly decrease in consumption rate and a constant rise in investment. The tension between investment and consumption escalated since the Chinese government launched its stimulus package to cope with the global financial crisis in 2008.

China's consumption rate, which rose and fell between 60% to 70% after the Reform and Opening-up, has witnessed a yearly decline since the beginning of 21st Century, from 63.7% in 2000 to 49.1% in 2010, reaching the lowest point since the Reform and Opening-up. Although there was a slight increase after 2011 (Figure 13), China's consumption rate has been 20% to 30% lower than the world's average level. For Japan and Korea, the consumption rate, even at their lowest points, were around 60-70%. Low consumption rate is mainly caused by low consumer spending, which dropped by 11.1%, from 47% in 2000 to 35.9% in 2010. Although increased slightly after 2011, the consumer spending in 2016 was merely 39%. In contrast, America's consumer spending was 70%, most of the European countries were 55% to 65%, most of the developing countries were 65% to 70%, and other Asian countries were 50% to 60% (Fig. 4).

Compared with the declining consumption rate, the rate of capital formation has increased by 13.4%, from 33.9% in 2000 to 47.3% in

2011, reaching its peak since the Reform and Opening-up. As shown in Figure 13, the investment rate started to rise above 40% since the beginning of 2003, and the rate has maintained its high level for 14 years. The rapid expansion of investment in 2009 caused investment rates to rise above 45%. Compared with other countries, China's investment rate has been twice as much as the world's average level[①] (Table 4). Admittedly, many emerging industrialized countries in East Asia had witnessed a high growth of investment, particularly during the process of industrialization. For instance, Japan and South Korea had for decades, maintained a high investment rate: Japan's investment rate had been 30.7% from 1946-2003, 36.2% from 1965-1973, a period of fast economic growth; South Korea's investment rate had been higher than Japan, having reached 40% at the peak of its economic growth. But neither Japan nor South Korea had seen the rate above 40% for 14 consecutive years.

---

① Certainly, considering the difference in the system of national accounts (SNA) and statistical approaches, we should be cautious when comparing the consumption or investment rate with that of the world level. Attention should be given to such problems as the underestimation of consumption rate. Consumption (% of GDP) includes both the commodity consumption and service consumption. The calculation of the former is based on information regarding sales volume of actual goods. Such a data is authentic and accessible online. However, the calculation of service consumption is largely based on assumption and estimation, which leads to the possibility of underestimation, particularly an underestimation of housing service consumption. Generally, the housing services are delivered in two forms: first, the rental services offered by the lessor and consumed by the tenant with rent; second, the purchased services offered and consumed by the property owner with virtual rent. In theory, the virtual rent of purchased property should be equal to the real rental price on market. The calculation of housing service consumption is supposed to be based on the real rental price, which is a common practice in many countries. However, in China, such calculation is actually based on property cost, namely the property cost multiplied by depreciation rate (2% to 4%). In recent years, with the rapid growth of house price, the rental price also rises quickly. In this regard, the calculation based on property cost will be lower than that based on real rental price. Besides, the rate of purchased house in higher in China (over 80% according to National Bureau of Statistics), which may cast doubts over the authenticity of data.

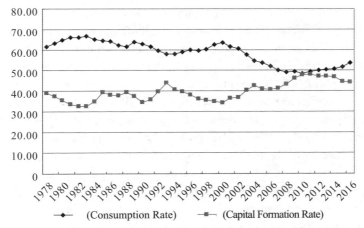

—●— (Consumption Rate)   —■— (Capital Formation Rate)

Fig. 13 China's Investment rate and Consumption Rate since Reform and Opening-up (%)

Source: National Bureau of Statistics of China.

Table 4 Consumption Rate and Investment Rate Across the World, 2015 (%)

	Consumption Rate	The Share of Consumer Rate	Investment Rate
China	51.1	37.1	45.4
Brazil	83.6	63.8	17.6
Germany	73.2	53.9	19.2
France	79.1	55.4	22.2
U.K.	84.4	65	17.2
India	69.4	59.1	32.9
Japan	76.4	56.6	23.9
Korea	64.1	49.1	28.9
Russia	69.6	52.1	22.4
America	82.5	68.1	20.3
High-income Countries	n.a.	59.6	21.4
Middle-income Countries	n.a.	54	31.1
Low-income Countries	n.a.	77.9	26.8
World's Average Level	n.a.	58	24.2

Source: World Bank WDI Database.

The most immediate cause of an unlikely faster growth of consumer consumption is closely related to China's distribution system. The growing tendency of distribution structure towards non-residential sectors has continued, and the declining status of the residential sector in national income distribution hasn't been changed.

First, labor remuneration (percentage of GDP by Income Approach), which has been on a decline over the past decades, dropped by 5.6%, from 53.1% in 1998 to 47.5% in 2016. Within the same period, net taxes on production rose by 0.8%, from 13.4% to 14.2% while the earned surplus by 5.6%, from 19% to 24.6% (Fig. 14). However, in a developed market, labor remuneration after primary distribution normally accounts for 50-60% of GDP. The decline of labor remuneration as a percentage of GDP was in part caused by the adjustment of statistics index (China revised its System of National Accounting in 2004, placing "income earned by the self-employed workers" originally under the category of "labor remuneration" under "earned surplus"). However, it is obvious that China's residential sectors are in less favorable conditions than government and enterprises during function distribution.

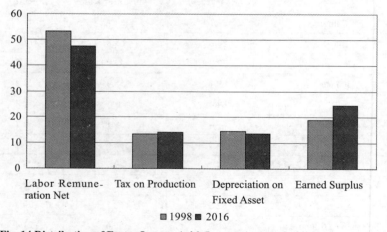

Fig. 14 Distribution of Factor Income (with Income Approach, %)

Source: Calculation of Provincial GDP with income approach, based on the statistics in China Statistical Yearbook.

The residential sector's share of income after primary distribution and disposable income has been on the decline over the past two decades, as shown in the cash flow statement offered by China Statistical Yearbook. According to Table 5, the residential sector's percentage of income after primary distribution dropped by 4%, from 65% to 61%, whereas the percentage of income after redistribution dropped by 5%, from 67% to 62%. In the same period, government share of redistribution rose by 2%, from 17% to 19% (share of primary distribution remained basically the same) while enterprise's share of primary distribution and redistribution rose by 4%, from 20% to 24% and from 16% to 20%.

Table 5 Income Distribution across Sectors of China's Economy

	Residential Sector: Primary Distribution	Government Sector: Primary Distribution	Enterprise Sector: Primary Distribution	Residential Sector: Redistribution	Government Sector: Redistribution	Enterprise Sector: Redistribution
1992	0.66	0.17	0.17	0.68	0.20	0.12
1993	0.63	0.17	0.20	0.65	0.20	0.16
1994	0.65	0.17	0.18	0.67	0.19	0.15
1995	0.65	0.15	0.20	0.67	0.17	0.16
1996	0.66	0.17	0.17	0.68	0.18	0.14
1997	0.66	0.17	0.17	0.69	0.18	0.13
1998	0.66	0.18	0.16	0.68	0.18	0.13
1999	0.65	0.17	0.18	0.67	0.18	0.15
2000	0.67	0.13	0.20	0.68	0.15	0.18
2001	0.66	0.13	0.21	0.66	0.15	0.19
2002	0.64	0.14	0.22	0.64	0.16	0.19
2003	0.64	0.14	0.22	0.64	0.16	0.20
2004	0.61	0.14	0.25	0.61	0.16	0.23
2005	0.61	0.14	0.25	0.61	0.18	0.22
2006	0.61	0.15	0.25	0.60	0.18	0.22
2007	0.60	0.15	0.26	0.59	0.19	0.22
2008	0.59	0.15	0.27	0.58	0.19	0.23
2009	0.61	0.15	0.25	0.61	0.18	0.21
2010	0.61	0.15	0.25	0.60	0.18	0.21
2011	0.61	0.15	0.24	0.61	0.19	0.20

(Contd.)

	Residential Sector: Primary Distribution	Government Sector: Primary Distribution	Enterprise Sector: Primary Distribution	Residential Sector: Redistribution	Government Sector: Redistribution	Enterprise Sector: Redistribution
2012	0.62	0.16	0.23	0.62	0.20	0.18
2013	0.61	0.15	0.24	0.61	0.19	0.20
2014	0.60	0.15	0.25	0.61	0.19	0.20
2015	0.61	0.15	0.24	0.62	0.19	0.20

Notes: Calculation based on data in China Statistical Yearbook.

A comparison between the growth of rural and urban income and the growth of GDP also reveals the declining share of residential sectors. As shown in Figure 15, from 1978 to 2015, China's GDP had grown at an annual rate of 9.7%, almost 29.3 times greater than in the past. In the same period, urban per capita disposable income and rural per capita net income were almost 13 and 14.1 times greater, growing at an annual rate of 7.4% and 7.6%. It is obvious that the growth of urban income is much lower than GDP growth. In a sense, the gap between national wealth and personal wealth marked the falling trend of the residential sector in the distribution of national income.

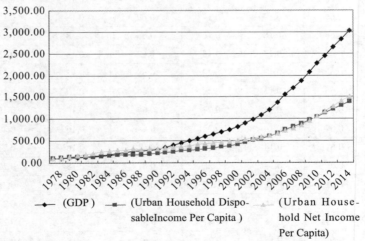

Fig. 15 China's Economic Growth and Resident Income Growth since the Reform and Opening-up

Notes: The index for both GDP and resident income is 100 in 1978.
Source: National Bureau of Statistics of China.

A further analysis would reveal that the falling status of the residential sector in distribution of national income is subject to many limitations such as the determination of factor return and redistribution of public income. In order to increase personal disposable income and then the consumer demands during the period of the 13th Five-year Plan, efforts should be made to balance the distribution system and directing income distribution toward the residential sector: first, workers input in negotiations over wages and welfare should be increased, so as to expand labor remuneration's share of factor distribution; second, farmers' right to land use should be ensured, particularly the rural collective construction land, which should be allowed to enter the market, and legally developed by farmers who can benefit from land value appreciation; third, regulation of income distribution should be strengthened. The system of individual income tax (reform is needed on the classified taxation systems) and redistribution of income from public property should also be further improved (improving state-owned capital operational budgeting and transferring state-owned capital to the social insurance fund).

4. Driving Force for Long-term Growth: from Depending on Total Factor Input to Depending on Increased Total Factor Productivity

Generally, there are two factors affecting the long-term growth of China's economy: the quantity of factors of production and total factor productivity. Certainly, increased amount of input will lead to a fast economic growth within a short period of time, but growth driven by input is subject to limitations such as insufficient supply of factors and diminishing marginal returns. The real driving force for economic growth stems not from the intensity of factors, but from the increased total factor productivity (TFP).

There has been a decline in the growth rate of total factor productivity over the past two decades, which dropped to −1.3% in 2015. In comparison, TFP of both America and European countries has been bouncing back steadily after a decline whereas that of India has kept rising (Table 6).

Table 6 TFP Growth Rate across the World (%)

	World	America	Europe	Japan	India	China
1999-2006	0.9	0.5	0.4	0.1	0.1	2.3
2007-2013	0.1	-0.2	-0.6	0.1	0.6	1.3
2013	0	-0.5	-0.2	0.7	0.9	0.2
2014	0	0.1	-0.1	-0.8	1.6	0.1
2015	-0.3	0.1	0.3	-0.1	1.9	-1.3

Source: The Conference Board Macro-economy Database.

A closer look at the contributions to economic growth would reveal that TFP growth rate contributed less to China's growth than labor quantity, labor quality and capital (Fig. 16). As a matter of fact, attempts had been made to analyze the source of China's growth from the perspective of TFP (based on growth accounting models and Paul R. Krugman's research on growth of Asian economy). Studies show that China's growth over the past three decades has been driven by the large-scale input of capital, energy, raw material and labor. Given the low contribution of TFP to economic growth, China is unlikely to sustain its current growth (Krugman, 1994; Young, 2000).

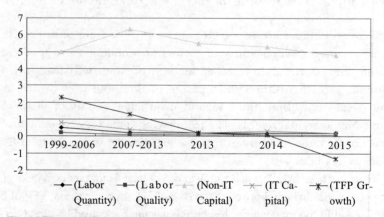

Fig. 16 Source of China's Economic Growth (%)

Source: The Conference Board Macro-economy Database.

The growth of China's labor productivity has fallen since the global financial crisis by 6.5%, from a peak of 13.1% in 2007 to 6.6% in 2015, with an annual rate of decrease being 0.8% (Fig. 17). What's more, China's output per unit of labor remained at a relatively low level, with $7,318 in 2015, far below the world average of $18,487, even lower than America's average of $ 98,990（Table 7）.

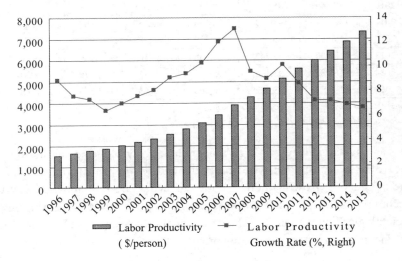

Fig. 17 China's Labor Productivity and Changes in its Growth Rate

Source: International Labor Organization.

Table 7 Output per Unit of Labor across the World, 2005 (at constant price $/person)

	World	America	Japan	Eurozone	India	China
1996	14,453	73,880	65,648	54,768	1,340	1,535
1997	14,792	75,782	66,174	56,470	1,372	1,652
1998	14,946	77,219	65,019	57,809	1,425	1,772
1999	15,180	79,411	65,700	59,144	1,524	1,885
2000	15,606	81,720	67,568	60,767	1,555	2,018
2001	15,601	82,459	67,759	61,469	1,574	2,172
2002	15,707	84,392	68,897	62,105	1,599	2,347
2003	15,864	86,318	70,124	62,885	1,669	2,561
2004	16,241	88,776	71,556	64,444	1,751	2,801
2005	16,497	90,072	72,209	64,992	1,872	3,088
2006	16,906	90,542	73,183	66,391	2,039	3,459
2007	17,310	91,773	74,157	68,007	2,218	3,912
2008	17,359	91,242	73,637	67,745	2,314	4,290

(Contd.)

	World	America	Japan	Eurozone	India	China
2009	16,963	92,560	70,477	64,946	2,503	4,674
2010	17,449	95,069	73,631	66,586	2,731	5,146
2011	17,711	95,724	74,108	67,559	2,909	5,586
2012	17,883	96,062	75,510	67,083	3,024	5,990
2013	18,107	97,748	75,958	67,164	3,189	6,423
2014	18,285	98,116	75,376	67,867	3,370	6,866
2015	18,487	98,990	76,068	68,631	3,559	7,318

Notes: Data for Eurozone are the average of its 19 member countries.
Source: International Labor Organization.

The sustainability of China's economic growth during the period of the 13th Five-year Plan will finally depend on the transformation from the exogenous growth to endogenous growth. The fundamental way to accomplish such transformation is promoting economic growth through technological innovation. To achieve this goal, two issues must be addressed: getting incentives right and getting prices right.

Getting incentives right

In general, the insufficiency of incentives found its expression in the following two aspects:

First, the system of intellectual property (IP) as an incentive is not fully-functioning. The IP system is one of the important protective measures for technological innovation. The malfunction of the IP system will reduce the spillover effect, preventing enterprises from innovation with their technologies. Although China has become more protective of intellectual property, its protection is far from sufficient, which imposes a limitation on the incentive function of the IP system.

Second, incentive mechanisms have to be improved for human capital in terms of the wages and intellectual property. Owners of human capital, such as entrepreneurs and scientists, assume most of the risks for technological innovation. Their creative efforts have to be recognized in terms of income and intellectual property distribution. However, the value of human capital to technological innovation is not given enough attention and owners of human capital, whose contribution and painstaking efforts are not respected in the process of distribution, were frustrating and discouraged them from taking risks. This has become a major barrier to technological innovation.

To further improve incentive mechanisms for innovation, more efforts should be made to build a more complete IP system as a deterrent to the breach of IP rights. Meanwhile, a talent incentive mechanism should be established to better evaluate and motivate innovative talents, who might be encouraged by such policies as "technology invested as capital stock" and "capitalization of technology".

Getting prices right

In a market economy, price, as a transmitter of market trend signal, plays an important role in regulating resource distribution. Economic growth in Japan, South Korea and China's Taiwan has proved that changes in the relative price of factors of production, if the market mechanism functions properly, prompts a transformation of growth model from being extensive to intensive. However, there has been too much government intervention in the market process in terms of factors distribution and price formation. In this regard, price is not a true reflection of the scarcity of factors, the relation between supply and demand as well as the damage of the environment, which to a certain extent lead to the price distortion. With such factors of production as land and capital being undervalued, cheaper tangible factors are invested for innovation. Such investments, which are under less pressure, are less motivated.

The key to cope with the problem is to get the price right, making the price a true reflection of the supply and demand by establishing an effective mechanism for pricing. In this way, enterprises will be able to make rational decision according to the market price, and the right price may regulate the behavior and expectation of enterprises for sustained innovation.

Apart from incentives and prices, the role of government in innovation should not be overlooked. Admittedly, the market won't be able to forecast all external effects. For instance, the innovation and upgrading of an enterprise will offer a pool of knowledge for other enterprises, or construction of infrastructural facilities will cause a decline in transaction cost and a rise in return on investment. External effects of this kind can't be completely coped with by the market and requires government intervention in industrial upgrading and technological innovation.

Still, there should not be too much intervention in the choice of industry and technology. As China has boosted its strategic emerging industries over the past few years, the measure of potentials of a certain sector has been based on the government's assumption and prediction of the supply and demand in the market. Even sector development plans are based on the government's judgment and prediction.

However, faced with a large amount of uncertainty, the government, due to its bounded rationality, might not be able to make correct judgment regarding economic trend. As a matter of fact, government judgment or control should never replace the regulatory mechanisms of the market. The rise and fall of PV industry in recent years is largely a result of bad government decisions and overlapping investment.

To avoid government failure, it is necessary to separate the optional industrial policy from the functional (Lall, 1994), direction intervention from indirect intervention. Industrial policy, in essence, is a safeguard against market failure, rather than a replacement of the market. In other words, during the implementation of industrial policy, the government should never attempt to replace the market. Rather, it should make efforts to enhance market trend signals and increase market activities.

Chinese Resident Income Distribution and Social Security System

Wang Zhen*

Since China initiated the Reform and Opening-up policy in late 1970s, its economy has seen rapid growth, with its GDP overtaking Japan in 2010 as the world's second largest economy before its share of U.S. GDP reaching 53.58% (Fig. 1). In terms of GDP Per Capita, China has become one of the countries with middle or high income. Some of its large cities and coastal regions in the east have ranked among the high-income economies (Fig. 2). However, the fast growth has led to the worsening condition of Chinese Resident income distribution and widening income gap between cities and rural areas, across regions and sectors. This is a major problem facing China's economy and society.

For the widening income disparities, efforts should be made to establish a well-developed social security system. For better serving the socialist market economy, China established a social security system with a focus on social insurance. The basic principle is to establish a multi-directional system with a wide coverage over basic needs and population. By 2013, a full coverage over China's regions and population has been accomplished. Admittedly, some of the problems in the system still need to be addressed and solved.

In this section, while offering an overview of China's social insurance system, including its establishment, evolvement and features, the author also analyzed the reform and improvement of the system.

---

* Wang Zhen, Researcher, Institute of Economics, Chinese Academy of Social Sciences.

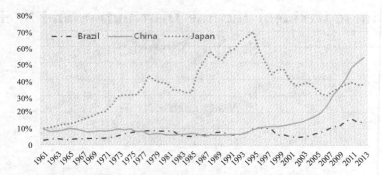

Fig. 1 China, Japan and Brazil——Catch-up Index Share of US GDP

Notes:

1. CUI Index refers to A Country's Share of US GDP.

2. Source: World Bank Database.

3. Current USD Price.

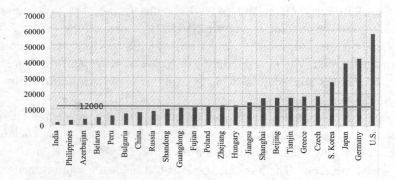

Fig. 2 GDP Per Capita 2015

Notes:

1. Current USD Price.

2. Source: World Bank Database, National Bureau of Statistics of China.

1. Resident Income Distribution in China since Reform and Opening-up

1.1 The Changing Pattern of Resident Income Distribution in China

The Gini Coefficient is a comprehensive measure of the income distribution of a nation's residents. A Gini coefficient of zero expresses absolute equality, where everyone has the same income while a Gini coefficient of 1 expresses complete inequality. However, in real practice, the Coefficient varies between 0 and 1, with 0.2 being considered as perfect equality, 0.2-0.3 as average equality, 0.3-0.4 as reasonable equality, 0.4-0.5 as disparity, 0.5 and above as wide disparity.

It should be noticed that the Gini Coefficient, which measures the inequality in total income, changes along with the change in the relative income of a population, instead of the change of a certain group. Normally, Gini Coefficient becomes lower when the total income of the low-income group increases, that of the high-income group is regulated and the size of middle-income group expands. However, if a group of people suffer from disease-induced poverty, their income may remain the same, but their conditions are worsening. Unless a special survey on the group is conducted, the Gini Coefficient won't be able to reflect the change in their conditions. What's more, even though the coefficient could be used as a measure of inequality and income distribution, it fails to present the source of inequality and the general feature of each of the groups. Therefore, studies on income disparity among different groups are based on the analysis of a very large database of Gini Coefficient, so as to find out the source of inequality by comparing the income of each group to the total income.

As was estimated by the World Bank, in the early period of Reform and Opening-up, China's Gini Coefficient was 0.2911 in 1981, which was reduced to 0.2764 in 1984, which expresses an average equality. Since China in the period was still a low-income developing country, Chinese residents' income, though relatively equal, remained at a very low level. Besides, urban residents had to purchase commodities with government-issued ration coupons due to the inadequate supply of economic products. Inspired by the idea of common prosperity, some areas and people under better conditions became richer than others, which resulted in the widening income disparity. China's Gini Coefficient in 1987 bounced back to 0.2985 from 1981, then grew to 0.3243 in 1990, marking a period of reasonable income distribution. Ever since then, the coefficient kept rising, though within a reasonable interval, to 0.3923 in 1999, being close to the international alert line. The coefficient rose to 0.4259 in 2002, and then 0.479 in 2003, above the international alert line. As was shown by the rising coefficient, the income distribution in China from 1984 to 2002 had gone from three stages: reasonable, acceptable and unequal.

As China's National Bureau of Statistics issued in 2013 the Gini

Coefficients since 2003, the coefficient has been used as a regular measure of economic growth and social development. Despite the coefficient offered by some social investigations being slightly different from that which was calculated by the Bureau of Statistics, the latter was more authoritative, because the Bureau's calculation was based on the analysis of voluminous data sets, while social investigation on random sampling. What's more, the statistics were issued on a year-by-year basis over a long time span. Social investigation wouldn't be able to ensure data continuity.

Therefore, the analysis of Gini Coefficients from 2003-2014 in this paper, is based on the data released in 2013 by the National Bureau of Statistics. According to the official statistics, China's Gini Coefficient was 0.479 in 2003, consistent with the rising tendency showed by the World Bank. Despite the difference in the manners of calculation, the structure of data released both by the Bureau and the World Bank revealed the fact that China's Gini Coefficient was higher than 4.0, the international alert line. From 2003 to 2008, the coefficient kept rising steadily, reaching the peak of 0.491 in 2008, not far from 0.5, the wide disparity line. Since 2009, Gini Coefficient had kept falling for seven consecutive years, reaching 0.462 in 2015, much lower than 2003.

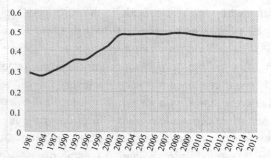

Fig. 3 The Changing Tendency of China's Gini Coefficient (1981-2015)

Notes: Data before 2003 was from the WDI 2016 from World Bank;
Data after 2003 was from China's National Bureau of Statistics.

The falling tendency of Gini Coefficient over the course of seven years might suggest a declining disparity in total income. Maybe it is safer to say that the zero growth of the coefficient since 2009 suggests that the disparity didn't keep widening.

It is worth noting that, China's Gini Coefficient, despite its falling tendency, is still above the international alert line in 2015, which means China is still a developing country with income disparity much wider than the rest of the world. According to WDI 2016, China's Gini Coefficients in 2010 was only lower than twenty countries, which, apart from Georgia, Israel and Vietnam, are all African or Latin-American countries.

1.2 Analysis on the Source of Residents' Income Disparity

First, the widening disparity was a result of marketization, the process in which factor allocation and income distribution were decided by the market. Since the Reform and Opening-up, labors and factors of production have been increasingly affected by marketization, and the rapid growth of non-public, private and foreign invested sectors caused further marketization factors of production. Labor remuneration, the main source of residents' income, was decided by marginal product of labor, which was subject to the influence of human capital. During the process of marketization, the difference in human capital of each individual caused the widening income disparity.

Second, the blockage of factor mobility is another cause of wealth gap. Factor of production, though increasingly exposed to marketization, were not be able to flow into a unified market. The flow of labor force, discouraged by the barriers across regions and sectors, was even slower than that of the capital. The flow of labor force between urban and rural areas was discouraged and blocked by China's household registration system. Labor policies during the period from 1989 to 1991 aimed at controlling the undirected flow of rural residents into cities. After 1992, efforts had been made to encourage rural workforce flowing into cities. However, from 1995 to 2000, particularly after the reform of state-owned enterprises, several provinces and cities adopted various measures to discourage the mobility of the rural labor force. Migrant farm workers, whose wages increased substantially in 2003, still found it difficult to be employed by public-owned enterprises. In contrast, capital flowed easier than labor force but the flow of capital was limited for many reasons, although many favorable terms had been offered to attract investment. Subject to government survillance and monopoly factor price is not totally determined by market, which brings a higher price or return on capital than that produced by its marginal output[1]. As one of the factors of production, capital may bring a higher price or more benefit than its marginal products, but the price of factors, which was supposed to be decided by the market, was subject to government control and monopoly. A bigger problem was caused by the unequal distribution of the resource compensation. Take Ordos for instance: there are 7000 billionaires in the area, most of whom became rich by selling natural resources like coal. Their ways to build wealth could be illegal, against government regulations or even tied up with corruption[2].

The predominant role of capital on the allocation of production factors. Since the Reform and Opening-up, China's fast economic growth benefited from the advantages of its labor force. However, compared with workforce, capital was rarely to be found, which caused a high rate of return on capital (ROC). Therefore, China's economic growth was characterized by a high rate of investment and ROC. The predominant role of capital reduced the share of labor remuneration in allocation. What's more, capital monopolized by a few investors even further widened the wealth gap.

Loopholes in the legal system increased the likelihood of income from illegal activities or misconduct. Along with economic growth, new income laws and regulations were passed to facilitate the distribution system. However, the loopholes in the legal system allowed someone to build wealth in inappropriate or illegal ways. As was mentioned above, the absence of tax on mining encouraged the people to benefit from selling resources. Besides, the increase of invisible income contributed to the worsening income inequality. If invisible income was taken into consideration, Gini Coefficient calculation based on the "total income of urban residents" would rise from 0.31-0.34 to 0.45-0.51. Unreported income accounted for 19% to 25% of China's GDP from 2002 to 2009[3].

As for the limited re-distributive ability, the amount of disposable

① Zhang Chewei, Zhao Wen, "Problems Facing China's Labor Remuneration Distribution: An Analysis and Calculation Based on Employment and Self-employment Economy", *Social Sciences in China*, No. 12, 2015.

② Li Qiang, "Social Classes and the Equality and Justice in Social Space", *Journal of Renmin University of China*, No. 1, 2012.

③ Bai Chongen, Tang Yanhua, Zhang Qiong, "An Estimation of the Scale of Invisible Income in China: An Interpretation Based on ELES and Data", *Economic Research Journal*, No. 6, 2015.

income was largely affected by primary distribution and redistribution. Taxation was supposed to be an important re-distributive method, but China's personal income tax was characterized by its regressive nature. Although the rich class in China had to pay high tax, the tax rate was relatively low. For example, the Gini Coefficient in 2009 was supposed to fall 0.018 after urban residents paid their personal income tax, but it actually dropped by 0.0129[1], which suggested that the regression of taxation policy weakened its re-distributive ability. Additionally, the re-distributive ability of the social security system was weakened by the boundaries within the system between the city and the rural area, one sector and the other. As the other important re-distributive measure, social security was supposed to narrow the wealth gap by offering social relief. However, the boundaries within the system made it difficult for the under-privileged to receive aid. Migrant workers had little access to social security in a city because such problems as the transfer and continuation of personal accounts prevented them from receiving benefit. Other forms of aids, such as the minimum living standard security, mainly targeted local residents, were not applicable to migrant workers.

Imbalance between urbanization and industrialization prevented the wealth gap from narrowing. The process of industrialization prompted the migration of surplus rural force to cities, which accelerated urbanization. China's urbanization, being discouraged by the household registration system, had undergone two stages: the stage of farmers becoming migrant workers and the stage of migrant workers becoming citizens. Public services, which were offered according to the status of one's household registration, posed barriers to the second stage of urbanization. In other words, migrant workers, although working in cities, had no access to urban public services but to that of the rural areas. Due to the huge difference in urban and rural public services, the wealth gap did not narrow along with the process of industrialization. As China became increasingly industrialized, groups of migrant workers expanded quickly, growing to 277.47 million in 2015, accounting for 35.8% of the total working population[2]. This further prevented the wealth gap from narrowing.

---

[1] Xu Jing, Yue Ximing, "The Effect of Taxes Inequality On Income Distribution", *Economics Information*, No. 6, 2014.

[2] *Statistical Communique of The People's Republic of China on the 2015 National Economic and Social Development*, http://www.gov.cn/xinwen/2016-02/29/content_5047274.htm.

2. A Social Security System with Universal Coverage

China's social security system, designed for the socialist market economy, includes social insurance, social relief, social welfare, Veteran's services, mutual aid and personal saving insurance[1].

2.1 China's Social Security in the Period of Planned Economy

China's current social security system evolved from the social security arrangement in the period of "planned economy". In this period, government regulated and controlled economic activities through administrative instructions and plans, which were supported by a corresponding system. According to the plan of "prioritizing heavy industry", China focused its resources in sectors of heavy industry, which gradually resulted in the urban-rural dual economic structure[2] of China. Accordingly, China's social security system in the period was also characterized by the dual structure: urban residents accessed social security according to their employment whereas the rural residents only had access to the benefits offered by collective economic organization. Government offered no fiscal support to social welfare in rural areas.

After 1950s, with the establishment of rural cooperative businesses, the system of People's Commune and village-level collective economic organization was formed in rural areas of China. To facilitate the system, rural social insurance policies, such as the "Five Guarantees Subsistence "(FGS) and "Rural Co-operative Medical Scheme"(RCMS) were adopted. FGS, which offers subsistence for minimum livelihood to those who had lost their abilities to work, was actually a relief system within the collective economic organizations. Unlike GGS, RCMS required personal premium for medical services and medicines, although it was also designed for the collective economic organizations.

Social security for urban residents was subdivided into different

---

[1] "Decision of the Central Committee of the Communist Party of China on Some Major Issues Concerning the Establishment of A System of Socialist Market Economy", *Communique of the Third Plenary Session of the 14th Central Committee of the CPC*, 1994.

[2] Lin Yifu, Cai Fang, Li Zhou, *The China Miracle: Development Strategy and Economic Reform*, Shanghai: Truth & Wisdom Press, Shanghai Sanlian Press, Shanghai Renmin Press, 1999.

categories, each designed for different occupations. The first category was for government or public service employees, who enjoyed free medical and pension services financially supported by the government. The second category was for employees of state-owned and collective enterprises. This type of social security requires premiums paid both by the enterprises and workers. The third type was for urban jobless residents. Generally, this group of people were not covered by any type of social security, but some of them could access partial welfare, like reimbursement for medical services if their spouses worked in government, public sector or enterprises.

The figure below presents the structure of social security system in the period of planned economy. The system, which evolved into types of welfare programs for different sectors, gradually lost its social relief function. In rural areas, FGS and RCMS were supported by collective economic organizations. In urban areas, workers' labor insurance evolved into enterprise welfare during the Cultural Revolution; social security for government or public sector employees were subject to the financial capability of each sector.

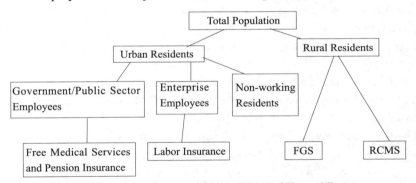

Fig. 4 Structure of Social Security System in the Period of Planned Economy

2.2 Social Security Reform from the Reform and Opening-up to Mid-1990s

The social security system was supported by the People's Commune and collective economy in rural areas, but in urban areas, social security evolved into enterprise welfare. The situation was changed in late 1970s, as China initiated its Reform and Opening-up. In rural areas, along with the collapse of the People's Commune, collective economy was replaced by a household responsibility system; in urban areas, state-owned enterprises started to make attempt towards concession, contracting and share-holding. The original social security system for urban residents, having lost its foundation, started to collapse.

In rural areas, due to lack of financial support from the collective economy, social security had lost its ability to offer welfare. RCMS coverage started to fall sharply from its peak of 90% in the mid-1970s, to 5% in 1983[1]. The medical-care system barely functioned until the establishment of the New RCMS in 2003.

Unlike RCMS, FGS had a stronger dependence on the collective economy whose collapse nearly cut off its finance. To solve the problem, central government decided that the FGS should be directly financed by farmers. Personal premiums were included in the fund for township planning and directly managed by town-ship government[2].

From the 1980s to early 1990s, issues caused by the reform of stated-owned enterprises, such as bankruptcy, lack of job opportunities, unemployment and increasing poverty in urban areas, began to emerge. Relief measures for the unemployed, the jobless and those who suffered from poverty were badly needed in urban areas[3]. In 1933, Shanghai established a guarantee program for the minimum livelihood of urban residents, which became the role model for China's Subsistence Security System[4].

At the same time, efforts had been made by local governments to develop a social-pool-plus-personal-accounts scheme (SPPPAS) for social insurance. In 1986, the State Council issued Interim Provision on *Implementing Labor Contract Systems in State-owned Enterprises*, in which the SPPPAS for

---

① Wang Lusheng, Zhang Licheng, "Lessons from China's Rural Co-operative Medical Scheme", *Chinese Health Economics*, 1996, No. 8, pp. 12-15.

② According to the *Notice on No Arbitrary Charges and Taxes for Farmers* issued by CPC Central Committee and State Council, "the fund for FGS, in principle, comes from taxation and fees required by law, but before the establishment of such a system, the fund shall be collected as fund for public activities". In 1991, the *Regulation on Farmer Bearing the Cost and Offering Labor* stipulated that "village reserve fund includes public accumulation fund, public welfare fund and administration. The public welfare fund will be used to finance FGS, poverty relief, cooperative medical insurance and other public welfare. Fund collected at the county level could be used as a source of finance for FGS".

③ Yang Lixiong, "An Overview of China's Minimum Livelihood Guarantee Program for Urban Residents: Problems and Policies", *Chinese Journal of Population Science*, 2004, No. 3, pp. 71-80.

④ *Decisions of the State Council of People's Republic of China on Reforming Urban Employees Pension Insurance*, 1991.

contracted workers was stipulated. The provision also required that "retired contracted workers be covered by social security systems, and the source of pension comes from both the enterprise and personal premiums". In 1991, the SPPPAS had covered all workers in state-owned enterprises.

The social security reform in the period, with an aim to facilitate the reform of state-owned enterprises, allowed the enterprises to lay down the heavy burden of employee welfare to increase its competitiveness. For government and public sectors that needed not to participate in market competition, no reform had been initiated, neither on the free medical service, nor the pension system.

2.3 Social Security System for the Socialist Market Economy

The aim of China's reform on the economic system, which was confirmed at the 14th CPC National Congress, was to establish a socialist market economy, whose framework was established at the Third Plenary Session of the 14th Central Committee of the CPC. Within the framework, the function, status and objective of social security reform were confirmed.

First, the objective was to establish a "multi-tiered social security system" which included social insurance, social relief, social welfare, Veteran's services, mutual aid and personal savings insurance.

Second, the emphasis of the reform, should be placed on old-age and medical insurance for urban workers, implementing the social-pool-plus-personal-accounts scheme. For rural pension insurance, the focus should also be placed both on family and community assistance.

Third, the way to maintain and increase the value of social security fund was to purchase government bonds.

The function of social security was to facilitate the reform of state-owned enterprises. The principles and framework for social security established at the Third Plenary Session of the 14th Central Committee of the CPC constituted the ground work and main body of China's current social security system. From the mid-1990s to 2000, China had established systems for Basic Pension Insurance, Urban Residents Basic Medical Insurance, Employment Injury Insurance, Unemployment Insurance and Maternity Insurance. Meanwhile, the Minimum Livelihood Security System was established in the form of social relief for urban residents.

2.4 A Social Security System with Universal Coverage

From the Reform and Opening-up to the early 21st Century, China's rural social security barely functioned. The basic principles for a social security system established at the 15th CPC National Congress still focused on rural areas and its function to reform state-owned enterprises. Ever since the 16th CPC National Congress, the purpose and principle for a new social security system had gradually changed. In the report delivered at the 16th CPC National Congress, the direction for new rural social security was confirmed as "a system that covers rural pension, medical-care and minimum livelihood". The outbreak of SARS in 2003 had reminded the Chinese government of the importance of building a social security system with universal coverage.

Over the decade that followed, China's efforts to build a new social security system had entered a new phase. In late 2003, NRCMS started to be implemented. The new scheme clarified the government's financial responsibility for rural social security. The financing model of the new scheme was designed as "government subsidy, collective relief and personal premium". The model also applied to the new pension scheme for rural workers initiated in 2009. The new FGS was also financially supported by the government. According to *Regulations on the Five Guarantees Subsistence* in Rural Areas issued in 2006, "finance for the five guarantees should be included in the government's budget", which meant that the "FGS" had become a form of government-financed social relief.

In this period, other forms of social relief, such as the guarantee program for minimum livelihood insurance and medial relief system had been established in both urban and rural areas. For jobless urban residents, Urban Residents Basic Medical Insurance and Urban Residents Pension System had been adopted.

With urban residents' pension system being established, China's social security system had achieved a universal coverage. So far, rural social security systems, apart from various forms of social relief, like FGS, Minimum Livelihood Guarantee and Medical Relief, also included the NRCMS and New Rural Pension Insurance. In contrast, urban social security mainly consists of pension insurance, medical insurance, unemployment insurance, employment injury insurance, as well as minimum livelihood guarantee and medical relief. Even jobless urban residents have access to pension insurance and medical insurance.

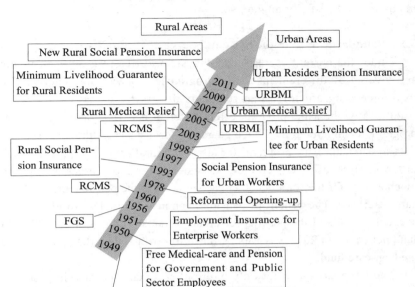

Fig. 5 Establishment of China's Social Security System

3. Challenges Facing China's Social Security System

Universal coverage means that any group of people in China has access to at least one type of social security. Admittedly, this is a great accomplishment of China. However, evolved from the planned economy and being used as a tool to facilitate reform of state-owned enterprises, China's current social security systems are still faced with challenges.

Most of the challenges can be traced to the two features of China's social security system: First, boundaries within the system and fragmentation of insurance programs; Second, heavy burden caused by invisible debt.

3.1 Fragmented Social Security System in China

One of the main characters of China's social security system is the fragmentation caused by the boundaries within the system. For instance, the benefits offered by the system, differs from region to region, from one group of people to another. The immobile, stationary nature of the system makes it impossible to transfer or migrate.

3.1.1 Boundaries Within the System: Source of Inequality

Under the current social security system, different groups of people are covered by different insurance programs, with varying benefits. The insurance program for urban residents differs from that of the rural. Additionally, the same program offers different benefits. Take social relief program, the minimum livelihood guarantee for instance. Although, basically the same in nature, the programs for urban and rural areas, are quite different in terms of benefits. Government subsistence for urban areas is twice as much as that for the rural. Another case in point is the pension and medical-care insurance. The benefit of pension insurance for jobless residents only accounts for 4% of the benefits for urban workers. The amount of NRCMS fund per capita in 2012 was ¥308.5, much lower than the urban pension and medical-care fund.

The boundaries are not only within the system, but also imposed on regions. The social fund for social security was raised on several levels: county, county-level city, city. There has been a huge gap in terms of the rate of premium, contribution bases and benefit bases on each level. Take pension insurance for instance: although the central government had decided the rate of premium for pension insurance, the actual rate at local level is decided by the average wage in the region, which contributed to the difference in premium rate. As for the benefit, the gaps are even wider across regions. Take the average pension benefit in 2012 for example: the highest benefit in some provinces was 2.15 times as much as the lowest, the second highest 1.78 times as much as the second lowest.

It is the same with social relief across regions. Take the minimum livelihood guarantee for instance: in 2012, the highest subsistence offered in some provinces was 2.27 and 2.45 times as much as the lowest, the second highest was 2.06 and 2.27 times as much as the second lowest. The disparity is more obvious in rural areas. The highest relief was 3.75 and 3.96 times as much as the lowest and the second highest was 3.72 and 2.79 times as much as the second lowest.

One of the fundamental principles for social security is that the level of social security should be consistent with the level of economic growth. As an important re-distributive measure, social security won't function properly if the income equality across regions can't be ensured. Boundaries within the social security systems, and across regions, has resulted in the difference in benefits, and has been a major source of social conflicts.

3.1.2 The Immobile and Stationary Nature of China's Social Security

Another problem with China's social security is its immobility. The stationary nature better suits a society with less population mobility. During the period of planned economy, population movement was under strict control by the government, and the migration of social security had not yet become a social problem. However, since the Reform and Opening-up, the migration of the rural population was encouraged by industrialization and urbanization. The number of migrant workers[1] had increased from 132 million in 2006 to 167 million in 2016, accounting for over 40% of the urban working population. This means nearly half of the workforce in urban areas, are migrant workers in pursuit of employment and life in the city. Migrant workers have become "an important part of industrial workers"[2].

The risks for migrant workers largely working in non-agricultural sectors are brought by an industrialized society. Since the model of social security should be consistent with the social risk, migrant workers should be covered in urban social security systems. Technically, migrant workers formally employed are allowed to participate in urban workers social insurance. However, surveys show that migrant workers are generally unwilling to participate in the social security program in his place of employment. Statistics show that, in 2016, the rate of migrant workers participated in pension, medical-care, employment injury and unemployment insurance was only 35.1%, 28.5%, 44.3% and 22.1%, much lower than the full coverage rate of urban workers in the same period. One of the major causes is the boundaries within the social security system and across the regions.

---

[1] According to National Bureau of Statistics, migrant workers refer to off-farm workers who work away from home. The migrant worker community include migrant workers both working away from home or those working in counties and towns near their hometown.

[2] *Decisions of the State Council of People's Republic of China on Coping with the Issue of Migrant Workers*, 2006.

Table 1 Migrant Works Covered by Urban Workers Basic Social Insurance (million persons)

	2011	2012	2013	2014	2015	2016
Total Number of Migrant Workers	158.63	163.36	166.1	168.21	168.84	169.34
Employment Injury Insurance	68.28	71.79	72.63	73.62	74.89	75.1
%	43.0%	43.9%	43.7%	43.8%	44.4%	44.3%
Pension Insurance	41.4	45.43	48.95	54.72	55.85	59.4
%	26.1%	27.8%	29.5%	32.5%	33.1%	35.1%
Medical-care Insurance	46.41	49.96	50.18	52.29	51.66	48.25
%	29.3%	30.6%	30.2%	31.1%	30.6%	28.5%
Unemployment Insurance	23.91	27.02	37.4	40.71	42.19	37.4
%	15.1%	16.5%	22.5%	24.2%	25.0%	22.1%

Notes: Migrant works refers to rural workforce who works away from home.
Source: Annual Statistics Issued by Ministry of Human Resources and Social Security.

3.2 The Burden of Invisible Debt and the Sustainability of China's Social Security

The burden of invisible debt is another major problem facing China's social security system. The term, also known as potential debt, refers to a debt which is not obvious but still has to be paid in the future. Invisible debts mainly occur in the social insurance programs.

The debts generated by the transformation of systems mainly manifest themselves in urban workers' pension programs. In the 1990s, when China started to build a social security system that facilitated its socialist market economy, the social pool plus personal account scheme had already been adopted. The issue of debt was not for employees who participated in the program after the establishment of new system, nor for those who already retired before the new system was established, but for those already employed waiting for retirement. Debts stemmed from their original social fund and personal premiums.

Such debts were supposed to be paid by government. However, local governments, facing financial troubles at the time, had to withdraw from personal accounts to raise the social pension fund, which caused the "empty account" issue. Although policies had been issued later which prevented the personal premium as pension fund, the problem still existed at the local level. The debts caused by "empty accounts" within the urban workers' pension system was estimated to be ¥1.4 to 0.5 trillion[①].

4. Reform and Improvement of China's Social Security System

As discussed above, there are two major problems facing China's social security system. The first is the fragmentation of the system–boundaries within the system and across regions resulted in equality and immobility that inhibited the function of social security. The other problem is invisible debt, which affects the sustainability of social security. To solve the aforementioned problems, the reform of social security should prioritize both equality and sustainability.

4.1 A Complete, Multi-tiered and Sustainable System for Providing Basic Social Security

Since the Reform and Opening-up, China's social security system had consisted of various programs for different groups of people, which resulted in the boundaries within the system and between regions. The existence of such boundaries led to the evolution of social security into social welfare for some people and a complete absence of social security for others. In urban areas, workers in government and public sectors were over-protected while rural residents barely had access to basic insurances. Although China's social security has accomplished a universal coverage in the 21st Century, people living in poverty still found it difficult to obtain basic insurances. To ensure "the basic insurances for everyone" is the first and foremost task for a well-developed system as well as for a moderately prosperous society.

A social security system, apart from its universal coverage, should be able to provide basic social security, which, unlike social welfare, is a social protection for the under-privileged. What's more, basic social security

---

① Gai Genlu, "Empty Accounts for Employees Pension Insurance", *China Social Security*, 2012, No. 6, pp. 36-37.
   Zhang Yingqin, Xiao Fei, "A Research on the Issue of Empty Accounts for China's Pension Insurance", *Ningxia Social Sciences*, 2011, No. 3, pp. 63-67.

is conducive to invigorate the society since over-protection may induce "laziness" that troubled European countries. Furthermore, basic social security may well-facilitate China's economic growth. For a country with a large population, an overly protective social security will not only cause heavy burdens for government but affect the labor market efficiency. Take social insurance programs for example: the source of funds comes mainly from employer and personal premiums. Raising benefits actually increases the personal premiums and the cost of inter-generational transfer from the currently employed to the already retired.

With basic insurances ensured, residents may participate in other insurance programs that best suit them. Therefore, China is in need of a multi-tiered social security system (Chinese counterpart of the multi-pillar system promoted by international society) that meets the demands of people from all walks of society. The first tier should be social relief that requires no premiums; the second should be social insurances with mandatory premiums; voluntary insurance should come third, in the form of annuity, business insurance or social welfare charities.

4.2 Equality to be Increased

Inequality caused by boundaries within social security system and between regions inhibited the function of social security and had become a major source of social conflicts. Middle or high income communities, such as government employees, workers in public sectors or enterprises, are better protected while the low-income group, like rural residents, migrant workers and jobless urban residents, are under-protected. This is a serious breach of the re-distributive duty of social security. A difference in benefits may also cause a conflict of interests between groups, which undermines social stability.

Suggestions were made regarding increasing equality of social security at the Third Plenary Session of the 18th Central Committee of the CPC: first, the integration of social security systems, like the integration of urban and rural insurance policy, minimum livelihood guarantees, so as to narrow the gap between rural and urban social security; second, reform on pension and medical-care insurance systems for government and public sector employees, in order to reduce the difference between the aforesaid employees and the enterprise workers; third, to eliminate regional differences in social security by increasing the level of social pooling.

4.3 Mobility to be Improved

Another way to promote equality is to increase the possibility of social insurance migration. The immobile nature of social security has become the major barrier to population movement. As proven by international experience, there are two ways to make social security easier to transfer: first, raising the level of social pooling, raising the social fund on a larger scale; second, establishing reasonable channels to allow the migration of social security data to different systems and regions.

In general, efforts should be made to promote the pooling for basic pension funds, the integration of pension and medical-care insurance in urban and rural areas and to improve the policies for social security data migration.

4.4 Sustainability to be Ensured

Invisible debt is another problem facing China's social security system. It directly threatens its sustainability. With the population aging faster than previously, and the burden of historical debts increasingly heavier, invisible debts posed a challenge to China's social security system. Although the government is fully responsible for the financing of social security, as was stipulated in the *Social Security Act*, the problem remained even after the debt was transferred. As a matter of fact, invisible debt is a common problem faced by all countries practicing PAYGO (or pay-as-you-go) in their social security systems.

First, "a portion of government capital should be allocated to fund social security". The effort aims at solving the problem of historical debts. The debts, as discussed above, were generated prior to Reform and Opening-up, particularly during the period of "planned economy" when workers received "low wages" but were offered "better welfare". In theory, the debts also contributed to the capital accumulation of state-owned enterprises. Therefore, it is reasonable to allocate a portion of government capital as the social security fund.

Second, improve the system of personal accounts while developing an incentive mechanism characterized by "more premiums, more benefits". Under the current pension insurance system, a "fully funded" plan is adopted for personal accounts, while the "defined contribution" plan is for the benefits. Compared with the PAYGO scheme, the system of personal accounts is free from the trouble of inter-generational transfer, hence from the invisible debts.

Third, regarding the benefit determination, importance should be attached to "actuarial balance" and the establishment of "a complete mechanism that regulates and determines the benefits for people from all walks of society", because the summarized income rate should be in line with the summarized cost rate so as to keep social security program in actuarial balance.

Fourth, higher returns on social security funds are another way to ensure sustainability. Social security funds, particularly the pension insurance fund, is accumulative in nature. Return on the accumulated investment is a major source of social security fund.

China's Health Insurance System and Its Relation to Labor Market

Yao Yu*

1. Introduction

As China enters a new period of growth, social and economic policies are being interpreted from new perspectives. Labor market theory, the central concern of economics, has been given new attention. Western scholars used to show their concern over China's unemployment generated by its large population and the quality of its employment. Over the past decades, much has been discussed about China's employment regarding the above-mentioned two topics. Despite many worries and concerns, the Chinese government has achieved great success in creating job opportunities and improving the quality of employment. Although the labor market is largely subject to the influence of macroeconomic policies, the influence of social policies should not be overlooked here. In what follows, I am about to take the example of China's medical insurance to show how social policy exerted positive influence over economic growth.

This research is a direct response to the practical demand of the current labor market, since both the old and new labor forces, even the retired ones, are expecting newer and better health-care policies. Being placed at the core of China's health-care system, medical insurance should be able to respond to the demand with rational policies and proper guidance in order that the labor market policy could cope with the new economic situation.

In this paper, the author will trace the history of medical insurance systems in China while discuss their connections and interactions with labor markets in each period.

* Yao Yu, Researcher, Institute of Economics, Chinese Academy of Social Sciences.

2. Literature Review

Studies on the relation between medical insurance systems and labor markets generally focus on the effects of changes in medical insurance systems on the demand for labor force, the rate of pay and labor mobility.

2.1 The Effect of Medical Insurance on Wages and Labor Demand

The most immediate effect of a medical insurance system is on the behavior of the insured person in seeking clinical advice. But in reality, it also affects the behavior of the worker and employer, because the medical insurance policy, particularly the medical insurance for urban workers, will cause a rise in labor cost. Employers must fulfill their legal obligation to offer medical-care to employees according to the wages they received (6% of the total wages will be paid by employer and 2% by the worker). However, it is difficult to estimate the number of uninsured workers who are informally employed. Up to now, scholars are more interested in how to offer social protection to such workers. Studies have been initiated on how employer and employee worked together to avoid paying for medical insurance or how the employers find themselves struggling to offer medical insurance to their workers.

2.2 The Effect of Medical Insurance on Labor Mobility

Statistics show that social security centers in coastal cities of China are often crowded with internal migratory population before or after the Spring Festival. Workers planning to leave the city would close their account for social insurance and withdraw the money beforehand. It was a common practice before the financial crisis in 2009[1]. Employers' attitudes towards offering medical insurance vary from city to city, sector to sector, depending on the actual practice of each company. As for workers, particularly those who earn high wages, medical insurance has been a big concern before

---

[1] Zheng Beifei, "Migratory Population covered by Employees Medical Insurance: Status and Measures", *Chinese Health Insurance*, No.1, 2015; Fan Shide, "A Study on Health Insurance Policy for Migratory Population in the Region of Yangtze River Delta", *China Population and Development Studies*, 2016, 38.

they change jobs. In this sense, medical insurance poses a barrier to labor mobility with it is immobile and region-bound nature[1]. Normally, the ability to attract a labor force depends on the wealth of medical-care resources in a given region[2], but a medical insurance system which requires the insured to reimburse their medical costs in a specified region often prevents the flow of a labor force into less developed regions[3]. The regional imbalance characterizing China's economic development has led to a huge difference in terms of the amount of reimbursement and the types medicines covered by medical insurance. The New Rural Co-operative Medical Scheme (NRCMS), which induces discrimination and limitation in terms of reimbursement across levels of health-care facilities, inhibits the flow of the rural labor force into towns and cities.

What's more, the popularization of the medical insurance could have affected the flow of a labor force between formal and informal labor markets. According to Liu Guoen, the "insurance and housing fund" stipulated in the Labor Law requires the employers to bear part of employees' insurance cost, which, while increasing the labor cost, inhibits the demand for a labor force. As for an informal labor market, the imperfect social security could prompt the flow of more labor into a formal market, which means that a formal market will suffer from a labor surplus whereas the informal will suffer from a labor shortage[4]. Some people who hold the opposite view believe that the popularization of mandatory medical insurance, particularly the insurance specifically tailored for different groups of people, will attract more labor by imposing limitations on the cost borne by the informal labor market.

2.3 The Influence of Medical Insurance on Employment and Retirement

According to Chinese law, workers may retire and access their pension once they reach the mandatory age for retirement. Early retirement is only

---

[1] Li Hongjuan, "A Study on the Regional Difference of Health Insurance for Urban Migratory Population", *Population and Society*, 2017.

[2] Wu Chuanjian, *The Mechanism for A Sustained System of Social and Health Insurance*, Economic Science Press, 2014.

[3] Qin Xuezheng, Liu Guoen, "An Overview of the Effect of Health Insurance on Labor Market", *Economics Information*, No.12, 2011.

[4] Ibid..

available under certain circumstances. Under such a system, workers are not allowed the freedom to choose when to retire or to choose among medical-care and pension systems. With the adoption of Social Endowment Insurance for Urban Residents in 2007, workers under the retirement age are allowed access to social medical insurances. This, to some extent, may affect the workers' decision to retire. For a long time, some workers have cheated their way into retirement by falsely reporting their age or illness[1]. The new form of medical insurance as well as its wide application allowed workers even more freedom in terms of early retirement. Admittedly, this may enable middle-aged or old-aged workers to make free choices as to when to retire, but it also directly affects the structure of a workforce in terms of age and ability[2].

In general, academic attentions have focused too much on the medical insurance system, with few studies on the history of the system or on its relation to the labor market. Although some researchers found that the relation between medical insurance and the labor market may prominently interfere with the flow of the workforce as well as the worker's decision to retire, the symbiotic relation between the two deserves a closer look[3].

3. Labor Markets and Corresponding Medical Insurance Systems in Chinese History

For the convenience of discussion, the author may focus on three periods since China's Reform and Opening-up: 1980-1992, the period of planned economy; 1992-2002, the period of transition from planned economy to socialist market economy; the period of socialist economy since 2002.

3.1 Labor Market and Medical Insurance Reform: 1980-1992

3.1.1 Continuation of the Labor System in the Period of Planned Economy

The labor market in the 1980s was characterized by the following

---

[1] Feng Jin, Hu Yan, "A Research on the Early Retirement of Urban Labor Force in China", *Chinese Journal of Population Science*, No.4, 2009.

[2] Wang Jun, Wang Guangzhou, "A Research Factors Affecting Urban Employees' Decision to Retire Early", *Chinese Journal of Population Science*, No.3, 2016.

[3] Qin Xuezheng, Liu Guoen, "An Overview of the Effect of Health Insurance on Labor Market", *Economics Information*, No.12, 2011.

features: (1) The labor force was organized, trained and deployed all by the government; (2) People were closely related to resource elements for social production, for which capital was placed in a place secondary to people; (3) Demand of state-owned enterprises, which were invigorated by the SOE Reform, for more labor force couldn't be met; (4) The contradiction between the needs of people who returned to cities after the Cultural Revolution and the demand of enterprises for a quality labor force made it difficult for people with no skills or low level skills to find a job. For these reasons, the government decided to leave the problem to the market. This period could be sub-divided into two stages:

In 1984, China made its first attempt to adopt the policy of labor contracts and to optimize the reorganization of the labor force. Workers with low level of skills were gradually sifted out and became part of the surplus work force. This was the first step toward a labor system reform and the formation of a labor market.

In 1986, the labor contract policy was formally adopted. According to the *Provisional Regulations for Adopting Labor Contract Policy in State-owned Enterprises* issued on 12th July 1986 by the State Council, permanent workers must be employed with a contract according to the national plan. Later, the policy was gradually extended to the community of directors and leaders in enterprises. Until then, the policy of labor contracts was implemented throughout all enterprises. This move abandoned the traditional way of employment adopted in state-owned enterprises for decades, leaving the issue of employment in the hands of the market. Transforming workers and directors into the employer and the employed in the market economy, this move could be regarded as a further attempt towards the establishment of a labor market.

3.1.2 A Desperate Need to Reform the Medical Insurance System in the Period of Planned Economy

Since China's Reform and Opening-up, a series of challenges were posed to the labor policy and the free medical service for urban workers as the country's economy evolved towards commodity economy. On the one hand, there had been an over-use of medical resources in the original medical-care system, since no individual had to pay for medical services, which caused the rapid increase of medical expense. On the other hand, the original system, which lacked the mechanism for risk dispersion, had different policies for enterprise workers, government employees and farmers, resulting in inequality, discrimination and more waste of medical resources.

In response to the government's call for being responsible for one's own profit and benefit during the economic reform, enterprises had to withstand the burden of paying social insurances, particularly the medical insurance for retired employees. What's more, with more flow of labor forces, the original labor and medical-care policies were unable to cope with the demands of economic development. In the meantime, with the household responsibility system being widely adopted, the collective economy in rural areas collapsed quickly, which cut off the financial support for the Rural Co-operative Medical Scheme. Without the agricultural cooperatives, the RCMS had lost its foundation. The pressing issues facing medical insurance in both city and rural areas were calling for an overhaul of the medical insurance systems of China.

3.1.3 A Barrier to Labor Mobility: Medical Insurance in Early Transitional Period

In the early period of Reform and Opening-up, the labor systems adopted by enterprises were still fixed and unchangeable, by which workers' labor insurance and free medical-care policy was adopted to cater to such a system. Starting from 1984, the economic reform had been placed on the government's agenda, followed by the reform of the labor system. By the time the policy of labor contracts was adopted in 1986, state-owned enterprises only assumed limited responsibilities for workers stipulated in the contract, which ran counter to the labor policy that took all around care of workers for free. Therefore in 1988, a preliminary reform was initiated on the free medical service policy in government and the labor-medical care policy in state-owned enterprises. Many of the laid-off employees from state-owned enterprises flowed into the labor market and invigorated the market. However, these employees, having lost the social insurance offered by the enterprises and having to face uncertainty in the future, found themselves with desperate desire for risk aversion, which put more pressure on the reform of the medical insurance system.

Meanwhile, rejuvenated by the reform, enterprises were faced with a contradiction between their demands for further development and the rigid, fixed employment policy. To solve the problem, enterprises started to hire urban citizens and rural workers as supplementary labor force,who barely had any access to welfare much as their employers wanted to help. The reasons behind the seemingly improbable issue were as follows: enterprises of the time were owned and managed by the government, which meant such things as human resource and payment were subject to unified government plans. Unless the employment issues were solved on a national scale, measures proposed to alleviate the job demands of a particular group or in a particular region, were unlikely to be adopted as universal policies, or there would be a possibility of bigger and more serious issues. Therefore, enterprises were unable to offer its supplementary workers welfare benefits or medical insurance programs as complete as that of their regular employees. Under such a situation, it was almost inevitable for employees without medical insurance to exit the labor market. The government policy, which apparently kept a balance between enterprises' demand for workforce and their need to reduce labor cost, also imposed limitations on individuals' career development and the formation of labor market.

3.2 Labor Market and Health Insurance Reform: 1992-2002

3.2.1 Labor System Reform and the Formation of Labor Market

Starting from 1992, state-owned enterprises began to initiate their "off-the-job" scheme and the "Less Employee and Higher Productivity (LEHP)" plan, which were motivated primarily by China's desperate need to establish modern systems for labor market and enterprises as the socialist market economy gained a political foot-hold in the country. With the LEHP plan being adopted, enterprises across the nation began to reduce a substantial portion of their labor force. While the laid-off employees contributed to the formation of labor market, the need to help enterprises overcome difficulties remained a headache for the government.

Along with the restructuring of state-owned enterprises in late 1990s, in simple terms, the demutualization and privatization of state-owned enterprises, workers had been separated from the system of public ownership and became those who had nothing to offer other than their labor — literally the labor force of market economy. This marked the formation of China's labor market.

3.2.2 Towards A Socialized Health Insurance System

In 1998, China initiated its preliminary reform on the free medical insurance scheme for government and public sectors employees and the labor medical-care scheme for workers of state-owned enterprises. Social insurances were introduced into the aforesaid schemes to regulate the behavior of both the provider and receiver of medial services. However, the reform had proceeded slowly until 1993 when the *Decisions on Major Issues Concerning Establishing Socialist Market Economy* (Decisions) was issued. It was stipulated in the Decisions that "the cost for urban employee's pension and medical insurance is borne by employer and employee, in the form of social pool plus personal account," which marked a further step towards a socialized system of basic medical insurance. In 1994, Zhenjiang (Jiangsu Province) and Jiujiang (Jiangxi Province) began their first attempt towards the "social pool plus personal account" scheme, which was officially ordained in 1998 by the State Council in its *Decisions on Establishing Basic Medical Insurance System for Urban Employees,* which called for joint efforts to ensure a universal coverage until 1999.

During this period, China's medical insurance system, once as a form of welfare and labor protection, based on government finance, gradually evolved into a system partially supported by the government and designed to facilitate the development of labor market. The main issues facing such a system were as follows: how to ensure equal access to medical resources in a society where huge gaps existed between the urban and rural areas and among different regions; how to provide low-cost yet efficient medical services in a society characterized by large population, slow economic growth, aging population, diverse diseases and rising medical cost. In general, how to ensure equality and efficiency. Such a system should be able to fulfill its obligation to satisfy the people's demand for medical services and to better facilitate the labor market. Either thrifty or extravagance in the use of medical insurance fund would be frowned upon and politically criticized.

China's medical insurance in this period took on various forms: apart from the urban employees medical insurance, there were also programs for farmers without land, the informally employed, as well as urban and rural residents.

3.2.3 The Basic Principle for Health Insurance Policies in the Period: to Facilitate the Development of Labor Market

Generally, the basic principle for the medical insurance system in this period was "low-cost, wide coverage, borne by employer and employee, and social pool plus personal account." The fundamental reason for building such a system, according to some scholars, was that China's financial capabilities were subject to limitations of many kinds. This is an assumption, the author believes, that can never prove true. The real reason was that China's medical insurance was not an exact equivalent of welfare, which was often manipulated by local officials for higher positions in the government. It was more of a social policy designed to better serve and facilitate labor market and local economy.

3.3 Labor Market and the Reform of Medical Insurance Systems after 2002

3.3.1 Labor Market Policy in the Socialist Market Economy

After the system of socialist market economy was established in China, particularly after China's entry into the WTO, a new form of labor market had been established by the central and local governments. New mechanisms for employment allowed the worker much freedom and more choices. The employment policies in this period were known as being "proactive" and "more proactive", which meant the purpose of such policies was to use macroeconomic policy to create more job opportunities while offering supportive measures for reemployment and entrepreneurship. The "proactive employment policies" over the past decades had evolved into different versions, each with a different focus and content.

—Version 1.0: The focus was placed on the unemployed;

—Version 2.0: The focus was placed on all employees. During its implementation, the Employment Promotion Act was enforced;

—Version 3.0: Characterized by being "more proactive" during its implementation, a series of measures were proposed for stable employment.

—Version 4.0: Characterized by being "more proactive" during its implementation, a series of measures were proposed for stable employment.

The emphasis was placed on further expansion of employment opportunities, and a complete set of policies were developed.

The highlight of Version 4.0, the most recent one, was its focus on encouraging both employment and entrepreneurship. The employment policies, from "free choices for the worker, regulated by the market demand and promoted by the government" to "encouraging employment and entrepreneurship", were consistent. Right now, the new leadership proposed the plan for "public participation in starting businesses and making innovations". With a focus on "starting business", the proactive employment policy 4.0 offered a detailed plan for employment under new circumstances.

In this period, China's labor market, with the usual aim to ensure employment, started to focus on the balance between the flexibility and quality of employment. Flexibility means that the enterprises have much freedom in choosing their employees and the right to be spared from intervention in the process. In simple terms, flexibility refers to all viable measures to promote employment. As for quality, it refers to workers' right to equal job opportunities, employment insurance, and the right not to be mistreated. However, the imbalance between flexibility and security has become an issue for the current labor market of China. On the one hand, employees in government and public service sectors are overprotected, which leads to labor immobility and fewer choices for the employer. On the other hand, employees in other sectors are under-protected and the over-flexibility caused an issue of rapid labor mobility.

3.3.2 Social Health Insurance as a Driving Force for Labor Market in the System of Socialist Market Economy

Along with the gradual perfection of medical insurance for urban workers, the CPC Central Committee and the State Council issued the *Decision on Further Strengthening the Medical Work in Rural Areas* (herein after referred to as the Decision), marking a further step toward a more complete system of medical insurance. The Decision calls for efforts to establish The New Rural Co-operative Medical Scheme and Rural Mutual Health Care Scheme. In 2003, the Ministry of Health issued the *Suggestions on Establishing A New Type of CMS in Rural Areas of China*, in which four provinces (including Yunnan) were designated as the pilot areas for the New CMS. The aim was to encourage the flow of surplus labor force in rural areas into the labor market by offering social health care to all. In this way, those who can't get insured in cities where they worked, can at least have access to the medical-care service in their hometown.

As the labor market in cities grew into maturity and the population of China became increasingly urbanized, the Chinese government started to pay attention to the access of the jobless in cities to medical-care after the problem with urban workers and farmers was solved. In 2007, the

State Council issued the *Guidance on Initiating the Pilot Scheme for Offering Basic Medical Insurance to Urban Residents*, which marked the establishment of a medical insurance system that covered all the population in China, including workers and residents in both cities and rural areas. The current medical insurance system includes Urban Employee Basic Medical Insurance, Urban Residents Basic Medical Insurance and New Rural Co-operative Medical Scheme, offering medical-care services to urban employees, urban residents and people living in rural areas.

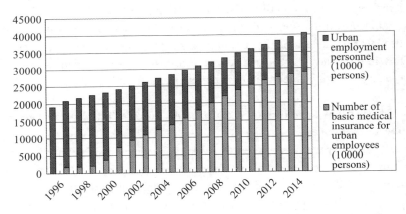

Fig. 1 The Number of Employed Persons and People with Medical Insurance Coverage, 1996-2016

With more encouraging measures being implemented and a more fierce competition between various medical-care systems, China's medical-care system is being perfected and its coverage rate increased. As shown in Figure 1, the number of people getting insured is growing as the number of employed persons is increasing. The growth of the former even surpassed that of the latter.

3.3.3 Basic Principles for Medical Insurance Policies during the Period

One of the basic principles was to attach equal importance to the account of the social insurance fund and individual accounts. Both accounts were managed separately, and both the maximum and minimum deductions for medical expenses were decided by the government. However, the scheme lacks direction regarding the extent to which each account should pay. The problem is to be decided by local, instead of the central government. Up to now, no regulations or policies have been proposed as to how to combine and manage both accounts. So far, there is no proven evidence to show that managing both accounts is a method without flaws, but the Chinese government resolved to take medical insurance as a social policy that facilitates economic development, which successfully avoided the argument over its efficiency.

Managing both accounts may clarify the responsibilities shared by the country and the individual. It may strengthen government control of medical expenses, promote equality and mutual help. Admittedly, there must be a viable preventive mechanism for this scheme, which means that public hospitals should become the central pillars for this medical insurance system. Only in this manner can the supervision of insurance funds and the hospital be ensured and the objective of the policy designer be achieved.

3.3.4 Medical Insurance System after 2002: Challenged, but not Inherently Flawed

With better welfare offered to workers, the labor market in this period witnessed unprecedented flow of labor force. In order to maintain labor mobility while avoiding the loss caused by regional competition for labor force, the central government has been cautious in advancing reforms in the area of medical insurance. Some of the following mechanisms, though seemingly harmful, are actually designed for the employees to have a better access to medical-care services.

3.3.4.1 The Immobile and Region-bound Nature of Medical Insurance

"Non-region bound" means that when an insured person changed his job or place of employment, or his medical insurance plan from one to the other, previous benefits could be retained, maintained or transferred. In this sense, the New Rural Co-operative Medical Scheme is characterized by its region-bound feature: first, people in rural areas can only get insured in their domicile, and their medical insurance can't be changed along with the change in his place of employment. Second, the deduction for medical expenses in other regions is higher than in ones' domicile, with a lower rate of reimbursement. Third, although the new policy allows workers to change their rural medical insurance into an urban one, the difference in fund-raising manners, the amount of funds and coverage makes it a difficult practice.

3.3.4.2 Complicated Catalogue Management

The mechanism for managing urban employees' medical insurance is characterized most prominently by the catalogue of medicines, medical services and facilities, designed for a better management of medical resources. In 2000, the first catalogue of medicine for urban employees' medical insurance was issued, before it was renewed in 2004 and is still used today. Since the use of the catalogue effectively curbed the waste of medical resources, China included the "Essential Medicines Agenda" into the medical-care reform in 2009. The catalogue of essential medicines, mainly for NRCMS and URBMI will play a more fundamental role than the existing one.

Admittedly, such catalogue management is faced with many problems: first, doctors' right to choose medicines for the patient was limited; second, the patients' right to access the latest medical technologies and services was limited; third, the new products of pharmaceutical companies, which were not listed in the catalogue, may hit a sales bottleneck. However, all such limitations were intended for a better control of labor mobility.

3.4 The Medical-care Reform and Labor Market under the New Circumstances

3.4.1 New Features of Labor Market

As the economic climate changes, China's current labor market exhibited new features: first, aging in the workforce. Twenty years after China adopted the "Family Planning Policy", the number of young workers started to decline while the percentage of the older workers began to rise. Rising dependency ratio caused a series of social problems. Second, the vanishing demographic dividend is calling more desperately for economic transition and upgrading. Faced with rising wages, labor costs and a more competitive market, enterprises have to accelerate their restructuring and upgrading, laying off employees that become surplus labor. Third, saturated traditional markets coexists with merging markets with a high threshold. Along with the development of a socialist market economy, many traditional markets become saturated, with their profitability gradually decreased. On the other hand, emerging markets in need of high-level talents impose high threshold on labor force.

Workers who become all the more health-conscious as their living conditions are improved, are expecting better working environments, and are particularly more sensitive to working conditions that might do harm to their health. They have more desire to avoid the risk in health and economic risks. However, as all industries become more mechanized and specialized, the pressure and stress in workplaces are increasing, posing challenges to workers' health. This is proven by the rising number of workers suffering from chronic diseases. That is why people's demand for medical resources is growing faster than economic growth.

3.4.2 Re-balancing the Flexibility and Security of Labor Market

Under the new economic situations, the need to balance the flexibility and security of the labor market has become a common sense. Economic transition requires labor mobility so as to increase the flexibility and to alleviate the pressure of employment caused by economic upgrading. Meanwhile, the desire of workers for better job protection has become stronger. The underprivileged community of migrant workers has expanded to include many college students, who, unlike migrant workers, have a different expectation for their employment. How to ensure the security and quality of their job has become as important issue as how to increase people's sense of fulfillment.

3.4.3 A New Type of Labor Market Featuring Rural-Urban Integration

With the rural and the urban being integrated, labor markets in both regions began to merge. The boundary between labor markets, once differentiated by educational background, was blurred. Labor mobility increased by urbanization also blurred the lines between the insured persons. The lack of data and information had caused overlapping in medical expense reimbursement. As a matter of fact, the medical insurance system based on classification of people could not cope with the process of urbanization and such classification, which may lead to discrimination and conflict between groups of people, may induce speculation, speculative behavior and moral risk. Increased mobility requires the medical insurance to be unbounded by locality and the medical-care system that divided the urban and the rural was becoming a barrier to labor mobility. Therefore, *Opinions of the CPC Central Committee and the State Council on Deepening the Health Care System Reform* addressed the need to "establish a medical-care system covering both the urban and the rural", to integrate the three types of basic medical insurance systems, to eliminate prejudice and discrimination in terms of the insured person's occupation, and to ensure a healthy and stable labor market.

3.4.4 The Influence of Medical Insurance System on Labor Market

On the one hand, the adoption of the New Rural Co-operative Medical Scheme obviously reduced the desire of rural labor to work away from home and encouraged rural workers to return to their hometown. On the other hand, without social security and welfare, migrant farm workers who find it difficult to live in cities, retreated from the labor market earlier than expected.

3.4.5 Influence of the New Labor Market on Health Insurance System

Previous experience shows that a well-developed system of social security is the key to solving labor market issues. Accordingly, medical-care systems should be developed under the same principle.

Just before the 19th CPC National Congress, efforts were made to establish a comprehensive health insurance system unbounded by locality. The purpose was to reduce the limitation on insurance transfer and to eliminate occupational prejudice through the integration of different insurance systems, so as to better serve the employed and ensure a healthy labor market.

4. Further Discussions

From the previous discussion on the influence of China's health insurance system on its labor market and economic transition, we can draw the following conclusions: first, principal contradiction of each period has always been the top concern of the government for building health insurance system; second, what China has pursued, was not the best, but the most appropriate health insurance system; third, China prefers the health insurance system adopted by less developed countries to those elaborate ones adopted by developed countries. These principles are simple in appearance, but difficult to practice in reality. In order to better understand China's choice, the following two aspects must first be understood:

4.1 Understanding Two "Relations"

4.1.1 The Relation between Health Insurance System and Worker's Decisions

A general and inclusive health-care system was not built in a day. Even the health-care in developed countries was basically shaped by the demands of the labor market and economic growth. The logic of China's health-care policy was based on domiciliary and occupational concerns. It is obvious that under a single health-care system, most of the employees, despite their hard work or long hours of working, may not be able to transfer their medical insurance from one system to another. This will discourage their further participation in the labor market. However, the change in labor policy may effectively affect the performance of the labor force[1].

Faced with health risks, workers would make different decisions as to the ways of offering their labor. For instance, a worker participating in NRCMS and URBMI would choose to shorten their working hours, which leads to a decrease in income. Price difference in medical services caused by the structural differences in the current health-care system will broaden the income gap between groups of people covered by different insurance policies.

4.1.2 The Relation between Welfare System and Moral Risk

On the patient's part, the insured person will have a sense of contentment only when his medical expense is lower or the quality of the medical service he received is higher than those who are not insured. In contrast, doctors may be exposed to temptations like maximizing his benefits by encouraging patients to spend more on medical services. Or doctors and patients may work together in insurance fraud. Too much attention to the convenience of the insured person will undoubtedly generate moral risk. Medical insurance agencies may choose to disperse the risk by hiring more people or increase the price for medical insurance. In either case, it is the worker who suffers greater loss.

The above-mentioned two relations must be regarded as the top concerns for the design of welfare system or even the best policies may induce

---

[1] Amartya Sen. *Development as Freedom*. Trans. Ren Ze, Yu Zhen. Beijing: China Renmin University Press, 2002.

negative attitudes toward them①.

4.2 The Chinese Interpretation of HiAP: A Case Study

"Health in All Policies" is the theme for the 8th Global Conference on Health Promotion organized by the WHO in June 2013. According to *Declaration of Helsinki* published at the conference, HiAP was defined as a strategy for addressing the complex factors that influence health and equity, with the aim of collaborating across sectors to achieve common goals. The idea of HiAP, first proposed in the the *Declaration of Alma-Ata* in 1978, focused too much attention on achieving the objective of health for all. Likewise, the Healthy Public Policy proposed in the *Ottawa Charter*, which was signed at the First International Conference on Health Promotion, requires all sectors to put health issues in first place. The conferences in 2005 and 2013 stressed the same principle. However, WHO policies hardly yielded any results in any country, despite the WHO acclaim for Finland's HiAP in Chronic Disease Control and Prevention, South Australia's Strategic Plan, Bhutan's National Happiness Index, and Swedish across-sectors experiences in reducing road injuries. All such cases are examples of success achieved in health sectors, instead of the social and economic sectors.

The Chinese government, however, placed the focus of its policy on developing the labor market and promoting economic transition. HiAP was interpreted by China as a tool for social policy, which in essence, was cross-sector governance, emphasizing joint efforts across sectors. While the objectives of other sectors have been achieved, the goal of promoting health was accomplished.

4.3 Conclusion

The development of the labor market is closely related to the change in health insurance systems. Both the labor market and the health insurance system are designed to meet the demand of economic growth in different periods. Since 1980s, China's medical-care system has fulfilled its

---

① Robert Nozick, *Anarchy, State, and Utopia*, Trans. Yao Dazhi, Beijing: China Social Sciences Press, 2008; Michael J, Sandel, *Liberalism and the Limits of Justice,* Trans. Wan Junren. Nanjing: Yilin Press, 2012.

responsibility for the transforming and developing labor market. Well-developed since the beginning of the 21th Century, health insurance system has exerted influence on the decisions of the labor force. Under the social and economic conditions of the new period, faced with the new features of the labor market, the challenges posed by the health-conscious people, the basic principles for China's medical-care system will continue to evolve and develop.

参考文献

白重恩、钱颖一、谢长泰：《中国的资本回报率》，《比较》
　　2007 年第 28 期。

蔡昉：《中国经济增长如何转向全要素生产率驱动型》，《中
　　国社会科学》2013 年第 1 期。

江小涓：《服务业增长：真实含义、多重影响和发展趋势》，
　　《经济研究》2011 年第 4 期。

杰黑米·里夫金：《第三次工业革命：新经济模式如何改变世
　　界》，中信出版社 2012 年版。

林毅夫：《新结构经济学：反思经济发展与政策的理论框
　　架》，北京大学出版社 2012 年版。

世界银行与国务院发展研究中心：《2030 年的中国：建设现
　　代、和谐、有创造力的高收入社会》，研究报告，2012 年。

王小鲁、樊纲、刘鹏：《中国经济增长方式转换和增长的可持
　　续性》，《经济研究》2009 年第 1 期。

吴敬琏：《中国增长模式抉择》，上海远东出版社 2009 年版。

熊彼特：《经济发展理论》，商务印书馆 1990 年版。

姚战琪：《生产率增长与要素再配置效应：中国的经验研

究》,《经济研究》2009 年第 11 期。

袁富华:《低碳经济约束下的中国潜在经济增长》,《经济研究》2010 年第 8 期。

中国经济增长前沿课题组:《中国经济长期增长路径、效率与潜在增长水平》,《经济研究》2012 年第 11 期。

Arrow, K. , "The economic implications of learning by doing", *Review of Economic Studies*, Vol. 29, No. 3, 1962, pp. 155 – 173.

Barlow D. , "Growth in Transition Economies: A Trade Policy Perspective", *Economics of Transition*, Vol. 14, No. 3, 2006, pp. 505 – 514.

Barro R. and Sala-i-Martin, X. , *Economic Growth*, 2nd edition, Cambridge, Massachusetts: MIT Press, 2004.

Blanchard, Olivier J. and Giavazzi, Francesco, Rebalancing growth in China: A three-handed approach, MIT Department of Economics Working Paper No. 05 – 32, 2006.

Blanchard, O. , Perotti, R. , "An Empirical Characterization of the Dynamic Effects of Changes in Government Spending and Taxes on Output", *Quarterly Journal of Economics*, Vol. 117, No. 4, 2002, pp. 1329 – 1368.

Boardman, Anthony E. , Claude Laurin and Aidan R. Vining, "Privatization in Canada: Operating and Stock Price Performance with International Comparisons", *Canadian Journal of Administrative Sciences*, Vol. 19, No. 2, 2002, pp. 137 – 154.

Bonoli, G. , *The Politics of Pension Reform: Institutions and Policy*

Change in Western Europe. – Cambridge University Press, 2000 〔http://assets.cambridge.org//97805217/72327/sample/97 80521772327ws.pdf; son baxılma-mart 2017〕.

Card D. and Krueger A. B. , *Myth and Measurement: the Economics of the Minimum Wage*, Princeton University Press: Princeton, 1995.

Card, David, "Using Regional Variation in Wages To Measure the Effects of the Federal Minimum Wage", *Industrial and Labor Relations Review*, Vol. 46, No. 1, 1992, pp. 22 – 37.

Card, David and Krueger, Alan B. , "Minimum Wages and Employment: A Case Study of the Fast Food Industry in New Jersey and Pennsylvania", National Bureau of Economic Research (Cambridge, MA) Working Paper No. 4509, October 1993.

Chaudhary M. Aslam and Amin Baber, "Impact of Trade Openness on Exports Growth, Imports Growth and Trade Balance of Pakistan", *Forman Journal of Economic Studies*, Vol. 8, 2012 (January-December), pp. 63 – 81.

Chihiro İnaba, "Effects on the Cross-country Difference in the Minimum Wage on International Trade, Growth and Unemployment", Kobe University, Discussion Paper series. July 2014.

Chua, Amy L. , "The Privatization-Nationalization Cycle: The Link between Markets and Ethnicity in Developing Countries", *Columbia Law Review*, Vol. 95, No. 2, 1995, pp. 223 – 303.

Chui M. , Levine P. , Murshed S. M. and Pearlman J. , "North-South Models of Growth and Trade", *Journal of Economics*

Surveys, Vol. 16, No. 2, 2002.

Clemens, J., and Wither, M., "The Minimum Wage and the Great Recession: Evidence of Effects on the Employment and Income Trajectories of Low-Skilled Workers", No. w20724, National Bureau of Economic Research, 2014.

De Castro Fernández, F., Hernández de Cos, "The Economic Effects of Exogenous Fiscal Shocks in Spain: A SVAR Approach", ecb working paper#647, 2006.

Dube A., "Minimum Wages and Aggregate Job Growth: Causal Effect or Statistical Abstract", IZA DP No. 7674, 2013.

Edelberg, W., Eichenbaum, M., Fisher, J., "Understanding the Effects of a Shock to Government Purchases", *Review of Economics Dynamics*, Vol. 2, No. 1, 1999, pp. 166 – 206.

Fatás, A., Mihov, I., "The Effects of Fiscal Policy on Consumption and Employment: Theory and Evidence", cepr discussion paper#2760, 2001.

Freeman, R., "Are Your Wages Set in Beijing?" *Journal of Economic Perspectives*, Vol. 9, No. 3, 1995, pp. 15 – 32.

Global Age Watch Index, 2015.

Gulaliyev M. G., Abasova S., Huseynova Sh, Azizova R., Yadigarov T., "Assessment of Impacts of the State Intervention in Foreign Trade on Economic Growth", *Revista Espacios*, Vol. 38, No. 47, 2017, p. 33.

Guriev, Sergei, and Andrei Rachinsky, "The Role of Oligarchs in Russian Capitalism", *Journal of Economic Perspectives*, Winter

2005, pp. 131 – 150.

Heppke-Falk, K. H. , Tenhofen, J. , Wolff, G. B. , "The Macroeconomic Effects of Exogenous Fiscal Policy Shocks in Germany: A Disaggregated Svar Analysis", deutsche bundesbank, discussion paper#41, 2006.

Holmstrom, Bengt, and Paul Milgrom, "Multi-task Principal-agent Analyses: Incentive Contracts, Asset Ownership and Job
Design", *Journal of Law, Economics and Organisation*, 7,
1991, pp. 24 – 52.

Jones, C. and Romer, P. , "The new Kaldor facts: Ideas, institutions, population, and human capital", *American Economic
Journal: Macroeconomics*, Vol. 2, No. 1, 2010, pp. 224 –
245.

Katz, Lawrence F. and Krueger, Alan B. , "The Effect of the
Minimum Wage on the Fast Food Industry", *Industrial and Labor
Relations Review*, Vol. 46, No. 1, October 1992, pp. 6 – 21.

Kobrin, Stephen J. , "Expropriation as an Attempt to Control Foreign Firms in LDCs: Trends from 1960 to 1979", *International
Studies Quarterly*, Vol. 28, No. 3, 1984, pp. 329 – 348.

Krugman, P. , "The myth of Asia's miracle", *Foreign Affairs*, No-
vember/December 1994, pp. 62 – 78.

Laffont, Jean-Jacques, Jean Tirole, "Privatization and Incentives", *Journal of Law, Economics, and Organization*, 7 (Special issue), 1991, pp. 84 – 105.

Lall, S. , "Industrial policy: The role of government in promoting industrial and technological development", *UNCTAD Review*, 1994, pp. 65 – 90.

Lester, Richard A. , "Employment Effects of Minimum Wages", *Industrial and Labor Relations Review*, January 1960, 13, pp. 254 – 264.

Lucas, R. , "On the mechanics of economic development", *Journal of Monetary Economics*, Vol. 22, No. 1, 1988, pp. 3 – 42.

Lustig N. and McLeod D. , "Minimum Wages and Poverty in Developing Countries: Some Empirical Evidence", Brookings Discussion Papers in International Economics, No. 125.

Manzano, Osmel, and Francisco Monaldi, "Forthcoming in Fall 2008", The Political Economy of Oil Production in Latin America. Economia.

Mara Faccio, *The American Economic Review*, Vol. 96, No. 1, Mar. , 2006, pp. 369 – 386.

Marc T. Law, "The Economics of Minimum Wages", The Fraser Institute, Public Policy Sources, Number 14 (https://www.fraserinstitute. org/sites/default/files/EconomicsofMinimumWage. pd).

Melbourne Mercer Global Pension Index (2016) [http://www.globalpensionindex. com; son baxılma-oktyabr 2016].

Minor, Michael S. , "The Demise of Expropriation as An Instrument of LDC Policy, 1980 – 1992", *Journal of International Business Studies*, Vol. 25, No. 1, 1994, pp. 177 – 188.

Mountford, A. , Uhlig, H. , "What are the Effects of Fiscal Policy Shocks?", Humboldt-Universität zu berlin working paper sfb# 649, 2005.

Muradov Ş. M. , *Müasir dünyada və Azərbaÿcanda gedən demo- qrafik dəyişikliklər: əsas meyillər və problemlər.* – Müasir mərhələdə Azərbaycanda demoqrafik inkişafın, məşğulluq və işsizliyin sosial-iqtisadi problemləri, Elmi-praktik konfransin materialları. – Bakı, 2003, s. 6 – 13.

Müzəffərli N. , *İqtisadiyyatın sosialyönlüyü sağçı və solçu sistemlərdə.* – Bakı, "Şərq-Qərb" Nəşriyyat evi, 2014.

Müzəffərli N. , İS (S) İ – 2015: İqtisadiyyatın liberallıq potensialı-Bakı, "Elm və Bilik" nəşriyyatı, 2017.

Müzəffərli, N. , *İqtisadi inkişaf və ictimai rifah.* – AMEA İqtisadiyyat İnstitutu, 2016 [http: //economics. com. az/in- dex. php/tedbirler/t-dbirl-r/item/694 – zhoerkaemli-alim-azhil- aeliyevin-90-illik-yubileyi-kidzhirilmishdir. html; son baxılma- yanvar 2017].

Müzəffərli, N. , *İqtisadiyyatın sosialyönlüyü sağçı və solçu sistemlərdə.* – Bakı, "Şərq-Qərb" Nəşriyyat Evi, 2014 [http: // economics. com. az/images/fotos/sag-solluq/N. Muzaffarli _ İqti- sadiyyatin_ Salliqi (Sollugu). pdf; son baxılma-fevral 2017].

Neumark D. , "Wasche Minimum Wage Effects on Employment and School Enrollment", *Journal of Business & Economic Statis- tics*, Vol. 13, No. 2, April 1995.

Neumark D. , "Employment Effects of Minimum Wages", IZA World of Labor, 2014, p. 6.

OECD, *Pension Markets in Focus*, 2016. – OECD Annual Report, 2016 [http: // www. oecd. org/daf/fin/private-pensions/pensionmarketsinfocus. htm; son baxılma-dekabr 2016].

OECD, *Taxing Wages* – 2011 – 2012. – OECD, 2013 [http: // www. keepeek. com//Digital-Asset-Management/oecd/taxation/taxing-wages – 2013 _ tax _ wages – 2013 – en#page18; son baxılma – sentyabr 2016].

Pallares-Miralles, M. , C. Romero and E. Whitehouse, *International Patterns of Pension Provision II: A Worldwide Overview of Facts and Figures.* – World Bank Discussion paper NO. 1211, June 2012 [http: //documents. worldbank. org/curated/en//143611468168560687/International-patterns-of-pension-provision-II-a-worldwide-overview-of-facts-and-figures; son baxılma-yanvar 2017].

Panagariya A. , "Miracles and Debacles: In Defense of Trade Openness", Columbia University, 2004.

Perotti, R. , "Estimating the Effects of Fiscal Policy in OECD Countries", University of Bocconi, working paper.

Radu Vranceanu, "Corporate Profit, Entrepreneurship Theory and Business Ethics", ESSEC Working Paper, Document de Recherche ESSEC/Centre de recherche de l'ESSEC. ISSN: 1291 – 9616. WP1308. 2013.

Raffaela Giordano, Sandro Momigliano, Stefano Neri, Roberto Perotti, "The Effects of Fiscal Policy in Italy: Evidence from a VAR Model", *European Journal of Political Economy*, 23,

2007, pp. 707 – 733.

Ramey, V. , Shapiro, M. , "Costly Capital Reallocation and the Effects of Government Spending", Carnegie Rochester Conference on Public Policy, 48, 1998, pp. 145 – 194.

Romer, P. , "Increasing returns and long run growth", *Journal of Political Economy*, Vol. 94, No. 5, 1986, pp. 1002 – 1037.

Sabia, J. J. , "Minimum Wages and Gross Domestic Product", *Contemporary Economic Policy*, Vol. 33, No. 4, 2015, pp. 587 – 605.

Samuel Kwabena Obeng, "An Empirical Analysis of the Relationship Between Minimum Wage, Investment and Economic Growth in Ghana", *African Journal of Economic Review*, Volume III, Issue 2, July 2015.

Shapiro, C. and Willig, R. D. , "Economic Rationales for the Scope of Privatization", In E. N. Suleiman and J. Waterbury (eds), *The Political Economy of Private Sector Reform and Privatization*, Boulder, C. O. : Westview Press.

Shleifer A. , "State Versus Private Ownership", *Journal of Economic Perspectives*, Vol. 12, 1998, pp. 133 – 150.

Slaughter, M. , "Globalization and Wages: A Tale of Two Perspectives", *World Economy*, Vol. 22, 1999, pp. 609 – 630.

Solow, R. , "A contribution to the theory of economic growth", *Quarterly Journal of Economics*, Vol. 70, No. 1, 1956, pp. 65 – 94.

Stabile Donald R. , *The Living Wage: Lessons from the History of*

Economic Thought, Northampton, MA: Edward Elgar, 2008, p. 176.

Stigler, George J. , "The Economics of Minimum Wage Legislation", *American Economic Review*, Vol. 36, No. 3, June 1946, pp. 358 – 365.

Swan, T. , "Economic growth and capital accumulation", *Economic Record*, Vol. 32, No. 2, 1956, pp. 334 – 361.

UN World Population Prospects, 2015.

UNDP, Is the Private Sector More Efficient? A Cautionary Tale// UNDP Global Centre for Public Service Excellence#08 – 01, Block A, 29 Heng Mui Keng Terrace, 119620, Singapore, 2015.

Villalonga, B. , "Privatization and Efficiency: Differentiating Ownership Effects from Political, Organizational, and Dynamic Effect", *Journal of Economic Behavior & Organization*, Vol. 42, No. 1, 2000, pp. 43 – 77.

Young, A. , Gold into base metals: Productivity growth in the Peoples Republic of China during the reform period, NBER Working Paper W7856, National Bureau of Economic Research, Cambridge, 2000.

Гюльалиев М. Г. . Оценка зависимости экономического роста отгосударственных финансов (сравнительный анализ Азербайджана и Грузии) //Інноваційна економ ка 1 – 2' 2017 [67] науково-виробничий журнал.